Deployment Fundamentals — Volume 6
Deploying Windows 10 Using Microsoft Deployment Toolkit

Mikael Nyström
Johan Arwidmark

PUBLISHED BY
Deployment Artist
http://deploymentartist.com

Warning and Disclaimer

Every effort has been made to make this book as complete and as accurate as possible, but no
warranty or fitness is implied. The information provided is on an "as is" basis. The authors and the
publisher shall have neither liability nor responsibility to any person or entity with respect to any
loss or damages arising from the information contained in this book.

Feedback Information

We'd like to hear from you! If you have any comments about how we could improve the quality
of this book, please don't hesitate to contact us by visiting http://deploymentfundamentals.com,
sending an email to feedback@deploymentfundamentals.com, or visiting our Facebook site
http://facebook.com/deploymentfundamentals.

Acknowledgments

This book would not exist without the support from our families. Thank you for your patience and understanding. We love you all.

Thank you, Chris Nelson. Without your tireless edits, this book would never have been completed.

Thank you, Eddie Hönig, for valuable advice and testing.

Special thanks to Michael Niehaus and Aaron Czechowski for putting up with all of our questions.

The following music was played (often loudly) during the writing of this book: Nightwish, Scooter, Linkin Park, Meatloaf, and Green Day. Chris also mentioned that he was listening to Ron Carter and Herbie Hancock while editing the book. ☺

Finally, we are deeply indebted to our many students, event attendees, and people who've reached out to us via social media. You've asked great questions, shared valuable information, and generally enriched our professional lives. We appreciate you more than we can express.

About the Authors

Mikael Nyström

Mikael is a Principal Technical Architect at TrueSec, with an extremely broad field of competence. He works in-depth with System Center suite, virtualization, cloud platforms, and operating system deployment. Mikael is a very popular instructor, is frequently used by Microsoft for partner training, and speaks at major conferences such as TechEd, Microsoft Ignite, MMS, and Techdays. He also spends a lot of time in communities, like deploymentbunny.com and itproffs.se. Mikael has been awarded Microsoft Most Valuable Professional (MVP) for more than eleven years.

Johan Arwidmark

Johan Arwidmark is a consultant and all-around geek specializing in Systems Management and Enterprise Windows Deployment Solutions. Johan also speaks at several conferences each year, including MMS and TechEd events around the world. He is actively involved in deployment communities like deploymentresearch.com and myitforum.com and has been awarded Microsoft Most Valuable Professional (MVP) for more than eleven years.

Contents

Introduction

Deployment Fundamentals – Volume 6 is the ultimate source for the working IT Pro who wants to build a real-world deployment solution for Windows 10 based on Microsoft Deployment Toolkit (MDT) and PowerShell.

This is a HOW TO GET IT DONE book, solely focusing on building deployment solutions with roots in the real world. In addition to the guidance provided, you also find a massive script repository in the book sample files.

Say Hello (Possibly Again) to ViaMonstra Inc.

In this book, we build a real-world Windows 10 deployment solution for the fictive ViaMonstra Inc. organization. ViaMonstra is a midsized company with two locations and 3000 employees. The locations are New York and Stockholm.

BTW, the name ViaMonstra comes from *Viam Monstra*, Latin, meaning "Show me the way." We thought it was a cool name to have. ☺

The famous ViaMonstra logo.

Structure of the Book

The first chapter is an introduction to the ViaMonstra infrastructure as well as the proof-of-concept environment we use.

The second chapter is a crash course in Windows deployment scenarios and terminology, followed by a chapter in the various tools used in Windows deployment solutions.

Chapter 4 is an introduction to Windows 10. Chapter 5 is a crash course in Office 2016 deployment, followed by a chapter on using PowerShell, with a focus on the features we use in this book.

Chapter 7 is about creating a base infrastructure for Windows 10 deployments, and Chapters 8–14 are all about using the infrastructure to create and deploy Windows 10 images.

Chapters 15–19 cover common deployment customizations, including adding support for BitLocker, enabling dynamic deployment rules, using the MDT database, and using web services.

At the end of the book, there are three appendices. In Appendix A, we have added a step-by-step for setting up the proof-of-concept environment used in this book. (Don't miss that. Hydration is always fun!) Appendix B provides instructions on how to build a distributed environment, and finally, Appendix C provides instructions on how to create a MSI-based package of Office 2016. (The Office 365 version of Office 2016 is covered in Chapter 5.)

How to Use This Book

We have packed this book with step-by-step guides, which means you can build your deployment solution as you read along.

In numbered steps, we have set all names and paths in bold typeface. We also have used a standard naming convention throughout the book when explaining what to do in each step. The steps normally are something like this:

1. On the **Advanced Properties** page, select the **Confirm** check box, and then click **OK**.

2. Review the assigned IP address by running the following command:

   ```
   Get-NetIPAddress
   ```

Code snippets and sample scripts are set in a different typeface like in the following example.

```
HideShell=NO
WSUSServer=http://wsus01.corp.viamonstra.com:8530
```

This book is not intended as a reference volume, covering every technology, acronym, or command-line switch known to man, but rather is designed to make sure you learn what you need to know to build a great Windows 10 deployment infrastructure based on Windows Server 2012 R2.

Sample Files

All sample files used in this book can be downloaded from http://deploymentfundamentals.com.

Additional Resources

In addition to all tips and tricks provided in this book, you can find extra resources like articles and video recordings on our blogs, http://deploymentresearch.com and http://deploymentbunny.com.

Topics Not Covered

This book does not cover VDI solutions or System Center deployment solutions

Chapter 1

Designing ViaMonstra Inc.

As you remember from the introduction, ViaMonstra Inc. is the fictive company we use throughout this book. In this chapter, we describe the company in more detail, as well as the proof-of-concept environment we use in our step-by-step guides.

ViaMonstra Inc.

ViaMonstra Inc. was invented for the very purpose of having a "real" company to build a deployment solution for. In the real world, these deployment solutions come from multiple consulting engagements we have done, consolidated into a single generic scenario.

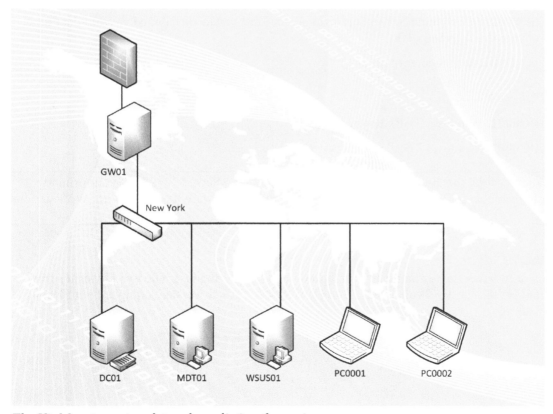

The ViaMonstra network topology, listing the various servers.

New York Site

As you learned in the introduction, ViaMonstra has 3000 employees and a single location. The datacenter is in New York. The New York site has the following servers related to software distribution and other supporting infrastructure. Detailed configuration of each server is found in the "Servers" section in this chapter.

Physical Servers

- **HV01.** Hyper-V Server

- **HV02.** Hyper-V Server

Virtual Servers

- **DC01.** Domain Controller, DNS, and DHCP

- **GW01.** Virtual Router (optional server used for Internet access)

- **MDT01.** Deployment Server

- **MDT02.** Deployment Server (optional server used for the distributed environment topic covered in Appendix B)

- **WSUS01.** Management Server

Virtual Clients

- **PC0001.** Windows 7 SP1 Enterprise x64

- **PC0002.** Windows 7 SP1 Enterprise x64

Note: When writing this book, we used Hyper-V in Windows Server 2012 R2 as our primary virtual platform, but all the guides also have been tested on VMware, both VMWare Workstations and ESXi.

Hardware

ViaMonstra Inc. uses server hardware kindly provided by HP (thanks). The two physical servers (HV01 and HV02) are HP Proliant ML350p Gen8 servers. All servers are equipped with local attached storage.

Server Software

For the server deployments there are not too many core applications to worry about. The following list describes ViaMonstra's software (in addition to Windows Server 2012 R2) that is used for the servers deployed in this book:

- Windows ADK 10

- BGInfo

- ConfigMgr 2012 R2 Toolkit

- MDT 2013 Update 2

- Visual C++ runtimes (2005–2015)

- Report Viewer 2008 SP1

- SQL Server 2014 Express SP1 with Tools

Servers

To build a replica of our infrastructure and run through the guides in this book, you can run all virtual machines on a single Hyper-V or VMware host with 16 GB of RAM and at least 500 GB free disk space.

As you read the book, you learn to install and configure the following servers for the New York site:

- **DC01. A Windows Server 2012 R2** machine, fully patched with the latest security updates, and configured as Active Directory Domain Controller, DNS Server, and DHCP Server in the **corp.viamonstra.com** domain.

    o   Server name: **DC01**

    o   IP Address: **192.168.1.200**

    o   Roles: **DNS, DHCP**, and **Domain Controller**

- **GW01. A Windows Server 2012 R2** machine, fully patched with the latest security updates, and configured as a workgroup server. This server is used as an optional virtual router that enables having all the other virtual machines on an isolated network, but still having Internet access.

    o   Server name: **GW01**

    o   IP Address: **192.168.1.1**

    o   Roles: **Routing and Remote Access (RRAS)**

- **MDT01.** A **Windows Server 2012 R2** machine, fully patched with the latest security updates, and configured as a member server in the **corp.viamonstra.com** domain.
  - o   Server name: **MDT01**
  - o   IP Address: **192.168.1.210**
  - o   Roles: **MDT 2013 Update 2** and **SQL Server 2014 SP1 Express with Tools**
- **MDT02.** An optional **Windows Server 2012 R2** machine, fully patched with the latest security updates, and configured as a member server in the **corp.viamonstra.com** domain.
  - o   Server name: **MDT02**
  - o   IP Address: **192.168.1.211**
  - o   Roles: **File Server**, and **WDS**
- **WSUS01.** A **Windows Server 2012 R2** machine, fully patched with the latest security updates, and configured as a member server in the **corp.viamonstra.com** domain.
  - o   Server name: **WSUS01**
  - o   IP Address: **192.168.1.240**
  - o   Roles: **WSUS**
  - o   Software: **SQL Server 2014 Express with SP1**

Chapter 2

Deployment Fundamentals

When working with Windows 10 deployment, there are a few terms you need to know. This chapter is a crash course in Microsoft deployment terminology and scenarios.

Deployment Scenarios

The deployment toolset we use, MDT, supports four scenarios for Windows 10 deployments. The scenarios are explained in detail in the next section, but here is quick summary:

- **In-place upgrade.** A new deployment scenario, available only for Windows 10. In this scenario, you simply upgrade an existing Windows 7 or Windows 8/8.1 machine exactly as it is to Windows 10.

- **New computer.** A bare metal deployment of a new machine.

- **Computer refresh.** A reinstall of the same machine (with user-state migration and an optional full WIM backup).

- **Computer replace.** A replacement of the old client with a new client (with user-state migration and an optional full WIM backup).

MDT also supports a special OEM scenario that you can use if you want to prepare an image in-house and then send it to an OEM for cloning. We do not describe that scenario in detail, but thought we should at least mention that it exists.

Real World Note: Deciding on using an OEM scenario is not an easy task. Even though useful in some cases, the OEM scenario really helps only when installing new computers. You still need to have a solution for refreshing existing machines, and you still need to create your reference images that you send to the OEM. Also, the turnaround time for new images is normally not "the next day." Make sure to dedicate plenty of time for a pilot project with your hardware vendor if thinking about using the OEM scenario.

In-Place Upgrade

The in-place upgrade scenario in Windows 10 is a very nice deployment addition when it can be used. First of all, it upgrades the system as it is, with all applications, data, and settings. There is no option for selecting what should be included. It's an all or nothing scenario. This means that you need to be quite happy with the current platform because the new Windows 10 machine will be exactly the same as before, except of course for now running Windows 10.

In addition, while in-place upgrades are nice, there are quite a few scenarios when you need to use the old-school deployment scenarios (new computer, refresh computer, and replace computer). Windows 10 in-place upgrades has the following limitations:

- You cannot use a custom reference image with applications installed. You have to use the default Microsoft image.

Real World Note: Even though you cannot use a custom image with applications, you can add updates, which is in fact what setup.exe does when dynamic update is enabled. In that scenario, setup.exe downloads the latest cumulative update, mounts a local copy of the WIM image, injects that update, and commits the changes. It then continues with the upgrade process.

If you patch the WIM manually, to avoid setup.exe from trying update the WIM image twice, you want to disable dynamic updates. But that also disables downloading out-of-box drivers from WU, so make sure to have a good driver management process for the upgrade (via MDT, of course).

- You cannot change from BIOS to UEFI (not supported by Microsoft) or do other disk layout changes.

- You cannot upgrade with (most) third-party disk-encryption software installed. (Currently, only one McAfee version works.)

- You cannot upgrade when (most) third-party antivirus software is installed.

- You cannot upgrade between architectures (e.g. x86 to x64)

- You cannot change the base operating system language.

- You cannot change to a lower edition (or SKU).

- You cannot upgrade a "boot from VHD" system.

- You cannot upgrade Windows To Go USB sticks.

Note: Upgrading WIMBoot/Compressed OS used to be a limitation, but that limitation was removed with Window 10 build 10041. It still requires sufficient disk space though.

The deployment process for the in-place upgrade scenario is as follows:

1. The setup starts on a machine running the operating system that is to be upgraded.

2. The operating system image is upgraded via the setup.exe /Auto Upgrade option.

3. Other application installations follow (as part of the task sequence, if added).

4. The machine is ready to be used.

New Computer

This scenario occurs when you have a blank machine you need to deploy, or an existing machine you want to wipe and redeploy without caring about any existing data. The setup starts from a boot media, using PXE, CD/DVD, USB, or ISO images. You also can generate a full offline media, including all the files needed for a client deployment. The target can be a physical computer, a virtual machine, a virtual disk running on a physical computer (Boot from VHD), or a USB stick (Windows To Go).

The deployment process for the new machine scenario is as follows:

1. The setup is started from boot media (PXE, CD/DVD, USB, or ISO).

2. System validations are run.

3. The operating system image is installed.

4. Other application installations follow (as part of the task sequence).

5. The machine is ready to be used.

Computer Refresh

Sometimes called *wipe-and-load*, this was the new "upgrade" for Windows 7 and Windows 8.1 deployments. The process is initiated on the running client. User data and settings are then backed up and restored as part of the deployment process. The target can be the same as for the new computer scenario except for the USB stick.

The deployment process for the wipe-and-load scenario is as follows:

1. The setup starts on a machine running the operating system that is to be upgraded.

2. System validations are run.

3. User state is saved locally (normally).

4. The operating system image is installed.

5. Other application installations follow.

6. User state is restored.

7. The machine is ready to use.

> **Real World Note:** In Windows 10, there is a similar feature built into the operating system named "Reset this PC." The core difference is that the Reset this PC feature does not restore legacy application settings, only the new Windows 10 applications, and it actually does not restore the application. It just reserves the application in the Start menu, and when you select the application, Reset this PC downloads it from the store.

Computer Replace

A computer replace is similar to the refresh scenario. But because we are replacing the machine, we divide this scenario into two main tasks: backup of the old client, and bare metal deployment of the new client. As with the refresh scenario, user data and settings are backed up and restored.

The deployment process for the replace scenario is as follows:

1. The setup starts on a machine running the operating system that is to be upgraded.

2. System validations are run.

3. The user state is saved on the server through a backup job.

4. Then the new computer is deployed as a bare metal deployment.

5. The previous backup is restored on the new computer.

Real World Note: Sometimes the computer replace scenario is used even if you would like to keep your old hardware. If the machine is using a third-party disk encryption system, it could be faster to treat the scenario as a replace to avoid decrypting the hard drive before deployment, or spending time getting refresh scenarios to work. This also applies when the disk partitioning layout is incorrect (BIOS vs UEFI).

Deployment Methods

In terms of actual deployment methods, nothing has changed with Windows 10. It still supports network deployment via both PXE and boot media, as well as completely standalone media. The standalone media can be either DVD or a USB stick.

Automation Level

Microsoft marketing sometimes has interesting ways of naming the deployment solutions. Names like MDT Lite Touch, or Zero Touch, are nothing but marketing names, and have nothing to do with the level of automation used. In fact, both solutions can be as manual, or as automated as you like it to be. For Windows 10 deployment, the solutions from Microsoft support the following automation levels:

- **Wizard driven.** Prompting for information during deployment.

- **Fully automated.** Prestaging information prior to starting the deployment.

- **Dynamic.** Local and/or backend systems generating information in real-time.

- **Hybrid.** Also called semi-automation, prestaging some information and prompting for other.

Images

Starting with Windows Vista, everything in terms of operating system deployment is image based. To give you an example, if you open the Windows 10 ISO and look in the Sources folder, you will find a file named install.wim. This is a ready-to-go sysprepped image of Windows 10. The Windows 10 images also support offline servicing, which enables you to add updates, language packs, drivers, and so forth.

Default Image

This is simple the default Microsoft image that you download from either Microsoft Developer Network (MSDN) or Volume Licensing Service Center (VLCS). This image is used for the in-place upgrade scenario and for building reference images.

Reference Images

With Windows 10, you don't really have to create a reference image because the image on the Windows 10 ISO/DVD is ready for deployment. However, you probably still want to create a reference image of Windows 10 for other reasons, such as speed of deployment and to add run-time components that other applications need.

In the long term, even with the Windows as a Service model, you will find that Windows 10 will require more and more updates, and using reference images greatly saves time on deployment. In general, we strongly recommend creating reference images from the beginning because changing methods along the road takes additional time.

> **Real World Note:** Even though not technically required for automated deployments, a good reference image makes your deployment easier; it is very well worth spending the extra hours making it perfect. Put it this way, even the tiniest error in the image cause a significant impact when you deploy the image to a few thousand machines.

We like the analogy of a house, where the reference image is the foundation. If you don't create a strong foundation, it doesn't matter how great the walls are. The structure will fail eventually. Ask the engineers who built the leaning tower of Pisa. They probably wished they had spent some extra time on the foundation. ☺

Thin Image

A thin image is an image without any applications. It may contain some basic settings, like customizations to the administrator profile or other operating system settings. When deploying thin images, the applications, drivers, and additional settings are installed or injected at deployment time. Even if this image type typically contains operating system components like .NET Framework, Internet Explorer, and updates from Microsoft Update, it's still considered a thin image. In general, a thin image is more suitable in a dynamic environment.

Thick Image

A thick image is an image with most applications included. The primary reason for creating this image type is deployment speed. Drivers and settings are still kept outside the image, with the rare exception of the new Windows To Go feature in Windows 10 where you do want to include drivers. In general, a thick image is more suitable in a static environment. Educational organizations typically use this type of image.

> **Real World Note:** If you do decide to use applications in the image, make sure that applications are Sysprep-aware. For example, never, ever, put third-party antivirus software in the reference image. It's the most common cause of Sysprep breaking. Other applications that don't fit in an image are applications that include unique identifiers.
>
> The main purpose of thicker images is to reduce deployment time. So if you have applications that require a manual installation, it makes sense to put those applications in the reference image. It's better to do it manually one time instead of a few thousand times.

Hybrid Image

A hybrid image is an image with only some features or applications included, with others being installed as part of the image deployment process. The primary reason for creating this image type also is for deployment speed. A hybrid image can sometimes provide you with the best of both worlds, decreasing deployment time, but providing flexibility. This is the most commonly used image type, and in this book, you use this image type.

Drivers

When deploying Windows to physical hardware, the setup requires drivers, and the various deployment solutions from Microsoft have slightly different ways of dealing with them. However, they do have a few things in common. The first thing is that you need to find the drivers.

Finding the Drivers

In a perfect world, there would be a single place where you could download ready-made drivers for all your hardware, but unfortunately all not hardware vendors are equal in the way they provide drivers. In this book, you learn to find drivers for HP, Lenovo, Dell, and Microsoft:

- **HP.** For HP hardware, we recommend using their SoftPaq Download Manager utility. This allows you to quickly select your hardware model(s) and the operating system for which you want the drivers.

- **Lenovo.** For Lenovo hardware, we recommend using their Lenovo ThinkVantage Update Retriever utility. It's quite similar to the HP tool.

- **Dell.** For Dell hardware, you don't need to use a separate utility because Dell provides ready-made CAB files with drivers for each model.

- **Microsoft.** For Microsoft hardware, you need to go to the Microsoft web site and download the drivers.

In general, you always want to start with each vendor's solution for getting drivers because these will be the only supported drivers from that vendor. But sometimes you simply cannot find the driver at the vendor site. If that happens, your second best option is to go to the vendor's vendor. For example, if you are looking for a driver to an Intel network card, go to Intel's web site.

Another option is to go to the Microsoft catalog site, which also contains drivers for most hardware.

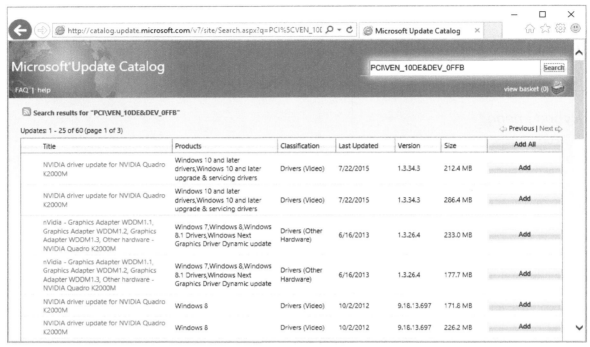

The Microsoft Update Catalog drivers for NVIDIA Quadro K2000M.

Driver Scenarios

A second thing related to drivers that Microsoft deployment solutions have in common is that the drivers are stored outside the image in a driver repository and are injected during deployment. There are three basic scenarios for driver injection that you should know about:

- **Total chaos.** The default method for injecting drivers. This method uses PnPID detection to figure out which drivers should be copied from the deployment server and injected during the deployment. In general, this method is useful if you have a very limited set of hardware models.

- **Added predictability.** This is a variant of the total chaos method, but you add additional filters to control which drivers are considered for injection. For example, if you have a driver repository that contains drivers for both Windows 7 and Windows 10, only Windows 10 drivers are considered for Windows 10 deployments and vice versa.

- **Total control.** This is a method in which you manually organize drivers in a logical structure, for example, by operating system, vendor, and model. You then configure the deployment solution to inject only the correct drivers for the correct model. This is the scenario we recommend that you use.

Real World Note: The scenario names are not official Microsoft terms. They are our own. ☺

Volume Activation

Since Windows Vista, all versions of Windows need to be activated. For an enterprise organization, you have a few different options for doing that. You can activate the Windows 10 client on-premise via Active Directory-Based Activation or the Key Management Service (KMS), and off-premise via Microsoft hosted activation services (online or via telephone).

Active Directory-Based Activation

If your activation server is running Windows Server 2012 or later, you can use the Active Directory-Based Activation service for your Windows 10 clients. The only requirement is that you have extended the Active Directory schema. Active Directory-Based Activation is configured by adding the Volume Activation Services role.

If you need to support older clients like Windows 7, you still need to use KMS. Like Active Directory-Based Activation, KMS is also configured by adding the Volume Activation Services role. If you cannot use Active Directory-Based Activation or KMS, you can also use Multiple Activation Keys (MAK) to activate the installations.

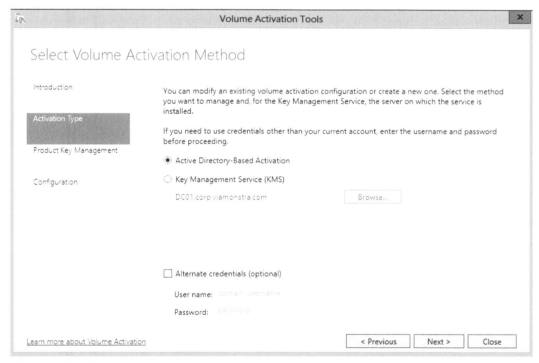

Configuring the activation type.

Key Management Service (KMS)

KMS allows enterprise organizations to enable activation of operating systems for Windows Vista and above. If you cannot use KMS, you also can use Multiple Activation Keys (MAK) to activate the installations. It's not uncommon for organizations to use both KMS and MAK licenses.

If running Windows 8.1 or Windows Server 2012 R2 (recommended) as your KMS host, you need to apply the https://support.microsoft.com/kb/3058168 hotfix on the KMS host in order to activate Windows 10.

You also can use an existing Windows 7 or Windows Server 2008 R2 KMS host to activate Windows 10 clients, but first you need to apply the https://support.microsoft.com/kb/3079821 hotfix on the KMS host.

> **Real World Note:** If running your KMS host on Windows Server 2008 R2, please upgrade to at least Windows Server 2012 R2. Windows Server 2008 R2 is a really old operating system.

Data Deduplication

Data deduplication was introduced in Windows Server 2012 and has been improved in Windows Server 2012 R2. The basic idea is to slice all files into chunks, basically remove everything that looks the same, and just keep one chunk, thereby saving space. In reality, it is a bit more complicated. In the R2 release, it is now possible to use data deduplication in conjunction with Hyper-V, primarily to improve Virtual Desktop Infrastructure (VDI) solutions. Data deduplication also works with Storage Spaces in clustered environments. The amount of space you save with data deduplication is in the area of 50–9x percent, but in the VDI scenario you also benefit significantly from the increased performance. Loading up a bunch of VDI machines is much faster if run on data-deduplicated spaces. The total amount of data that needs to be read is much smaller and most of it will be the same, so it stays in the cache during the expansion of the data.

Chapter 3

Tools of the Trade

Microsoft has a lot of utilities and kits available to help with deployment. Some of them are only "plumbing," such as foundation components used by the deployment solutions, and some of them are in fact the deployment solution. In this chapter, you learn about the various tools available and what roles they play in the deployment processes.

Windows Assessment and Deployment Kit (ADK) 10

Windows ADK 10 contains the core assessment and deployment tools, including most of the nifty command-line utilities that Microsoft's deployment solutions use in the background. ADK contains tools and technologies like the Deployment Image Servicing and Management (DISM), Windows System Image Manager (WSIM), Windows Imaging and Configuration Designer (WICD), User State Migration Tool (USMT), Volume Activation Management Tool (VAMT), Windows PE, Windows Assessment Toolkit, Windows Assessment Services – Client, Windows Performance Toolkit, and Application Compatibility Toolkit (ACT).

Real World Note: Please note that the deployment tools included in the ADK are nothing but supporting infrastructure and are not to be used as a deployment solution. We still meet too many customers who tried to build their own deployment solutions based on the ADK (and former WAIK) tools. Never, ever do that, please…

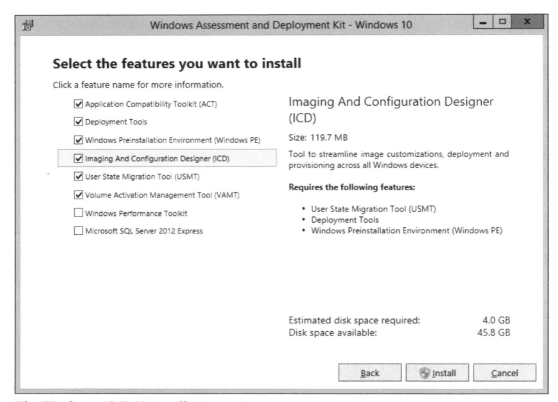

The Windows ADK 10 installation options.

Note: If you install Windows ADK 10 on a server, you don't get the Windows Assessment Toolkit and Windows Assessment Services – Client. But if you install Windows ADK 10 on a client, you do.

Deployment Image Servicing and Management (DISM)

Unofficially dubbed (by us) as the most difficult acronym to remember, DISM is used for servicing boot images and operating system images. You also can use PowerShell to call the DISM functions; for example, you can run this PowerShell command to see all available DISM functions:

```
Get-Command -Module Dism
```

Real World Note: Even though we recommend using the PowerShell cmdlets of DISM when you can, please note that the dism.exe file has features that are not yet supported by the PowerShell DISM cmdlets.

DISM supports servicing both online and offline images. An example is installing the Microsoft .NET Framework 3.5.1 online in Windows 10. "Online" here means starting the installation in the running operating system, not that you get the software online. The /LimitAccess switch configures DISM to get the files only from a local source.

```
Dism.exe /Online /Enable-Feature /FeatureName:NetFX3 /All
/Source:D:\Sources\SxS /LimitAccess
```

In the preceding command, the D:\Sources\SxS folder is pointing to the Window 10 installation media, where the .NET Framework setup files are stored.

The equivalent PowerShell command would be like this:

```
Enable-WindowsOptionalFeature -FeatureName NetFX3 -LimitAccess
-Source D:\Sources\SxS -Online
```

Windows System Image Manager (WSIM)

WSIM is the authoring tool for Unattend.xml files. When using MDT, you don't have to use this tool very often because MDT takes care of updating the Unattend.xml file for you. However, it is useful for enabling components in the Windows operating system that are not available in the MDT Deployment Workbench.

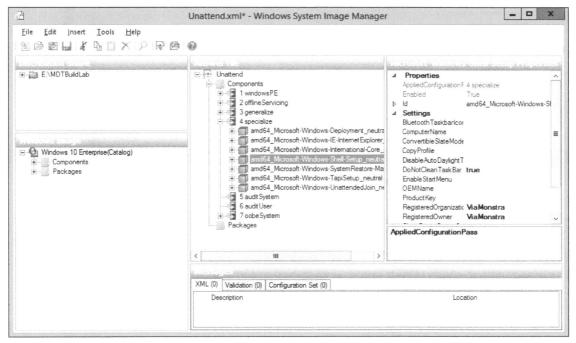

Windows 10 answer file opened in WSIM.

Windows Imaging and Configuration Designer (Windows ICD)

With Windows 10 deployment, there is a new option available called *provisioning packages*. You can think of this as an uber version of Unattend.xml, in which you also can set policies and attach file assets. These packages are only for Windows 10, and you create these packages using Windows ICD, which is part of Windows ADK 10.

Real World Note: While provisioning packages is a very interesting technology, it's also a very 1.0 feature. That means there are quite a few bugs, and the integration with other deployment solutions like MDT or ConfigMgr is nonexistent.

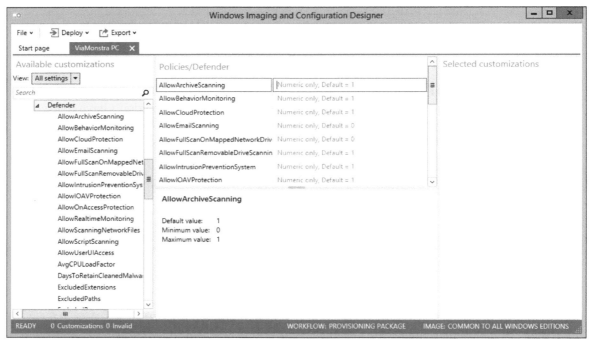

WICD showing the Windows 10 settings for Windows Defender in a provisioning package.

Volume Activation Management Tool (VAMT)

If you don't use KMS, you can still manage your MAKs centrally by using the Volume Activation Management Tool (VAMT) from Microsoft. With this tool, you can install and manage product keys throughout the organization. The VAMT tool also can activate on behalf of clients without internet access, acting as a MAK proxy. VAMT also enables online activation (proxy-activation) of an Active Directory-based object. Even if you use KMS, you can still use VAMT to view, change, and modify activation on Windows machines. It also handles Office activation and Active Directory-based activation.

Windows ADK 10 includes VAMT version 3.1 (the same version as in Windows ADK 8.1), which stores its data in a SQL Server database. There is also a VAMT PowerShell module for command-line operations.

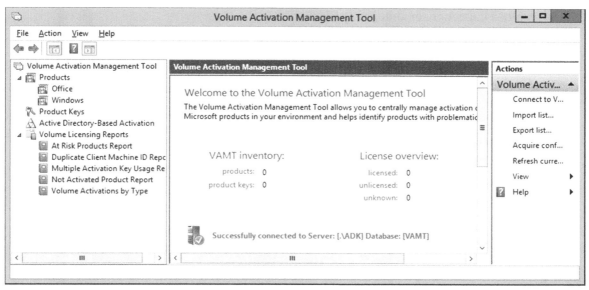

The updated Volume Activation Management Tool.

Windows Preinstallation Environment (Windows PE)

Windows PE, or WinPE, is a "Lite" version of Windows 10 and was created to act as a deployment platform. Windows PE replaces the DOS or Linux boot disks that ruled the deployment solutions in the late 1990s and early 2000s.

The key thing to know about Windows PE is that, like the operating system, it needs drivers. It requires Windows 10-type drivers, at the very least network and storage drivers. Luckily Windows PE in Windows ADK 10 has the same inbox drivers as Windows 10, which means much of your hardware will work out of the box.

Application Compatibility Toolkit (ACT)

ACT is a toolkit for inventory and application compatibility management. Its functionality overlaps a bit with Microsoft Assessment and Planning (MAP) Toolkit, but its real strength is on the application compatibility side.

ACT is really a collection, or suite, of applications:

- **Application Compatibility Manager (ACM).** The main application used for inventory and to set up the database for storing inventory data.

- **Compatibility Administrator.** The application used to create fixes (shims) for applications that do not work by default in Windows 10. There are two versions of the application, one for fixing 32-bit applications and one for fixing 64-bit applications.

- **Standard User Analyzer.** A tool that helps find issues and create fixes for running applications as a standard user.

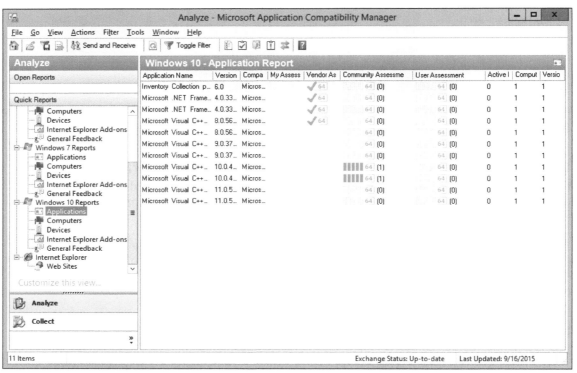

Application Compatibility Manager listing inventoried applications and their compatibility levels.

Microsoft Assessment and Planning Toolkit (MAP) Toolkit

The MAP Toolkit is an application that helps you prepare for infrastructure upgrades. It helps you inventory your hardware and verifies that you are good to go. Version 9.3 has full support for Windows 10.

Real World Note: The reports and information in MAP are not only useful for engineers and technicians. They also can help "convert" technical data into business language, making the information easy to understand for less technical people.

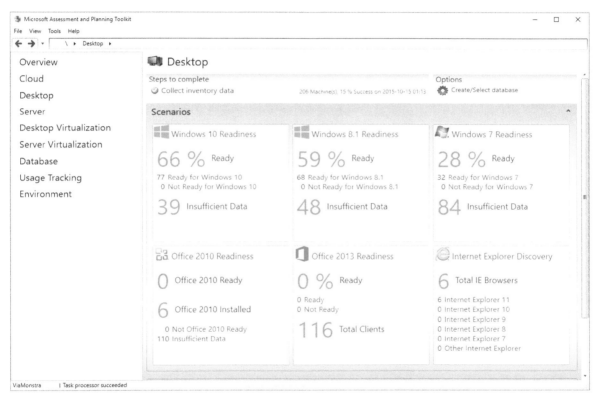

The desktop inventory results view in MAP.

Security Compliance Manager (SCM)

SCM is a utility used to create baseline security settings for the Windows client environment. The baselines also can be exported and then deployed via MDT. SCM also has updated templates for Windows 10.

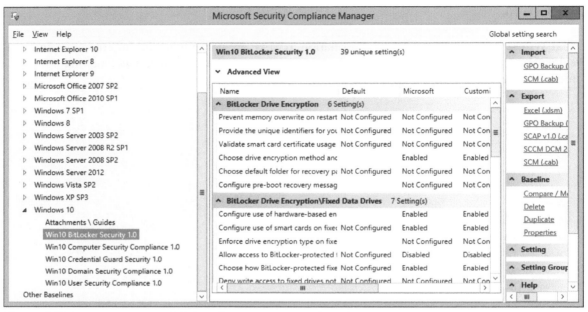

Using SCM to create or modify Windows 10 security baselines.

Windows Deployment Services (WDS)

Windows Deployment Services (WDS) has been updated and improved in many ways. The improvements can be divided into two categories, the one you can see and the ones you cannot see. Most of the changes are related to management and increased performance. In Windows Server 2012 or later, WDS also can be used for the Network Unlock feature (BitLocker).

> **Real World Note:** We don't consider WDS to be a deployment solution. It's far too limited to be called a solution. Rather, it is a critical deployment piece used by other deployment solutions like MDT. This means that even if you should not use WDS as your deployment solution, you still need to use it indirectly, as supporting infrastructure. Without the WDS infrastructure, you will not be able to PXE boot or use multicast when needed.

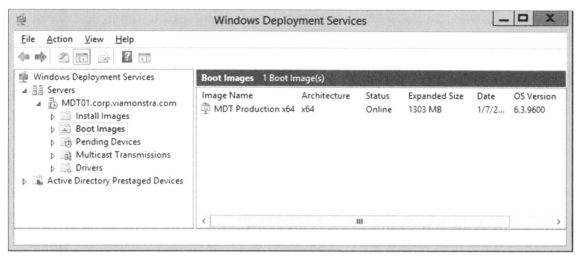

The WDS console, with a boot image from MDT added.

Microsoft Deployment Toolkit (MDT)

MDT is a free deployment solution from Microsoft. It provides end-to-end guidance, best practices, and tools for planning, building, and deploying Windows operating systems. MDT builds on top of core deployment tools in ADK, adds guidance, reduces complexity, and adds critical features for an enterprise-ready deployment solution.

MDT has two main parts: the first is called Lite Touch, which is a standalone deployment solution, and the other is called Zero Touch, which is an extension to System Center Configuration Manager (ConfigMgr).

Real World Note: "Lite Touch" and "Zero Touch" are just marketing names for the two solutions that MDT supports, and the naming has nothing to do with the level of automation. The standalone MDT solution (Lite Touch) can be fully automated if you want, and the solution integration with ConfigMgr can be configured to prompt for information.

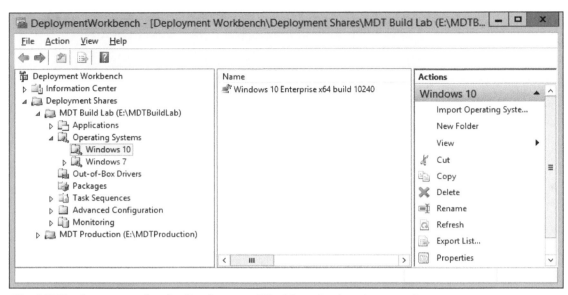

The MDT admin console, the Deployment Workbench, showing a task sequences.

Lite Touch Components

To master MDT Lite Touch quickly, it's valuable to first learn what the major components are and what they are used for. In addition to the Deployment Workbench, which is a Microsoft Management Console MMC 3.0 snap-in, used to administer MDT Lite Touch, there are quite a few terms that you need to know about.

Deployment Share

One or more shared folders on the server contain all the setup files and scripts needed for the deployment solution. The folder is the deployment share. It also holds the configuration files (called rules) that are gathered when a machine is deployed. These configuration files can reach out to other sources, like a database, external script, or web server, to get additional settings for the deployment.

Rules

The rules (CustomSettings.ini and Bootstrap.ini) make up the brain of MDT, the mastermind if you will. The rules control the Windows Deployment Wizard on the client and, for example, can provide the following settings to the machine being deployed:

- Computer name

- Domain to Join, and OU in Active Directory to hold the computer object

- Whether to enable BitLocker

- Regional settings

- And literally hundreds of additional settings

Later in this chapter, in the "The Rules Explained" section, you learn more details about the rules.

Boot Images

Boot images are the WinPE-based images that are used to start the deployment. They can be started from a CD/DVD, an ISO file, a USB device, or over the network using a PXE server. The boot images connect to the deployment share on the server and start the deployment.

Operating Systems

Using the Deployment Workbench, you import the operating systems you want to deploy. In this book, we use Windows 10, but MDT 2013 Update 2 also supports deploying Windows 7, Windows 8, Windows 8.1, Windows Server 2008 R2, Windows Server 2012, Windows Server 2012 R2, and Windows Server 2016 Technical Preview 4.

You can import either the full source (like the contents of the Windows 10 ISO file) or a custom image that you have created. The full source operating systems are primarily used to create reference images and for the new in-place upgrade scenario.

Applications

Using the Deployment Workbench, you also add the applications you want to deploy. MDT supports virtually every executable Windows file type. It can be a standard .exe file with command-line switches for an unattended install; it also can be a Windows Installer (MSI) package, a batch file, a VBScript, or a PowerShell script. In fact, it can be just about anything that can be executed unattended. MDT also supports the new universal applications in Windows 10.

Real World Note: You cannot add an application just anywhere in the task sequence. It needs to be in the state restore phase (or after). We get quite a number of email messages from people who tried to install the application during the WinPE phase, and that doesn't work.

Drivers Repository

You also use the Deployment Workbench to import the drivers your hardware needs into a repository that lives on the server, not in the image. The default behavior in MDT Lite Touch is to do a PnP ID scan during the WinPE phase, match that list with the drivers in the repository, and then download and inject the matching drivers during deployment.

Real World Note: Some devices do need a full application to work, in addition to the core driver, and these driver applications have to be added as normal applications in MDT.

Packages

With the Deployment Workbench, you can add any Microsoft packages that you want to use. The most commonly added packages are language packs, and the Deployment Workbench Packages node works fine for those. You also can add security and other updates this way. However, we generally recommend that you use WSUS for operating system updates because package administration in MDT can be quite time-consuming. The rare exceptions are critical hotfixes that are not available via WSUS, packages for the boot image, or any other package that needs to be deployed before the WSUS update process starts (for example updates to the Windows Update agent).

Task Sequences

Task sequences are the heart and soul of the deployment solution. When creating a task sequence, you need to select a template. The templates are located in the Templates folder in the MDT installation directory, and they determine which default actions are present in the sequence.

You can think of a task sequence as a list of actions that need to be executed in a certain order. Each action also can have conditions. Some example actions follow:

- **Gather.** Reads configuration settings from the deployment server

- **Format and Partition.** Creates the partition(s) and formats them

- **Inject Drivers.** Finds out which drivers the machine needs and downloads them from the central drivers repository

- **Apply Operating System.** Runs DISM to apply the operating system image

- **Windows Update.** Connects to a WSUS server (or Microsoft Update if no WSUS server is specified) and updates the machine

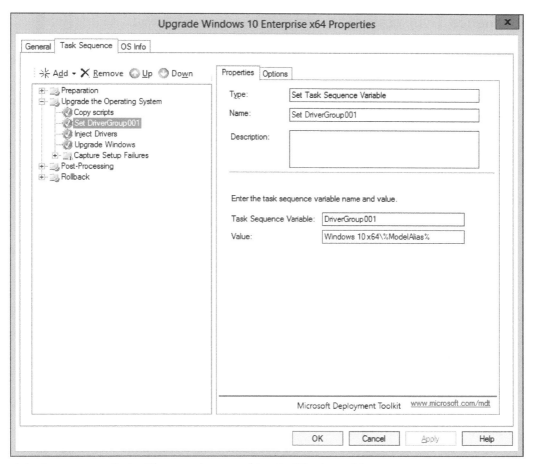

A task sequence that will upgrade a machine to Windows 10.

Task Sequence Templates

MDT comes with eleven default task sequence templates. You also can create your own templates. As long as you store them in the Templates folder, they will be available when you create a new task sequence.

- **Sysprep and Capture task sequence.** Runs Sysprep and captures an image of a reference computer.

> **Real World Note:** We don't recommend using the Sysprep and Capture task sequence. The primary reason is that you are supposed to use an automated process when creating reference images, as described in this book, and the Sysprep and Capture task sequence also tends to break as soon as the image is slightly different from what the task sequence expects. You have been warned. ☺

- **Standard Client task sequence.** The most used task sequence. Used for creating reference images, as well as for deploying clients in production.

- **Standard Client Replace task sequence.** Used to run USMT backup for client deployments and the optional full WIM backup action. Can also be used to do a secure wipe of a machine that is going to be decommissioned.

- **Standard Client Upgrade task sequence.** Used to run the in-place upgrade scenario for Windows 10 (only).

- **Custom task sequence.** As the name implies, a custom task sequence with only one default action (one Install Application action).

- **Litetouch OEM task sequence.** Used to pre-load operating system images on the computer hard drive. Typically used by computer OEMs, but some enterprise organizations also use this feature.

- **Standard Server task sequence.** The default task sequence for deploying operating system images to servers. The main difference between this template and the Standard Client task sequence template is that it does not contain any USMT actions (because USMT is not supported on servers).

- **Standard Server Upgrade task sequence.** Used to run the in-place upgrade scenario for Windows Server 2016 (only). Currently the upgrade is not recommend for Windows Server 2016.

- **Post OS Installation task sequence.** A task sequence prepared to run actions after the operating system has been deployed. Very useful for server deployments and various hydration solutions, but not often used for client deployments.

- **Deploy to VHD Client task sequence.** Similar to the Standard Client task sequence template, but also creates a virtual hard disk (VHD) file on the target computer and deploys the image to the VHD file.

- **Deploy to VHD Server task sequence.** Same as the Deploy to VHD Client task sequence, but for servers.

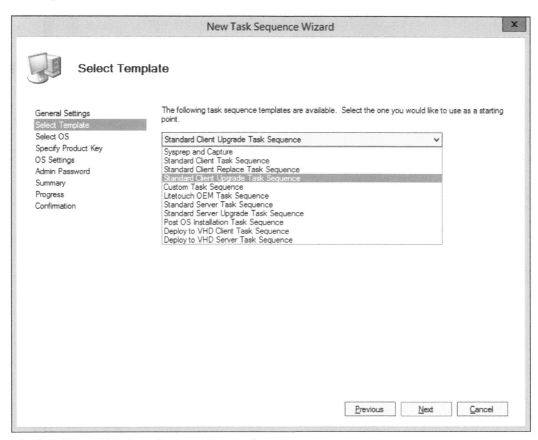

The MDT Lite Touch task sequence templates.

Selection Profiles

Available in the Advanced Configuration node, selection profiles provide a generic way in MDT to filter content in the Deployment Workbench.

Logging

MDT uses a lot of log files during operating system deployments. By default, the logs are client side, but by configuring the deployment settings, which is recommended and what you do in this book, you can have MDT store them on the server, as well.

Monitoring

On the deployment share, you also can enable monitoring. After doing that, you will see all running deployments in the Monitor node in the Deployment Workbench.

Windows Server Update Services (WSUS)

WSUS is a server role in Windows Server 2012 R2 that enables you to maintain a local repository of Microsoft updates and then distribute them to machines on your network. WSUS offers approval control and reporting of the update status in your environment.

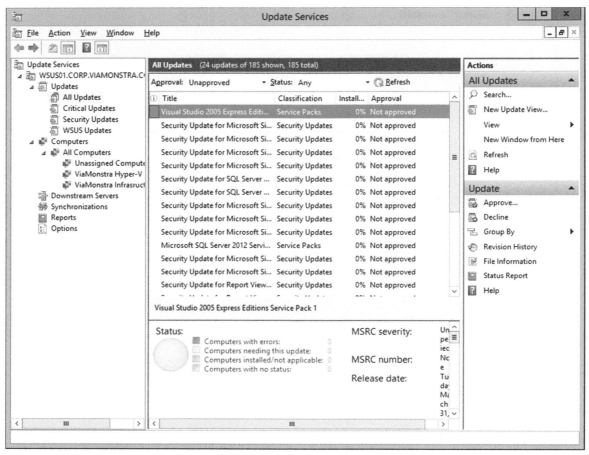

The Windows Server Update Services console.

Microsoft Desktop Optimization Pack (MDOP)

MDOP is a suite of extra utilities for both Windows Server and Windows Clients. MDOP used to be an extra license on top of software assurance, but is now included in the software assurance license, which we think is very nice. The utilities included in MDOP are the following:

- Microsoft Application Virtualization (App-V)

- Microsoft User Experience Virtualization (UE-V)

- Microsoft Advanced Group Policy Management (AGPM)

- Microsoft BitLocker Administration and Monitoring (MBAM)
- Microsoft Diagnostics and Recovery Toolset (DaRT)

We do not use all of the MDOP features in this book, but we are using DaRT, UE-V, and App-V.

Microsoft Diagnostics and Recovery Toolset (DaRT)

DaRT provides additional tools that extend WinPE to help you troubleshoot and repair your machines. MDT offers an easy way to add DaRT to your boot images. The most commonly used feature for operating system deployment is the remote connection feature, which allows you to connect to a running deployment while the machine is still in the WinPE phase.

For security reasons, MDT does not enable all DaRT features in the boot image, only the following:

- **Crash Analyzer.** Allows you examine memory dump files, for example to find the driver that caused a computer to fail

- **File Restore.** Allows you to restore files that were accidentally deleted or that were too big to fit in the Recycle Bin

- **Disk Commander.** Used to recover and repair disk partitions or volumes

- **Disk Wipe.** Allows you securely (U.S. Department of Defense standards) wipe a disk

- **Explorer.** Allows you to browse for files on the machine

- **Solution Wizard.** A wizard that helps you determine which tool to use when you are new to the DaRT tools

- **TCP/IP Config.** Used for networking configuration

- **Search.** Allows you to search for files on the machine

Real World Note: It's the DartConfig.dat in MDT that restricts the number of tools from DaRT being available. If you want to use another feature, you can create another DartConfig.dat file using the DaRT Recovery Image feature.

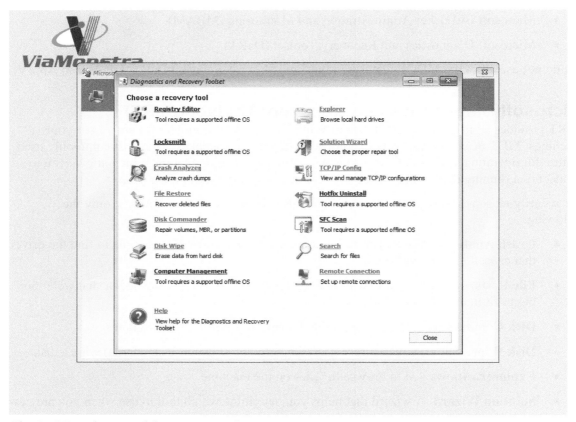

The DaRT tools started from an MDT boot image.

Microsoft User Experience Virtualization (UE-V)

UE-V allows your users to roam their Windows and application settings between devices. The feature basically saves settings in files or registry settings for Windows and applications and saves them in a network location such as the user's home directory or a directory that you designate.

UE-V uses an agent to roam the settings, and the agent uses XML templates that define which settings should roam, for example, a background image in Windows 10. The actual synchronization is based on triggers or can be run as a schedule task. It also can occur, for example, when an application starts and closes, or when you lock and unlock a machine.

In UE-V, there is also a graphical user interface, Company Settings Center, available for end users. From there, users can see exactly which settings are being roamed for which applications, as well as manually trigger a synchronization.

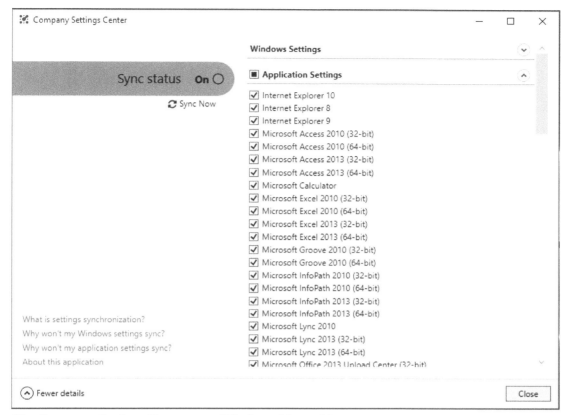

The Company Settings Center on a Windows 10 machine.

Microsoft Application Virtualization (App-V)

Application virtualization is a term for software technologies that improve portability and compatibility of applications. This is done by isolating the application from the Windows operating system in a virtual bubble. For the end user, the application appears to be installed on the machine, but it's not really installed, but just available for the end user to start it. Application virtualization in general allows for faster application deployment and updates, and it also minimizes conflicts between applications.

Microsoft's solution for application virtualization is App-V, and the version that fully supports Windows 10 is App-V 5.1.

Chapter 4

Windows 10

Windows 10 is a major update to say at least. In this chapter, we highlight the most important changes.

Windows 10 Editions

There are quite a few editions of Windows 10 available, and in this book, we focus only on the Windows 10 Pro and Windows 10 Enterprise editions. That being said, there are other editions of Windows 10 that may be of interest to you.

A machine installed with Windows 10 Enterprise.

Windows 10 Home

Windows 10 Home is the consumer-focused desktop edition, meaning probably not for you. It's the Windows version your grandmother will buy, well unless she works in IT, too. ☺

Windows 10 Mobile

Then there is the Windows 10 Mobile edition, the version to be used on smaller, mobile, touch-centric devices like smartphones and small tablets, also called *phablets*. They are like big phones, but in general are used for playing videos, checking email, and so forth.

Windows 10 Pro

The Pro version is the desktop edition for PCs, larger tablets, and 2-in-1s. This one may look like the Windows 10 Home version, but has additional business features, like joining legacy Active Directory domains.

Windows 10 Enterprise

Windows 10 Enterprise is the version we recommend for organizations. It builds on Windows 10 Pro, adding more security features and management capabilities. As with prior versions of Windows, active Software Assurance customers in volume licensing can upgrade to Windows 10 Enterprise as part of their existing Software Assurance benefits.

In Windows 10 Enterprise, you also get access to features like AppLocker, DirectAccess, Windows To Go, and more.

Windows 10 Enterprise LTSB

Windows 10 Enterprise also comes in a Long Time Servicing Branch (LTSB) edition, which is intended for mission-critical machines like hospital equipment or rocket launchers. This version does not receive updates (new features) as often as the normal Windows 10 Enterprise and also is missing native universal applications, Microsoft Edge, and access to the Microsoft Store. This is not the version to deploy for normal machines in your organization.

Windows 10 Mobile Enterprise

Like the Enterprise version of windows, Mobile Enterprise adds productivity, security, and mobile device management features, but obviously is for phones and small tablets. This edition is available to volume licensing customers.

Windows 10 Education

Windows 10 Education has the same feature set as Windows 10 Enterprise. It's just licensed differently and, as the name implies, targeted for educational organizations.

Windows 10 IoT

This edition is a very small version of Windows 10, intended for devices such as robot vacuum cleaners, controller devices, or any industrial application where you need a small and very cheap computer. This edition is used for devices like the $35 dollar Raspberry Pi 2 computer and has a very small footprint.

Windows as a Service

With Windows 10, Microsoft is changing to a Windows as a Service model. What this means is that Microsoft provides not only security updates on a regular basis, but also new features every once in a while. These new features releases, commonly referred to as service releases, will be released 2–3 times per year for the "normal" Windows 10 editions, and less frequently for the Windows 10 Enterprise LTSB version. The exact frequency for the LTSB editions are not yet known, but from what we've heard, you can expect yearly updates, rather than almost quarterly updates for the other Windows 10 editions.

The new service model also changes how updates are released and tested compared with previous releases of Windows. Updates for Windows 10 (and Office 2016) are released in a ring-based approach.

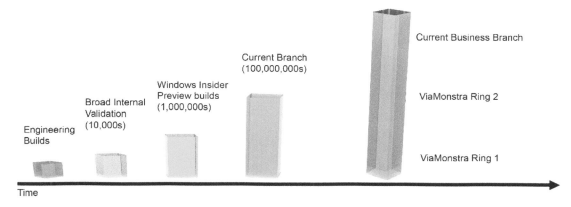

Timeline of Windows as a Service and the numbers for testers for each step.

When using a ring-based approach, as with Windows 10, you get the following timeline for how updates are tested and released:

1. Updates are created and released internally within Microsoft for initial testing.

2. After the initial, engineering build release, the updates are delivered for a broad validation, still inside Microsoft. Updates are being tested by tens of thousands of people at this point.

3. After that, the updates goes out to the people signed up for the Microsoft Insider Preview program, meaning the updates are now being tested by the millions of insiders.

4. When the insider tests are done, the updates becomes available for organizations and users with Windows 10 configured for the current branch (CB), that is, with system not configured to defer updates.

5. Finally, the updates reach the users and organizations that are following the current business branch (CBB), that is, have configured their environments to defer updates. Within the current business branch, organizations typically deploy updates in waves, or rings, starting with smaller pilots and then expanding after the pilot tests have been successful.

Real World Note: Because most organizations are using either WSUS or ConfigMgr to release updates internally, the actual release cycles of the updates are not the same as the updates actually being installed. When using WSUS or ConfigMgr, an administrator must still approve the updates before machines get it. Obviously, updates are not available for approval until released.

Windows Store for Business

In November 2015, the new Windows Store for Business was launched, adding support for bulk application acquisition as well as a private store. Microsoft also added flexible distribution options for distributing content and applications to your Windows 10 devices.

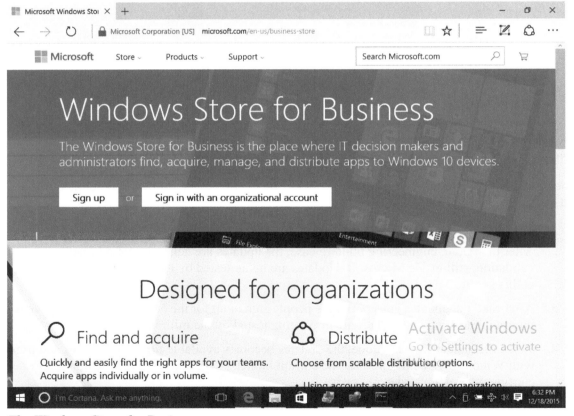

The Windows Store for Business.

Windows Update for Business

As with the Windows Store for Business, Windows Update for Business also was released in November 2015, together with the Windows 10 v.1511 release. Using group policies, you can control deployment and validation groups, also known as *update rings*. This feature also uses the peer-to-peer delivery built into Windows 10 to make bandwidth usage efficient.

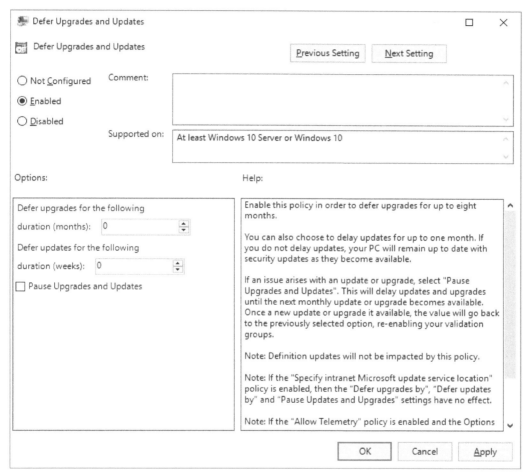

The updated Defer Upgrades and Updates settings for Windows Update for Business.

New or Improved OS Functions

Covering all the changes in Windows 10 would require a complete book of its own, but here is a summary of the most important changes.

User Interface Changes

In addition to the obvious Start menu in Windows 10, we highlight some of the user interface changes in Windows 10.

Start Menu

You cannot miss the new Start menu in Windows 10, which you can resize and customize. Like the Windows 8 and 8.1 Start menu, it also can be customized during deployment and via group policy (Windows 10 Enterprise and Education editions).

Action Center (Notifications)

In the Windows 10 system tray, you find a shortcut to the Action Center, also called Notification Center. It is a convenient collection of shortcuts not only for notification messages, but also for shortcuts to Tablet Mode (full screen), network connections, and other settings.

Settings

In Windows 10, if you open the old control panel, you see that most settings are gone. They are instead moved to Settings, or PC Settings as it was in Windows 8.1 and earlier builds of Windows 10.

You also will notice that many of the configuration wizards have changed, as well. As an example, if you select to join Windows 10 to a legacy Active Directory domain, you see that the wizard is quite different from the one in previous versions of Windows. You type mostly the same information, but you still can't control much from here. Therefore, we recommend using PowerShell when you can because it gives you more control, like selecting what OU in Active Directory to put the machine into.

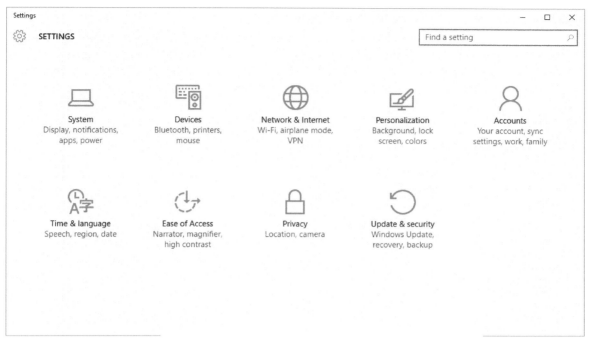

Settings in Windows 10.

Universal Applications

The Windows 10 platform enables a new class of applications, *universal applications*. These are applications intended to be written only once, with one set of business logic, but still work on the various device form factors that are available. You also find several universal applications built into Windows 10, like Calculator (except for the Windows 10 Enterprise LTSB edition in which it is still the old calculator).

A universal application looks like any other desktop application in Windows 10, can run in a window, and is installed and updated via the Microsoft Store.

Windows Management and Virtual Desktops

In Windows 10, there are more keyboard shortcuts than ever. Some of them you can use to control Windows behavior, as well as virtual desktops, which is a feature that allows you to have multiple instances of Windows running on a separate (virtual) desktop.

You still have the classic Alt + Tab to switch between applications in the current desktop, but there is also Windows logo key + Tab, which gives you both access to the task view as well as access to virtual desktops. You can also the following shortcuts:

- **Windows logo key + Ctrl + Left/Right.** Toggle between virtual desktops
- **Windows logo key + Ctrl + D.** Create a new virtual desktop
- **Windows logo key + Ctrl + F4.** Close the current virtual desktop

Console Changes (Command and PowerShell)

In Windows 10, you find more changes to the various consoles than the past ten years combined. For example, you can use shortcuts to copy and paste (Ctrl + C and Ctrl + V), set transparency, resize the window, have the text flow, search, and select by column. These changes are both for the Command prompt as well as for the PowerShell prompt.

Some of the new console options in Windows 10.

Cortana

Then, of course, you find Cortana, your built-in Windows 10 personal assistant.

Security Enhancements

Security is a core tenant in Windows 10, with protection against modern security threats. Quite frankly, there has never been a time during which securing an operating system was more important than it is now.

Microsoft Passport

Microsoft Passport can be used to replace passwords with strong two-factor authentication that consists of an enrolled device and Windows Hello (biometric) or PIN.

Windows Hello

Windows Hello is biometric authentication that lets you unlock your Windows 10 device with your fingerprint, iris, or face. The fine print states that Windows Hello requires specialized hardware such as Intel's RealSense 3D camera.

Health Attestation Service

This is a feature that came with Windows 8.1 but is improved vastly in Windows 10. This is a feature that allows Windows 10 to perform a health and send the results to the cloud before gaining access to internal resources. This checks features like SecureBoot, DEP, BitLocker, AV status, patch level, and so on. For more details, see the information on MSDN: https://msdn.microsoft.com/en-us/library/windows/hardware/dn934876%28v=vs.85%29.aspx.

Virtual Secure Mode (VSM)

We're guessing that most of you have heard about passing-the-hash attacks and the tool Mimikatz. NT LAN Manager (NTLM) has known security issues that allow some fortunate ones to get access to an NTLM hash of an administrator account. When a hacker has access to this hash, well, the hacker can use the hash to access resources that administrator account has access to.

In Windows 10, Microsoft did something pretty cool. VSM can isolate the Local Security Authority (LSA), used to authenticate and log users on to the local system, within a virtual machine running a core OS subset on Hyper-V. This means that a regular Windows user is not able to gain access to the hash of a user because they aren't allowed to communicate with LSA.

Device Guard

Device Guard works pretty much like AppLocker, but is actually a hardware-assisted application locker that allows only signed applications to run on a system. This feature is in Windows Enterprise only and requires UEFI and virtualization support in BIOS (Intel VT-X or AMD-V).

Also, with Device Guard, the kernel is running in Virtual Secure Mode.

Hyper-V in Windows 10

Another feature in Windows 10 that has improved quite a bit is Hyper-V. You will find a lot of nice enhancements in this release.

Integration Services Updated Through Windows Update

First, with Windows 10 Hyper-V, Microsoft provides virtual machine driver updates via Windows Update. That means you now don't need to have the VM integration services match the host version. You simply need the latest version of the integration services.

Secure Boot for Linux

Microsoft is pushing hard to bring more and more support for Linux operating systems, such as dynamic memory and other features. With Hyper-V vNext, Microsoft provides Secure Boot support for Linux that works with Ubuntu 14.04 (and later) and SUSE Linux Enterprise Server 12.

Hot-Adding NICs and Memory

Windows 10 allows for hot addition and removal of network adapters and memory in Hyper-V. For adding memory on the fly, the virtual machine has to be a generation 2 VM and the Hyper-V host must be running Windows 10 (or Windows Server 2016).

Virtual Network Adapter Identification

This feature allows you to name a network adapter when adding it on the Hyper-V host, and you can then pick up that name, using PowerShell for example, inside the virtual machine.

Production Checkpoints

Production checkpoints allow you to easily create "point-in-time" images of a virtual machine. The change, compared with the old saved states, is that these production checkpoints can be restored later on in a way that is completely supported for all production workloads.

For production checkpoints, the Volume Snapshot Service (VSS) is used inside Windows virtual machines. And if you are using Linux virtual machines, they will flush their file system buffers to create a file system-consistent checkpoint.

Support for Alternate Credentials

When connecting to other Hyper-V hosts, you now can specify credentials.

PowerShell Direct

PowerShell Direct is a new feature to Windows Management Framework version 5 that enables Windows hosts to run PowerShell commands against a Hyper-V guest. Think of this as PowerShell remoting without having to enable remoting on the guest operating system. Your guest doesn't have to configure the firewall to permit remoting. You don't even need a network card.

Connected Standby

Also, we did not list it here, but in Windows 10, Hyper-V is compatible with Connected Standby When the Hyper-V role is enabled on a computer that uses the Always On/Always Connected (AOAC) power model, the Connected Standby power state is now available and works as expected.

Nested Virtual Machines

Because Windows 10 is Windows as a Service, some of the new features have already been deployed to the Windows Insider program. One of the new features is the ability to run Hyper-V in Hyper-V, i.e. nested virtual machines (from Windows 10 build 10565). We think that is pretty cool.

Chapter 5

Deploying Office 2016

Microsoft Office 2016 was released on September 22, 2016, and is now available both as a standalone MSI deployment and via the Office 365 offerings. In this chapter, you get a crash course in how the Office 2016 deployment via Office 365 process works. This information serves as a foundation for adding Office 2016 to the Windows 10 reference image, which you do in Chapter 8.

Using the Office 2016 Deployment Tool

The Office 2016 Deployment Tool allows you to customize and manage Office 2016 Click-to-Run deployments. This includes configuring installation sources, product and language combinations, and also deployment configuration options for Office Click-to-Run.

After you download the Office 2016 Deployment Tool, running it extracts two files to a folder you specify. The download link is https://www.microsoft.com/en-us/download/details.aspx?id=49117.

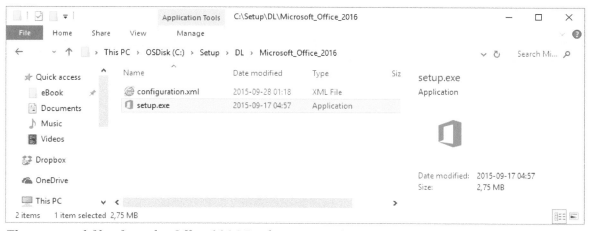

The extracted files from the Office 2016 Deployment Tool.

Configuration Files

Office 2016 uses two configuration files: one to download Office 2016, and one to install or configure Office. In the Office 2016 Deployment Tool download, you already get a sample configuration file, which you need to modify; however, you need to start by creating a download XML file that is used to download or update the installation source with the latest version of Office 2016.

Real World Note: You can find a reference for the Click-to-Run configuration.xml file on TechNet: https://technet.microsoft.com/en-us/library/jj219426.aspx.

The following is a sample download XML file for the x86 edition of Office 2016 (Click-to-Run). In this example, we changed the branch from the default current branch for business plan (the default plan for Office 365 Pro Plus subscribers) to current branch.

```
<Configuration>
 <Add SourcePath="C:\Setup\DL\Microsoft_Office_2016"
OfficeClientEdition="32" Branch="Current" >
   <Product ID="O365ProPlusRetail">
     <Language ID="en-us" />
   </Product>
   <Product ID="VisioProRetail">
     <Language ID="en-us" />
   </Product>
 </Add>
</Configuration>
```

Download Office 2016

Once you have created the download.xml file, to download the latest version of Office 2016, you simply run the following command:

```
C:\Setup\DL\Microsoft_Office_2016\Setup.exe /download
C:\Setup\DL\Microsoft_Office_2016\download.xml
```

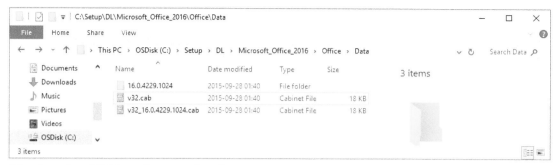

The download folder after running Setup.exe.

Install Office 2016

When Office 2016 is downloaded, you need to modify the configuration XML file, which you use to actually install Office 2016. Below you find a sample configuration XML file for the x86 edition of Office 2016 (Click-to-Run).

```
<Configuration>
 <Add SourcePath="C:\Minint\O365Inst" OfficeClientEdition="32"
Branch="Current" >
   <Product ID="O365ProPlusRetail">
     <Language ID="en-us" />
   </Product>
   <Product ID="VisioProRetail">
     <Language ID="en-us" />
   </Product>
 </Add>
 <Updates Enabled="TRUE" Branch="Current"/>
 <Display Level="None" AcceptEULA="TRUE" />
 <Logging Level="Standard" Path="%temp%" />
 <Property Name="AUTOACTIVATE" Value="1" />
</Configuration>
```

After the configuration file is modified, you simply run the following command:

```
Setup.exe /configure configuration.xml
```

Chapter 6
Using PowerShell

Throughout the various guides in this book, you use quite a few PowerShell scripts. If you are new into PowerShell, we highly recommend reading through this chapter which covers the core PowerShell basics used in this book.

> **Note:** This chapter is not a complete reference guide to PowerShell 5.0 (preview), which is the version used in Windows 10. It is closer to the "super-quick crash course" that will get you into a state where you can use PowerShell without banging your head against the keyboard (or wall) too many times. ☺

Get-Help, Update-Help, and Online Help

The very first PowerShell cmdlet every IT administrator should learn is Get-Help. The Get-Help cmdlet works exactly like it sounds: it gives you help information about cmdlets. For example, if you want to know how the Get-WmiObject cmdlet works, you can type:

```
Get-Help -Name Get-WmiObject
```

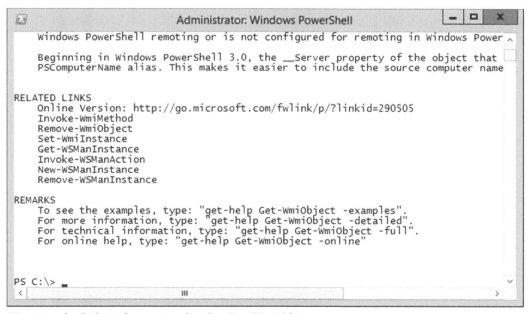

Viewing the help information for the Get-WmiObject.

Real World Note: The first time you run Get-Help on a new server, it wants to download/update the help documentation. To avoid this, you can make a habit of always running Update-Help when you deploy a new server.

Updating the Documentation

The Update-Help cmdlet makes sure your help documentation is downloaded and up to date. To update the documentation, you simply run the cmdlet as-is:

```
Update-Help
```

Enhanced Online Help

Enhanced online help is another very nice feature. Let's assume that you prefer to read about a certain command on TechNet. Well, that's an easy thing to do. This command fires up Internet Explorer and connects you to the help page at TechNet:

```
Get-Help Get-WmiObject -Online
```

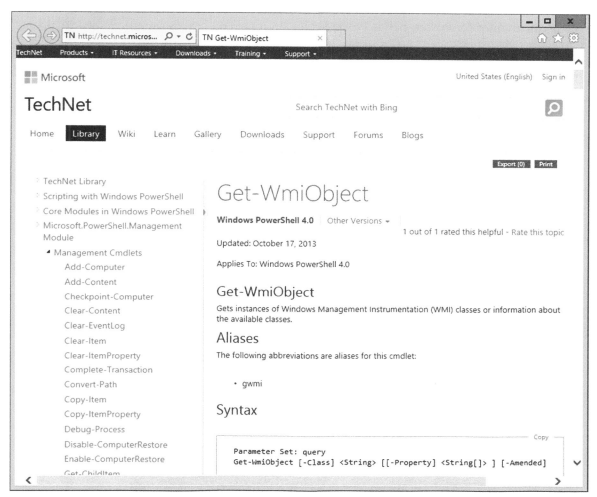

Running Get-Help Get-WmiObject -Online.

PowerShell ISE

The premier editor for PowerShell is PowerShell ISE. It has IntelliSense, auto-complete, snippets, help access, the works.

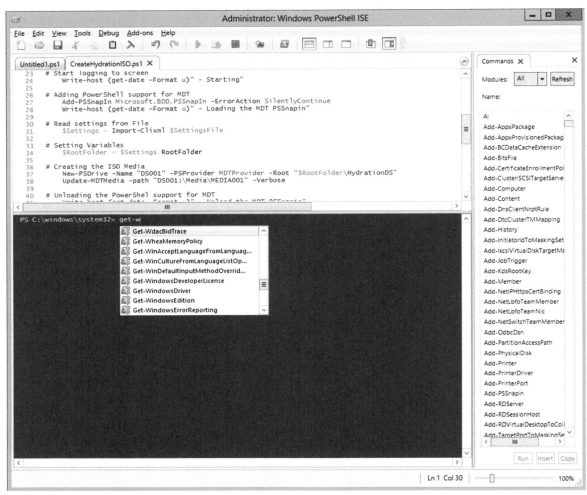

ISE showing IntelliSense.

Showing Commands

Another cool feature in PowerShell is the ability to graphically display cmdlets, or options for the cmdlets, using the Show-Command cmdlet:

```
Show-Command
```

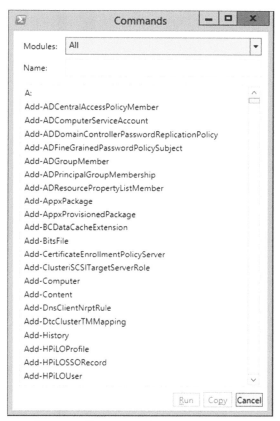

Displaying all commands.

Or why not display the available options for a single cmdlet?

```
Show-Command New-NetIPaddress
```

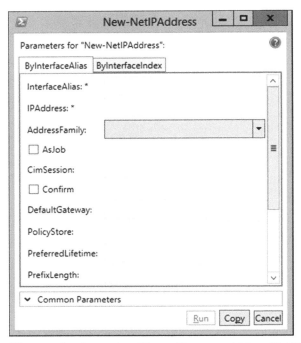

The result of running Show-Command New-NetIPaddress.

Verbose Output

When running commands, you often can get verbose output by simply adding the -Verbose switch to the command. We say "often" because not all cmdlets give you additional output. It depends on how the cmdlet is written, but many commands do give you additional detail.

```
PS C:\> Remove-Item C:\Setup\ISO -Verbose
VERBOSE: Performing the operation "Remove Directory" on target "C:\Setup\ISO".
PS C:\>
```

Verbose output from the Remove-Item cmdlet.

Get – Filter – Set!

Let's start with a common scenario: You need to change, add, or remove a setting on all items that match a specific criterion. It could be something like changing the DNS client setting on all servers that are located on a network, or it could be adding a component to a list of Windows Server 2012 R2 servers, restarting all servers that are in a "restart pending" mode, or ejecting a mounted ISO from a set of VMs.

In PowerShell, Get/Filter/Set operations translate to using Get- cmdlets to find items, maybe use the -Filter function to further filter the result, and finally use Set- cmdlets to do a configuration. Please note that this is not always the case because PowerShell uses many different verbs for similar operations.

Get!

Most Get- cmdlets work the same way. If you don't specify a name, the cmdlet gives you all items in that location. So here are some examples:

> **Note:** Remember that most server configuration operations require that you run the PowerShell prompt elevated.

- Show all the network adapters:

  ```
  Get-NetAdapter
  ```

- Show all virtual machines:

  ```
  Get-VM
  ```

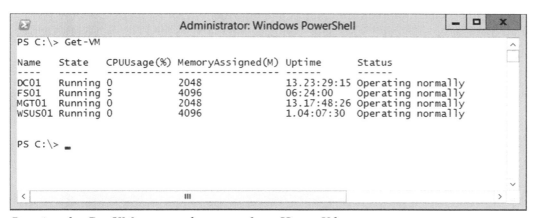

Running the Get-VM command on one of our Hyper-V hosts.

- Show the content in the file C:\Setup\Scripts\AddReversDNSZone.txt:

  ```
  Get-Content C:\Setup\Scripts\AddReversDNSZone.txt
  ```

- Show the WMI information in WIN32_ComputerSystem:

  ```
  Get-WmiObject -Class:Win32_ComputerSystem
  ```

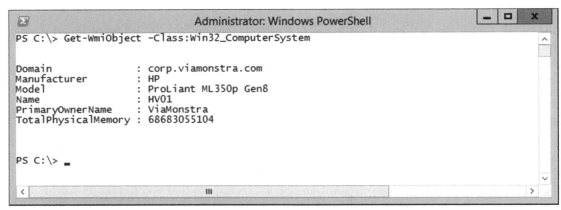

Data returned from Get-WmiObject Win32_ComputerSystem.

The information that is shown to you is not everything that is retrieved. It is just part of the object, so let's bring the rest into view by adding | Select-Object * at the end:

```
Get-WmiObject -Class:Win32_ComputerSystem | Select-Object *
```

It is also possible to execute multiple Get- cmdlets and pipe them in a chain. Let's assume you need to see all MAC addresses in all VMs. Get-VM gets you the VMs, and Get-NetWorkAdapter gets you information regarding MAC addresses. This gives you the answer:

```
Get-VM | Get-VMNetworkAdapter
```

With the new output format Out-GridView, you get a really good view of the data, and you can even sort and filter data with it. Add | Out-GridView at the end, and you get this:

```
Get-VM | Get-VMNetworkAdapter | Out-GridView
```

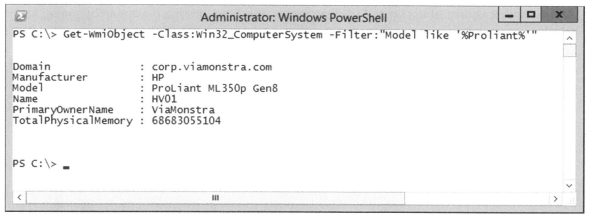

Running the Get-VM | Out-GridView command on one of our Hyper-V hosts.

Filter!

There are two basic ways to filter data. First, you can use a built-in -Filter function in the cmdlet (if it has one). In general, if the cmdlet you are using has a -Filter function, we recommend using it because it is easy and fast. Here is an example with a cmdlet (Get-WmiObject) that has the -Filter function:

```
Get-WmiObject -Class:Win32_ComputerSystem -Filter:"Model like
'%Proliant%'"
```

```
PS C:\> Get-WmiObject -Class:Win32_ComputerSystem -Filter:"Model like '%Proliant%'"


Domain               : corp.viamonstra.com
Manufacturer         : HP
Model                : ProLiant ML350p Gen8
Name                 : HV01
PrimaryOwnerName     : ViaMonstra
TotalPhysicalMemory  : 68683055104


PS C:\> _
```

Filtering the Get-WmiObject command.

In some cases, the cmdlet does not have the -Filter function, and that leads us to the second option, which is to pipe all data from the Get- cmdlet into another cmdlet, such as the Where-Object cmdlet. To pipe the output to another cmdlet, you use any of the PowerShell cmdlets that can refine your output. There is a bunch of them, but the most commonly used ones for filtering are Where-Object, Select-Object, Select-String, and ForEach-Object. Here is an example with Where-Object:

```
Get-VM | Where-Object {$_.State -eq 'Running'}
```

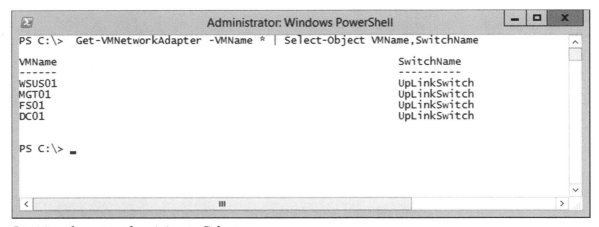

Filtering using Where-Object.

Here is another variant of the second filtering option, this time limiting the output by piping to Select:

```
Get-VMNetworkAdapter -VMName * | Select-Object VMName, SwitchName
```

Limiting the output by piping to Select.

New and Set

The New- cmdlets allow you to create items, and the Set- cmdlets allow you to configure settings on items. Because you now know how to use Get-, it's rather easy to configure items.

- Creating a new VM:

  ```
  New-VM MDT01 -Path D:\VMs
  ```

- Changing the name of a VM:

  ```
  Set-VM MDT01 -NewVMName MDT02
  ```

- Combining Get- and Set- to configure a VM's memory settings (the command is wrapped and should be one line):

  ```
  Get-VM -Name MDT01 | Set-VM -StaticMemory
  -MemoryStartupBytes 4GB
  ```

Variables

When creating scripts, it is useful to use variables. In PowerShell, you also can use them interactively, which saves a lot of typing. By using variables, you can put a long Get- command in one simple variable. The cool thing with variables is that the item you have in your variable is not just an item; it also is the complete object. You can see that by adding a trailing "." to the end of the variable and then using the Tab key to browse through all the properties behind the object.

In this example, we assigned the $MyVM variable to a VM named MGT01 and then typed $MyVM + Tab to find all available properties:

```
$MyVM = Get-VM -VMName MDT01
$MyVM.MemoryStartup
```

Setting and using the custom $MyVM variable in PowerShell.

String Quoting and Escape Sequences

When variables are used in this book, you sometimes see single quotation marks used, sometimes double quotation marks, and sometimes combinations of them with escape sequences. So, what's the difference? Well, both kinds of quotation marks, or "quotes," are used to delimit string values, and for most scenarios, we recommend using single quotes. But let us explain when to use which.

Using Single Quotes

For most commands, PowerShell does a pretty good job of figuring out the type of a value. For example, with the following command, PowerShell thinks "ViaMonstra" is a string based on the content and its position in the command:

```
Write-Output -InputObject ViaMonstra
```

But if you add another word, like "Datacenter" in the following example, then PowerShell gets confused and does not correctly detect "Datacenter" as belonging together with "ViaMonstra". As a result, PowerShell throws an error.

```
Write-Output -InputObject ViaMonstra Datacenter
```

To avoid problems with type detection, you can tell PowerShell that ViaMonstra Datacenter is a string by adding single quotes around it, like this:

```
Write-Output -InputObject 'ViaMonstra Datacenter'
```

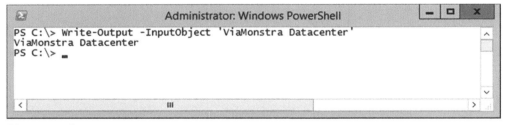

Using single quotes.

Single quotes display the text in between them literally, even if you are using a variable, like $MyData:

```
$MyData = 'is king!'
Write-Output -InputObject 'ViaMonstra Datacenter $MyData'
```

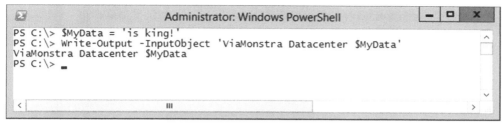

Single quotes making PowerShell display the text literally.

Using Double Quotes

What if you want to display the value of $MyData instead of the variable name? That's a job for double quotes:

```
$MyData = "is king!"
Write-Output -InputObject "ViaMonstra Datacenter $MyData"
```

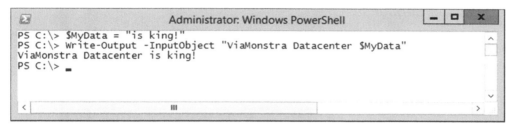

Displaying the variable's value.

Another situation in which double quotes are useful is when you need to delimit a string within the string, like this:

```
$SQLQuery = "SELECT * FROM ComputerSettings WHERE OSDComputerName
LIKE '%MDT%'"
```

Using Escapes

Another technique you can use is the *escape*, a back quote (`). The escape forces PowerShell to treat the following character literally, as opposed to interpreting it in any way. For example:

```
$DiskType = 'SSD'
Write-Output -InputObject "Our new $DiskType disk was `$1000"
```

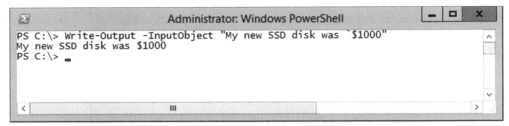

Using an escape to force PowerShell to treat the $ character literally.

Another example in which the escape character is useful is when dealing with drive letters. PowerShell really doesn't like it if you use a colon (:) in a string unless you use an escape character:

```
$DriveLetter = 'D'
Write-Host "Drive letter is $DriveLetter`:"
```

Using Special Escape Sequences

A following list provides examples of using a back quote escape together with another character to represent a special character that cannot otherwise be represented in a string.

- `n. New line
- `r. Carriage return
- `t. Tab
- `a. Alert
- `b. Backspace
- `". Double quote
- `'. Single quote
- ``. Back quote
- `0. Null

Here is an example:

```
Write-Host "First line. `nSecond line."
```

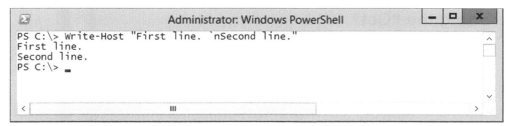

Combining double quotes and a special escape sequence.

Set-ExecutionPolicy and Get-ExecutionPolicy

To control the level of security surrounding PowerShell scripts, you use the Set-ExecutionPolicy cmdlet. You also can use the Get-ExecutionPolicy cmdlet to read the current setting on a server. In Windows Server 2012 R2, there are six options:

- **Restricted.** The default execution policy. Scripts are not allowed to run, but you can run commands interactively.

- **All Signed.** Only scripts that are signed by a trusted publisher are allowed to run.

- **Remote Signed.** Scripts that are created locally are allowed to run. Scripts created remotely are allowed to run only if they are signed by a trusted publisher.

- **Unrestricted.** Allows all scripts to run. If you run an unsigned script that was downloaded from the Internet, however, you are prompted for permission before it runs.

- **Bypass.** Allows all scripts to run, and there are no warnings or prompts.

- **Undefined.** Removes the currently assigned execution policy from the current scope (unless set in a group policy).

Building Blocks to Create Great Scripts

When using PowerShell, you quickly realize that creating a collection of useful scripts is very handy, and with the repository you get with the book sample files, you are off to a very good start.

That being said, when you start writing your own scripts, there are a few building blocks that will help you create better scripts.

Step One: Doing the "Get"

You already learned the basics of the Get- cmdlet earlier in this chapter, and using Get- is a safe and very practical way to start using PowerShell. In the following snippet, you find some additional examples based on the Get-VM cmdlet. The first line gets all VMs; the second line lists all VMs that are turned off; and the third line does the same thing but also starts all of them.

```
Get-VM
Get-VM | Where-Object -Property State -EQ -Value "Off"
Get-VM | Where-Object -Property State -EQ -Value "Off" | Start-VM
```

Step Two: Using Parameters as Input in Your Script

The Param block can be used to make a script act like a cmdlet. We will present some questions that we then "convert" into variables that can be used in the script.

> **Note:** The Param block needs to be at the beginning of the script to work.

In the next example, you learn to use a few different Param blocks, with different conditions and validation settings:

```
Param(
[Parameter(Mandatory=$True,HelpMessage="First Name")]
[ValidateLength(3,20)]
$FirstName,

[Parameter(Mandatory=$True,HelpMessage="Last Name")]
[ValidateLength(3,20)]
$LastName,

[Parameter(Mandatory=$False,HelpMessage="Department")]
[ValidateSet("Sales","Store","Management")]
$Department = "Store"
)

$FirstName
$LastName
$Department
```

The first parameter asks for the name. It's a mandatory parameter (required), and the name needs to be at least 3 characters long but no longer than 20 characters.

The second parameter is the same, but that will be stored in the $LastName variable instead of in the $FirstName variable.

The third parameter is a bit different. First, it is optional; second, it has a default value; and third, it allows only Sales, Store, or Management as valid options. Because we do that, we also can tab choose values on the command line when we run the script, which is very nice.

Step Three: Ifs and Buts

This step is basically the same as the preceding one, but we add "If" and "Switch" blocks. In the following example, the "If" block checks whether you work in Sales, and the "Switch" block checks all the different countries for various pieces of information. In general, if you need a single exclusion, we recommend using an "If" block; but if you need to check multiple settings, the "Switch" block is a better option.

```
Param(
[Parameter(Mandatory=$True,HelpMessage="First Name")]
[ValidateLength(3,20)]
$FirstName,

[Parameter(Mandatory=$True,HelpMessage="Last Name")]
[ValidateLength(3,20)]
$LastName,

[Parameter(Mandatory=$True,HelpMessage="Department")]
[ValidateSet("Sales","Store","Management")]
$Department,

[Parameter(Mandatory=$True,HelpMessage="Department")]
[ValidateSet("Sweden","Norway","Finland")]
$Country
)

$FirstName
$LastName
$Department

If($Department -like "Sales")
    {
        Write-Host "Sales is fun"
    }
Else
    {
        Write-Host "You are working in $Department"
    }

Switch($Country)
{
```

```
Sweden
    {
        Write-Host "Contact Johan for salary discussions"
    }
Norway
    {
        Write-Host "Contact Harold for salary discussions"
    }
Finland
    {
        Write-Host "Contact Linus for salary discussions"
    }
Default
    {
        Write-Host "Epic fail..."
        Break
    }
}
```

Step Four: Reading Data from an XML File Instead of Typing Everything

Even though it's nice to have all the details on the command line and use Param, you will soon find that it gets quite boring typing 192.168.1.1 as the default gateway every time you build a new VM using PowerShell. To avoid that, you can store commonly used parameters in an XML file and read in the data like this:

```
$SettingsFile = ".\XMLSettings.xml"
[xml]$Settings = Get-Content $SettingsFile -Verbose

$name = $Settings.Settings.Defaults.Name
Write-Host $Name
```

From the file that looks like this:

```
<Settings>
<Defaults>
  <Name>Frank</Name>
</Defaults>
</Settings>
```

Step Five: Where Am I?

Writing scripts is great fun, but after a while you realize that hardcoding the location is a bad practice, especially when you need to move the script and the data with it somewhere else.

To find the location from where you are running the script, you can use the built-in variable $MyInvocation and then Split-Path. See this example:

```
$CurrentPath = $MyInvocation.MyCommand.Path | Split-Path -Parent
Write-Host "Running this from $ CurrentPath"

$ScriptName = $MyInvocation.MyCommand.Path | Split-Path -Leaf
Write-Host "I can feel my name is… $ScriptName"
```

Running Executables in PowerShell

From time to time you need to call other executables in your PowerShell scripts, and if you have never done it before, it can be a bit challenging. For example, if you are used to old school batch files, you know you could simply run:

```
C:\Downloads\Setup.exe
```

Or if the path has spaces in it, you put it in quotes, like this:

```
"C:\Program Files\Internet Explorer\iexplore.exe"
```

The problem is that PowerShell won't like that one bit. Instead you either have to lead in with an "&" or use Invoke-Item cmdlet. This means that either of these commands works:

```
& "C:\Program Files\Internet Explorer\iexplore.exe"

Invoke-Item "C:\Program Files\Internet Explorer\iexplore.exe"
```

The preceding also works with parameters. For example:

```
Invoke-Item "C:\Program Files\Internet Explorer\iexplore.exe"
http://viamonstra.com
```

Or, with multiple parameters (open viamonstra.com in InPrivate mode):

```
Invoke-Item "C:\Program Files\Internet Explorer\iexplore.exe"
http://viamonstra.com -private
```

You also can use the Start-Process cmdlet. One of the cool things about Start-Process is that you can use parameters to specify options, such as loading a user profile, starting the process in a new window, or using alternate credentials. Here is an example that starts Notepad, maximizes the window, and waits until you close Notepad:

```
Start-Process Notepad -Wait -WindowStyle Maximized
```

Another (technical) option is to use Invoke-Expression, but generally you want to avoid that. Invoke-Expression is useful for some scenarios, such as creating new scripts at runtime, but for running other executables, we don't recommend using it.

Using Write-Host (or Not)

During the last months of 2013, there was a somewhat big discussion going on whether you should use Write-Host, Write-OutPut, Write-Verbose, or any of the other cmdlets when displaying data in your scripts. It all started when Jeffrey Snover, the original architect behind PowerShell, issued a statement on his blog (http://www.jsnover.com/blog). The statement was the following:

Using Write-Host is almost always wrong.

Then the post continued on and explained why it is that way. The shorthand version is that using Write-Host in scripts interferes with automation, such as when you have multiple scripts that are used together for a large task.

Jeffrey continued to say that the correct cmdlet to use is Write-Output or Write-Verbose. Write-Output is useful to convey the results because Write-Output displays the results to the screen when you run your script by itself; but, it also allows your script to be used in a pipeline (or foreach loop) and have the results used by other scripts/cmdlets. Write-Verbose is useful for conveying comforting information to the user.

That being said, we believe that Write-Host is not all bad. It's faster and simpler to use, and it can be very useful when creating small scripts not intended for automation, like temporary scripts, or when you want to generate a user experience (UX) for the user running the script. Write-Host does have the ability to colorize text.

Support for Windows PE

Okay, we just have to mention support for Windows PE. It's not really new in Windows 10 because PowerShell has been available for Windows PE (WinPE) since version 4.0, but still, it's both cool and useful to have the support for PowerShell in WinPE. For example, when deploying servers, it's much easier to add code for dealing with hardware or the operating system compared with using VBScript. Assume you would like to know more about the hardware. Just fire up PowerShell and type:

```
Get-WmiObject -Class:Win32_ComputerSystem
```

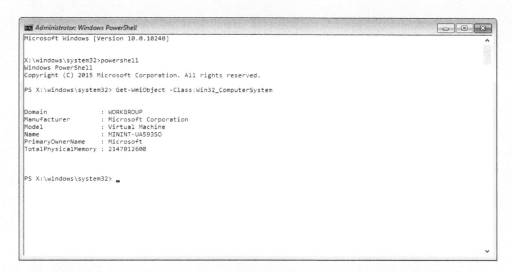

Running PowerShell commands in Windows PE.

Chapter 7

Preparing Your Infrastructure for OS Deployment

In the Chapter 1, you learned about the ViaMonstra environment. It is now time to start preparing the infrastructure. In this chapter, you learn about configuring the legacy Active Directory and why it's still important, as well as the following step-by-step configurations:

- Create service accounts, groups, and sample users
- Install Volume Activation Services
- Configure Active Directory permissions
- Update your ADMX files
- Preparation for BitLocker and Virtual Secure Mode
- Prepare the MDT01 server and WSUS01 server

Step-by-Step Guide Requirements

If you want to run the step-by-step guides in this chapter, you need a lab environment configured as outlined in Chapter 1 and Appendix A. In this chapter, you use the following virtual machines:

DC01   WSUS01   MDT01

The VMs used in this chapter.

> **Note:** You also need to have downloaded the setup files and book sample files, as outlined in Appendix A. This files will be used in the various guides in this and later chapters.

Why Do You Need a Legacy Active Directory?

Active Directory is needed for quite a few things in a modern datacenter; basically, it is the central repository for identity and access control. Many of the features in Windows 10 require Active Directory, and having Active Directory also helps manage the environment more easily. A commonly used feature is Group Policy to configure machines and users centrally, and you can use Active Directory as a way to have a trusted connection when using remote PowerShell. But there is new functionality in Windows 10 that could lead you to have Azure Active Directory instead or a hybrid solution. Let's say that you work for an education organization and have 1,000 staff users and 10,000 students. In this case, you could have all student computers joined into Azure Active Directory, managed using Windows 10's built-in Mobile Device Management Agent, and the staff being managed by on-premise resources. It is possible to manage Windows 10 in so many new ways, so because you managed computers one way "back in the days" does not mean it should still be that way.

Create the Service Accounts

ViaMonstra uses a role-based model for configuring permissions for its various service accounts. It's now time to create the service and administrator accounts that the ViaMonstra infrastructure needs. In this guide, we assume you have copied the book sample files to C:\Setup on DC01.

> **Real World Note:** As you learned in Appendix A, in addition to copying the downloaded files over the network to the various servers used in this book, or via RDP (slow), one easy way to copy setup or sample files to a virtual machine is simply to mount the ISO file on the virtual machine. To create an ISO file of the downloaded setup files, you can open a Deployment and Imaging Tools Environment prompt and run the following command to create an ISO file: oscdimg.exe -u2 C:\Setup C:\ISO\SetupFiles.iso.

1. On **DC01**, log on as **Administrator** in the **VIAMONSTRA** domain using a password of **P@ssw0rd**, and open an elevated **PowerShell prompt**.

2. Create the **MDT Build Account** by running the following command (the command is wrapped and should be one line):

    ```
    C:\Setup\Scripts\New-VIAServiceAccount.ps1 -AccountName
    MDT_BA -AccountDescription "MDT Build Account"
    -AccountType ServiceAccount -Password "P@ssw0rd"
    ```

3. Create the **MDT Join Account** by running the following command (the command is wrapped and should be one line):

    ```
    C:\Setup\Scripts\New-VIAServiceAccount.ps1 -AccountName
    MDT_JD -AccountDescription "MDT Join Domain Account"
    -AccountType ServiceAccount -Password "P@ssw0rd"
    ```

4. Verify the configuration via PowerShell by running the following command:

    ```
    Get-ADUser -Filter 'Name -like "*MDT*"'
    ```

Result after running Get-ADUser.

Create the Sample Users

As in any real environment, you need a few users. To do this, you use a PowerShell script that reads a .csv file to create some sample users:

1. On **DC01**, open an elevated **PowerShell prompt**.

2. Create the ViaMonstra users by running the following command (the command is wrapped and should be one line):

```
C:\setup\Scripts\Set-VIAADDSAccounts.ps1 –BaseOU
"ViaMonstra" -SettingsFile C:\Setup\Settings\Settings.xml
```

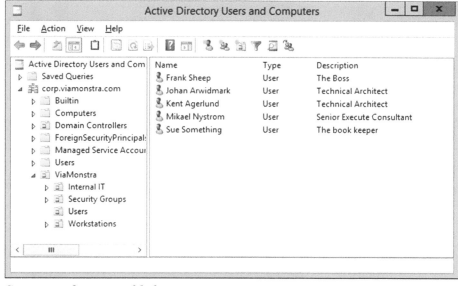

Some sample users added.

Create the Sample Groups

As in any real environment, you need a few groups. To do this, you use a PowerShell script that reads an XML file to create some sample users:

1. On **DC01**, open an elevated **PowerShell prompt**.

2. Create the ViaMonstra groups by running the following command (the command is wrapped and should be one line):

```
C:\setup\Scripts\Set-VIAADDSGroups.ps1 -BaseOU "ViaMonstra"
-SettingsFile C:\Setup\Settings\Settings.xml
```

Add Sample Users to Sample Groups

As in any real environment, users are members of different groups. To accomplish this, you use a PowerShell script that reads an .XML file to add users to groups:

1. On **DC01**, open an elevated **PowerShell prompt**.

2. Add the ViaMonstra users to the sample groups by running the following command (the command is wrapped and should be one line):

```
C:\setup\Scripts\Set-VIAADDSUserGroupMemberShip.ps1 -BaseOU
"ViaMonstra" -SettingsFile C:\Setup\Settings\Settings.xml
```

Install Volume Activation Services

Because the ViaMonstra network uses both Windows 7 and Windows 10 clients, we recommend using Active Directory-Based Activation for the new Windows 10 client, but also having the KMS service configured to support existing Windows 7 clients and any machines that are not part of the corp.viamonstra.com domain.

No matter whether you are using Active Directory-Based Activation, KMS, or both, a Windows 10/Windows Server 2012 R2 KMS host key is used. For Active Directory-Based Activation, the key is used to create the Active Directory-Based Activation object in Active Directory. In the KMS scenario, it's simply used to configure the KMS host.

Note: Make sure to get the Windows 10 KMS host key named "Windows Srv 2012 R2 DataCtr/Std KMS for Windows 10" on the VLCS site. There is also a Windows 10-only key that can be installed only on KMS hosts running the Windows 10 operating system.

---

1. On **DC01**, to support Windows 10 activation on a Windows Server 2012 R2 host, download and extract the **KB 3058168** (https://support.microsoft.com/en-us/kb/3058168) hotfix in the **C:\Setup\DL\KB3058168** folder.

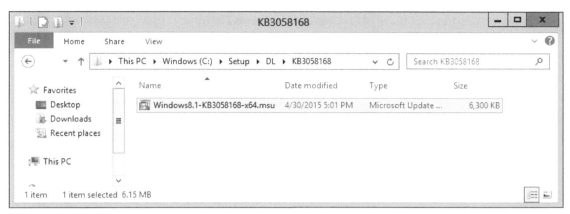

The KB 3058168 hotfix downloaded and extracted.

2.   Install **KB 3058168** (Windows8.1-KB3058168-x64.msu) using the default settings, and then restart **DC01**.

Note: The KB 3058168 hotfix requires that you have the April 2014 update rollup for Windows Server 2012 R2 (KB 2919355) installed, but if you followed our guide in Appendix A, you are already good to go.

---

3.   After restarting **DC01**, log on as **Administrator** in the **VIAMONSTRA** domain, and open an elevated **PowerShell prompt**.

4.   Install Volume Activation Services by running the following command (the command is wrapped and should be one line):

```
Install-WindowsFeature -Name VolumeActivation
-IncludeManagementTools
```

5.   Using **Server Manager**, select the **VA Services** node, right-click **DC01**, and select **Volume Activation Tools**.

6.   On the **Introduction** page, click **Next**.

7.   On the **Activation Type** page, select **Active Directory-Based Activation** and click **Next**.

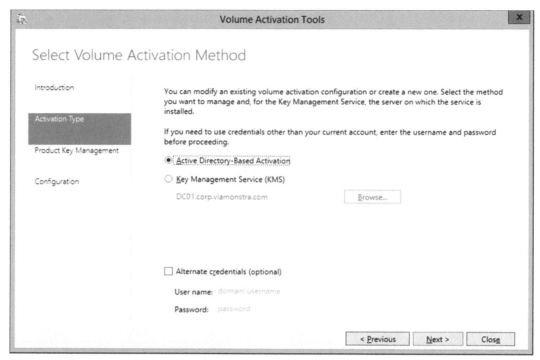

Selecting Active Directory-Based Activation.

8. On the **Product Key Management** page, in the **Install your KMS host key** text box, type your KMS product key. Select the **Enter a display name for your new Activation Object (optional)** check box, type in **Windows Server 2012 R2 CSVLK**, and click **Next**.

9. On the **Product Key Management** page, select **Activate online** and click **Commit**.

10. In the **Volume Activation Tools** dialog box, click **Yes**.

11. On the **Product Key Management** page, click **Close**.

12. Repeat step 5–11, but this time, on the **Activation Type** page, select the **Key Management Service (KMS)** option.

Real World Note: Even if your organization has decided on migrating all machine to Windows 10, you will likely still have to support Windows 7, at least for a little while. That's why you have to enable KMS in addition to the Active Directory-Based Activation.

Configure Active Directory Permissions

The MDT_JD account created earlier is used to join deployed computers to the domain. For this to work, the MDT_JD account needs to have permissions to the organizational unit. In these steps, you run a script that assigns the correct permissions:

1. On **DC01**, log on as **VIAMONSTRA\Administrator**, and open an elevated **PowerShell prompt**.

2. Set the Active Directory permissions by running the following command (the command is wrapped and should be one line):

    ```
    C:\Setup\Scripts\Set-VIAOUPermissions.ps1
    -Account MDT_JD
    -TargetOU "OU=Workstations,OU=ViaMonstra"
    ```

Update Your ADMX Files

In order to configure your Windows 10 clients with one or more group policies, you need to add the Windows 10 ADMX templates in your environment. This is done by creating a central repository for group policy templates. In this guide we assume you have copied the downloaded Windows 10 ADMX files to DC01, either by simply copying the entire C:\Setup folder from your host machine, or by creating an ISO file, and mount it in the virtual machine.

1. On **DC01**, install the **Windows 10 ADMX templates** (Windows10-ADMX.msi) using the default settings.

2. Using **File Explorer**, copy the **C:\Windows\PolicyDefinitions** folder to **C:\Windows\SYSVOL\domain\Policies**.

3. Using **File Explorer**, navigate to the **C:\Program Files (x86)\Microsoft Group Policy\Windows 10\PolicyDefinitions** folder, and copy the contents to the following folder (replacing the existing files):

    C:\Windows\SYSVOL\domain\Policies\PolicyDefinitions

4. Using **File Explorer**, navigate to the **C:\Windows\SYSVOL\domain\Policies\PolicyDefinitions** folder and then delete the **LocationProviderADM.admx** and **LocationProviderADM.adml** files.

Real World Note: The LocationProviderADM.admx file was renamed Microsoft-Windows-Geolocation-WLPAdm.admx in Windows 10. That's why you need to delete the files. If you want to learn more, see: https://support.microsoft.com/en-us/kb/3077013.

Create a Separate OU for Windows 10 Machines

When starting your Windows 10 pilots, we recommend starting by adding the first Windows 10 clients to a separate OU to which the existing group policies don't apply. We often find that organizations have quite a few group policies that have been inherited for years, sometimes several hundred policies, and you really don't know what's going to happen when they are applied to a Windows 10 machine. So instead of spending endless hours trying to figure out which settings work and then create a filter for each operating system, just to find out that most of these old group policy settings aren't really useful anyway.

This is your chance to start over, and we strongly recommend that you take this opportunity. By creating a new OU and block Group Policy Inheritance, you can create just those policies that are needed. That is usually in the range of 5 to 10, maybe even 20.

Also, if you are going to use System Center Configuration Manager or the built-in MDM Agent in Windows 10 (or maybe Windows Intune or something like that), you may not need many policies at all. If the machines are joined into Azure Active Directory, you don't need to work on OUs because the machines are not in your legacy Active Directory anyway.

Preparation for BitLocker

To enable BitLocker to store the recovery key and TPM information in Active Directory, you need to create a group policy for it in Active Directory. Because you are running Windows Server 2012, you don't need to extend the schema, but you do need to set the appropriate permissions in Active Directory.

Add the BitLocker Drive Encryption Administration Utilities

In Windows Server 2012 R2 (as well as in Windows Server 2012 and Windows Server 2008 R2), you also have access to a toolkit that will make your BitLocker life a bit easier, and we recommend that you add this toolkit to your server:

1. On **DC01**, start an elevated **PowerShell prompt** (run as administrator).

2. Add the BitLocker Drive Encryption Administration Utilities by running the following command:

   ```
   C:\Setup\Scripts\Install-VIARoles.ps1 -Role BitLockerAdmin
   ```

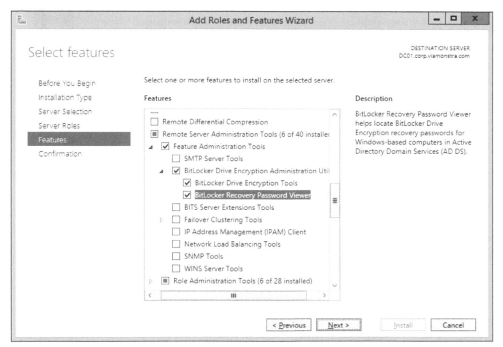

The BitLocker Drive Encryption Administration Utilities added by the PowerShell script.

Create the BitLocker Group Policy

In these steps, you enable the backup of BitLocker and TPM recovery information to Active Directory. You also enable the policy for TPM platform validation profile.

1. On **DC01**, using **Group Policy Management**, right-click the **ViaMonstra / Workstations** OU, and select **Create a GPO in this domain, and Link it here**.

2. Assign the name **BitLocker Policy** to the new group policy.

3. Expand the **Workstations** OU, right-click the **BitLocker Policy**, and select **Edit**.

4. In the **Computer Configuration / Policies / Administrative Templates / Windows Components / BitLocker Drive Encryption / Operating System Drives** node, enable the **Choose how BitLocker-protected operating system drives can be recovered** policy, and configure the following settings:

   a. **Allow data recovery agent** (default)

   b. **Save BitLocker recovery information to Active Directory Domain Services** (default)

   c. **Do not enable BitLocker until recovery information is stored in AD DS for operating system drives**

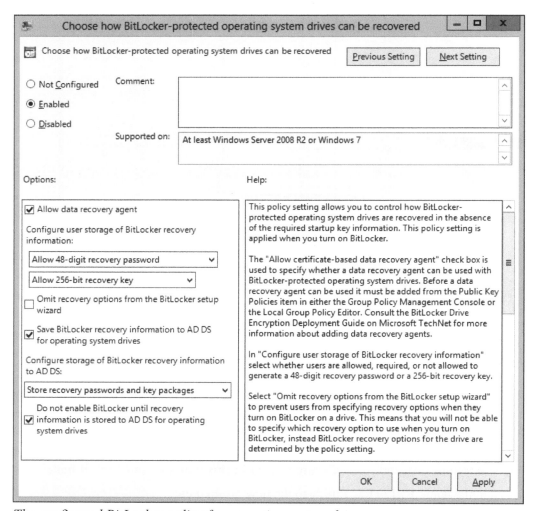

The configured BitLocker policy for operating system drives.

5. In the **Computer Configuration / Policies / Administrative Templates / Windows Components / BitLocker Drive Encryption / Operating System Drives** node, enable the following policies:

   o **Configure TPM platform validation profile for BIOS-based firmware configurations**

   o **Configure TPM platform validation profile (Windows Vista, Windows Server 2008, Windows 7, Windows Server 2008 R2)**

Real World Note: Even though we don't configure BitLocker for any Windows 7 machines in this chapter, we still recommend enabling support for Windows 7. Most organizations are likely to have a mix of Windows 7, Windows 8/8.1, and Windows 10, at least for a while. ☺

---

o   **Configure TPM platform validation profile for native UEFI firmware configurations**

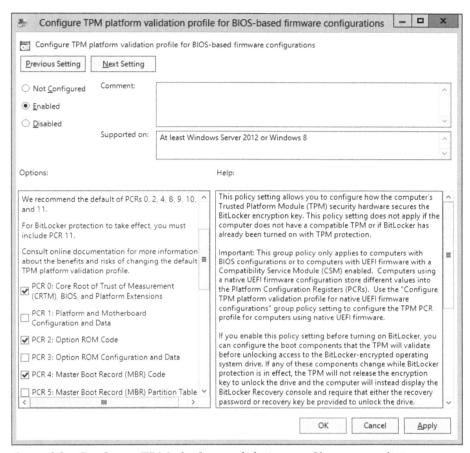

One of the Configure TPM platform validation profile group policies.

6. In the **Computer Configuration / Policies / Administrative Templates / System / Trusted Platform Module Services** node, enable the **Turn on TPM backup to Active Directory Domain Services** policy.

Real World Note: If you consistently get the error "Windows BitLocker Drive Encryption Information. The system boot information has changed since BitLocker was enabled. You must supply a BitLocker recovery password to start this system." after encrypting a computer with BitLocker, you might have to relax the various "Configure TPM platform validation profile" group policies, as well. This depends on what hardware you are using. For the hardware used for this book, we didn't need to; however, we have run into other hardware where this was needed, such as when using docking stations.

Set Permissions in Active Directory for BitLocker

In addition to the group policy created previously, you need to configure permissions in Active Directory to be able to store the TPM recovery information. In these steps, we assume you have downloaded the Add-TPMSelfWriteACE.vbs script from Microsoft (http://go.microsoft.com/fwlink/?LinkId=167133) to the C:\Setup\ BitLocker and TPM folder on DC01.

1. On **DC01**, start an elevated **PowerShell prompt** (run as administrator).

2. Configure the Active Directory permissions for BitLocker by running the following command:

```
cscript.exe C:\Setup\Scripts\Add-TPMSelfWriteACE.vbs
```

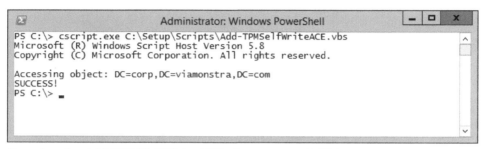

Running the Add-TPMSelfWriteACE.vbs script on DC01.

Preparation for Virtual Secure Mode

If you plan to use Virtual Secure Mode to increase the security in Windows 10 (and you should really consider doing so, as it's a very nice feature), you need to make sure you have configured a group policy to allow for that. In addition to the policy, your Windows 10 clients must be configured for Secure Boot (UEFI enabled), and have the Hyper-V role installed.

To enable Virtual Secure Mode, you do the following:

1. On **DC01**, using **Group Policy Management**, right-click the **ViaMonstra / Workstations** OU, and select **Create a GPO in this domain, and Link it here**.

2. Assign the name **Enable Virtual Secure Mode** to the new group policy.

3. Expand the **Workstations** OU, right-click the **Enable Virtual Secure Mode**, and select **Edit**.

4. In the **Computer Configuration / Policies / Administrative Templates / System / Device Guard** node, enable the **Turn On Virtualization Based Security** policy, and configure the following settings:

   o   Select Platform Security Level: **Secure Boot**

   o   Enable Credential Guard

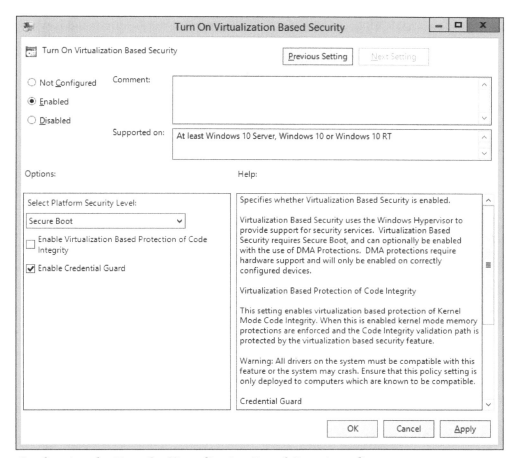

Configuring the Turn On Virtualization Based Security policy.

Configuring MDT01

In this section, you configure the MDT01 deployment server.

Install Windows ADK 10

In this guide, we assume you have copied the book sample files and the Windows ADK 10 setup files to C:\Setup on MDT01. Again, the easiest way to do this is simply copy the entire C:\Setup folder from your host machine (created in Appendix A), or create an ISO of the folder that you mount in the MDT01 virtual machine.

1. On **MDT01**, log on as **Administrator** in the **VIAMONSTRA** domain using a password of **P@ssw0rd**, and open an elevated **PowerShell prompt**.

2. Install **Windows ADK 10** by running the following command (the command is wrapped and should be one line):

```
C:\Setup\Scripts\Invoke-VIAInstallADK.ps1 -Setup
C:\Setup\DL\Windows_ADK_10\adksetup.exe -Role MDT
```

3. The unattended Windows ADK 10 setup runs without a visible UI. But you can view the setup progress by reviewing the Windows ADK 10 setup logs in **C:\Users\Administrator.VIAMONSTRA\AppData\Local\Temp\adk**.

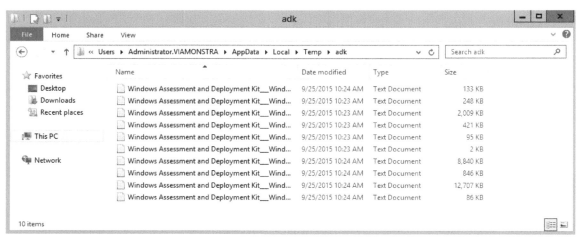

The Windows ADK 10 setup log files.

Install MDT 2013 Update 2

In this guide, we assume you have copied the book sample files and the MDT 2013 Update 2 setup files to C:\Setup on MDT01.

1. On **MDT01**, install **MDT 2013 Update 2** by running the following command (the command is wrapped and should be one line):

```
C:\Setup\Scripts\Invoke-VIAInstallMDT.ps1 -Setup C:\Setup\
DL\MDT_2013_U2\MicrosoftDeploymentToolkit2013_x64.msi
-Role Full
```

2. Verify the installation by running the following command (the command is wrapped and should be one line):

```
Get-WmiObject -Class Win32_Product -Filter "Name LIKE
'%Toolkit 2013%'"
```

```
PS C:\> Get-WmiObject -Class Win32_Product -Filter "Name LIKE '%Toolkit 2013%'"

IdentifyingNumber : {F172B6C7-45DD-4C22-A5BF-1B2C084CADEF}
Name              : Microsoft Deployment Toolkit 2013 Update 2 (6.3.8330.1000)
Vendor            : Microsoft Corporation
Version           : 6.3.8330.1000
Caption           : Microsoft Deployment Toolkit 2013 Update 2 (6.3.8330.1000)


PS C:\> _
```

Verifying the MDT setup.

Install ConfigMgr 2012 R2 Toolkit

In this guide, we assume you have copied the ConfigMgr 2012 R2 Toolkit setup files to C:\Setup on MDT01. The toolkit includes CMTrace, which is great for reading MDT log files.

1. On **MDT01**, install **ConfigMgr 2012 R2 Toolkit** by running the following command (the command is wrapped and should be one line):

   ```
   C:\Setup\Scripts\Invoke-VIAInstallCMToolkit.ps1 -Setup
   'C:\Setup\DL\ConfigMgr 2012 R2 Toolkit\ConfigMgrTools.msi'
   -Role Full
   ```

2. On the **Start screen**, type in **CMTrace** and start it.

3. Click **Yes** in the dialog box asking whether you want to use this program for log files.

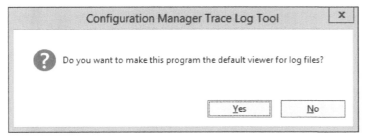

The Configuration Manager Trace Log Tool dialog box.

Add WDS and Data Deduplication to the MDT01 Virtual Machine

In this guide, you use PowerShell to install WDS and data deduplication:

1. On **MDT01**, install **WDS** by running the following command:

   ```
   C:\Setup\Scripts\Install-VIARoles.ps1 -Role DEPL
   ```

2. Configure **WDS** by running the following command (the command is wrapped and should be one line):

```
C:\Setup\Scripts\Set-VIARoles.ps1 -Role DEPL -Path
"E:\RemoteInstall"
```

Configuring WSUS01

Windows Server Update Services (WSUS) is a critical infrastructure component in any network. WSUS needs a database and can use either the Windows Internal Database built into Windows Server 2012 R2 or a SQL Server database (either the full or express version). ViaMonstra has decided to use the free SQL Server 2014 SP1 Express database for WSUS.

In this section, you configure the WSUS01 server.

> **Note:** To support Windows 10 feature upgrades, you need to install the https://support.microsoft.com/en-us/kb/3095113 hotfix on WSUS01.

Install Report Viewer 2008 SP1

In this guide, we assume you have copied the book sample files and Report Viewer 2008 SP1 to C:\Setup on WSUS01. WSUS also requires Report Viewer 2008 SP1. Although the SQL Server 2012 SP1 Express setup does install the Report Viewer, it is version 2012, and WSUS still requires Report Viewer 2008 SP1 in Windows Server 2012 R2.

1. On **WSUS01**, install **Report Viewer 2008 SP1** by running the following command (the command is wrapped and should be one line):

```
C:\Setup\Scripts\Invoke-VIAInstallReportViewer.ps1 -Setup
"C:\Setup\DL\Report_Viewer_2008_SP1\ReportViewer.exe"
```

2. Verify that **Report Viewer 2008 SP1** was installed on WSUS01 by running the following command (the command is wrapped and should be one line):

```
Get-WmiObject -Class Win32_Product -Filter
"Name LIKE '%Report%'"
```

Report Viewer 2008 SP1 installed on WSUS01.

Install SQL Server 2014 SP1 Express with Tools

In this guide, we assume you have copied the book sample files and SQL Server 2014 SP1 Express with Tools copied to C:\Setup\DL on WSUS01.

1. On **WSUS01**, install **SQL Server 2014 SP1 Express SP1 with Tools** by running the following command from an elevated **PowerShell prompt** (the command is wrapped and should be one line):

    ```
    C:\Setup\Scripts\Invoke-VIAInstallSQLServerExpress.ps1
    -Setup
    "C:\Setup\DL\SQL_2014_Express_SP1\SQLEXPRWT_x64_ENU.exe"
    -SQLINSTANCENAME "SQLExpress" -SQLINSTANCEDIR "E:\SQLDB"
    ```

2. Check whether **SQL Server** is started by running the following command:

    ```
    Get-Process -Name *SQL*
    ```

    You should get a process called **sqlservr**. (Yes, it's named like that.)

```
PS C:\> Get-Process -Name *SQL*

Handles  NPM(K)    PM(K)     WS(K) VM(M)   CPU(s)     Id ProcessName
-------  ------    -----     ----- -----   ------     -- -----------
     89      10     1340      3908    25     0.03   3104 sqlbrowser
    566      75   206260    128244  -651     1.31   3144 sqlservr
    101       9     1488      5576    41     0.03   1640 sqlwriter


PS C:\> _
```

Verifying the SQL Server 2014 SP1 Express services on WSUS01.

3. As a best practice, you should limit the amount of memory that SQL is allowed to consume. That prevents the system from being memory starved. To limit the amount of memory, run the following script from an elevated **PowerShell prompt**:

    ```
    C:\Setup\Scripts\Set-VIASQLMemoryConfiguration.ps1
    -SQLInstance SQLEXPRESS
    ```

Add Windows Server Software Update Services (WSUS)

Note: Before starting these steps, make sure that WSUS01 can access the Internet. One very easy way to do that is by running the Test-NetConnection command with no parameters. The default behavior for that command is to verify access to internetbeacon.msedge.net.

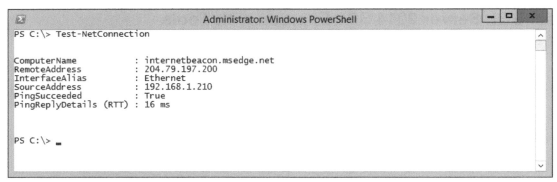

Verifying Internet access on WSUS01.

1. Install **Windows Update Server Services** by running the following command from an elevated **PowerShell prompt**:

    ```
    C:\Setup\Scripts\Install-VIARoles.ps1 -Role WSUS
    ```

2. Start the **WSUS Postinstall** process by running the following command:

    ```
    C:\Setup\Scripts\Set-VIARoles.ps1 -Role WSUS -Path "E:\WSUS"
    ```

3. Verify that the **Windows Server Update Services** has started by running the following command:

    ```
    Get-Process -Name *WSUS*
    ```

    You should see a process called WsusService.

Configure Windows Server Update Services (WSUS)

Using PowerShell, you can configure the entire WSUS server configuration. The scripts you are about to run perform the following tasks:

*   Configure WSUS to download from Microsoft Update

*   Set update languages, classifications, and products

*   Create the target groups

*   Create the default approval rule

*   Set the synchronization schedule and perform a synchronization

In the following steps, you configure the preceding settings using multiple PowerShell scripts. To understand the scripts better, please open and review them before you run them.

1. On **WSUS01**, configure WSUS with basic settings and perform the initial sync by running the following command from an elevated **PowerShell prompt**:

    ```
    C:\Setup\Scripts\Configure-VIAPostWSUSPart1.ps1
    ```

2. Configure WSUS for products, classifications, second sync settings and decline superseded patches by running the following command from an elevated **PowerShell prompt**:

    ```
    C:\Setup\Scripts\Configure-VIAPostWSUSPart2.ps1
    ```

3. Create the **ViaMonstra Default Approval Rule** by running the following command from an elevated **PowerShell prompt**:

    ```
    C:\Setup\Scripts\Configure-VIAPostWSUSPart3.ps1
    ```

4. Run the **ViaMonstra Default Approval Rule** by running the following command from an elevated **PowerShell prompt**:

    ```
    C:\Setup\Scripts\Configure-VIAPostWSUSPart4.ps1
    ```

Note: The last script, Configure-VIAPostWSUSPart4.ps1, also initiates the actual download of the updates, which takes some time.

5. Verify the WSUS configuration for **Update Categories** by running the following command from an elevated **PowerShell prompt** (the command is wrapped and should be one line):

    ```
    (Get-WSUSServer -Name WSUS01 -Port
    8530).GetSubscription().GetUpdateCategories() |
    Select-Object Title
    ```

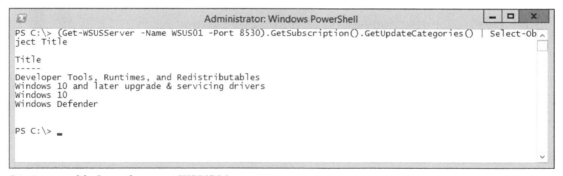

Listing enabled products on WSUS01.

6. Verify the WSUS configured target groups by running the following command following command from an elevated **PowerShell prompt** (the command is wrapped and should be one line):

    ```
    (Get-WSUSServer -Name WSUS01 -Port
    8530).GetComputerTargetGroups()
    ```

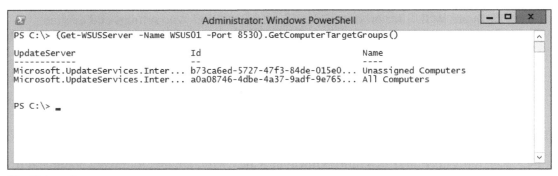

Verifying the target groups.

7. Verify the WSUS approval rules by running the following command from an elevated **PowerShell prompt** (the command is wrapped and should be one line):

```
(Get-WSUSServer -Name WSUS01 -Port
8530).GetInstallApprovalRules()
```

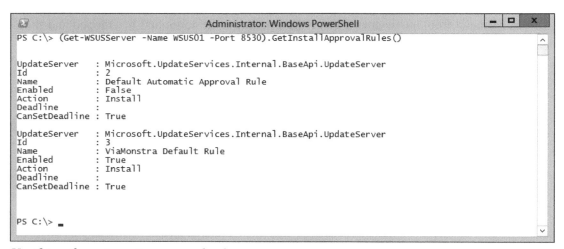

Verifying the automatic approval rules.

Additional Verification of the WSUS Configuration

The installation and the main configuration is now done, and in addition to the checks you ran in PowerShell earlier, you also can review the setup via Server Manager.

1. On **WSUS01**, using **Server Manager**, select the **WSUS** section, right-click **WSUS01**, and select **Windows Server Update Services**.

> **Note:** If the Windows Server Update Services Configuration Wizard appears the first time, just click Cancel. WSUS is (most times) not smart enough to figure out that it is already configured.

2. Browse through the configuration, and you should see that it is fully configured now.

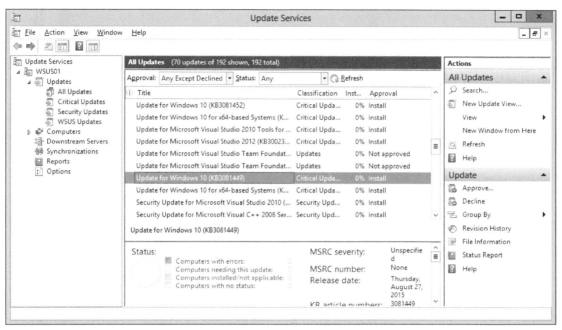

The WSUS console populated with updates.

Chapter 8

Setting Up MDT for Reference Image Builds

In Chapter 2, you learned what a reference image is and why you need one. Now it is time to import the operating system, create the task sequence, and prepare the reference image build environment. In this chapter, you do the following:

- Create a deployment share for reference image creation

- Import the Windows 10 operating system

- Import applications to include in your reference image

- Create the Windows 10 reference image task sequence

- Configure the deployment share rules and settings

Step-by-Step Guide Requirements

If you want to run the step-by-step guides in this chapter, you need a lab environment configured as outlined in Chapter 1 and Appendix A. In this chapter, you use the following virtual machines:

DC01   WSUS01   MDT01

The VMs used in this chapter.

The Reference Image

The reference image described in this book is designed primarily for deploying to physical machines. However, the reference image is created on a virtual platform before being automatically sysprepped and captured to a WIM file. The reasons for creating the reference image on a virtual platform are the following:

- You reduce development time and can use snapshots to test different configurations quickly.

- You rule out hardware issues. You simply get the best possible image, and if you have a problem, it's not likely to be hardware related.

- You make sure that no unwanted applications are installed as part of a driver install, but not removed by the Sysprep process.

- It's very easy to move between lab, test, and production.

Setting up the MDT Build Lab Deployment Share

As you learned in Chapter 2, there is no longer a hard requirement to create reference images with Windows 10; however, to reduce the time for deployment, you create a reference image that has a few base applications in it, as well as all the latest updates installed.

Because reference images should be deployed only to virtual machines and have specific settings (rules), you create use a separate deployment share for this process.

Create the MDT Build Lab Deployment Share

1. On **MDT01**, log on as **Administrator** in the **VIAMONSTRA** domain using a password of **P@ssw0rd**, and open an elevated **PowerShell prompt**.

2. Create the deployment share by running the following command (the command is wrapped and should be one line):

```
C:\Setup\Scripts\New-VIAMDTBuildLabDS.ps1 -Path
"E:\MDTBuildLab" -Description "MDT Build Lab"
```

3. From the **Start screen**, start the **Deployment Workbench** and review the **MDT Build Lab** deployment share. You should find folders in **Operating Systems** and in **Task Sequences**.

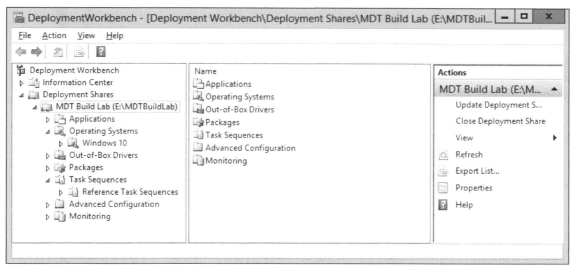

The MDT Build Lab deployment share showing the folders created.

Configure the MDT Build Lab Deployment Share

The newly created deployment share needs to be configured. Items that need to be configured are Bootstrap.ini, CustomSettings.ini, the names of the ISO images, and the names of the WIM files.

1. On **MDT01**, open an elevated **PowerShell prompt**.

2. Configure the deployment share by running the following command (the command is wrapped and should be one line):

```
C:\Setup\Scripts\Set-VIAMDTBuildLabDS.ps1 -Path
"E:\MDTBuildLab"
```

> **Note:** The Set-VIAMDTBuildLabDS.ps1 script also copies a sample set of deployment rules (CustomSettings.ini).

Configure the MDT Build Lab Deployment Share for Updates

To get the updates into your reference image, the most reliable solution is to use a local WSUS server.

If you have set up the WSUS01 server in your environment, use these steps to configure MDT to use it; otherwise, simply skip these steps, and MDT will use Microsoft Update directly.

1. On **MDT01**, using the **Deployment Workbench**, right-click the **MDT Build Lab** deployment share and select **Properties**.

2. In the **Rules** tab, remove the comment (;) from the WSUSServer line and type in your WSUS server (WSUS01):

```
WSUSServer=http://wsus01.corp.viamonstra.com:8530
```

3.   Click **OK** to save the changes.

Alternative Ways to Add Updates

Because Windows 10 has cumulative updates, you can simply download the latest cumulative update (and the latest servicing stack update) and import them into the packages node in MDT.

The packages will then be injected to the offline Windows installation after the WIM image has been applied in the WinPE phase. MDT calls DISM to do the job, and this way the operating system is patched at first boot.

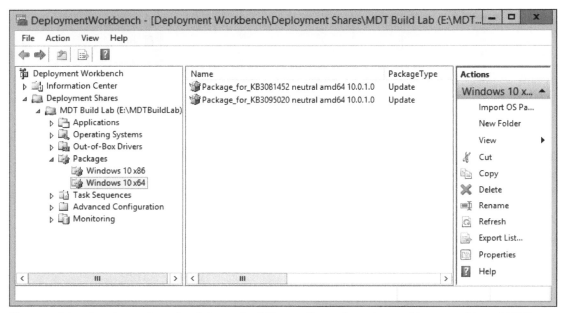

Two updates has been download from the Microsoft catalog site and imported into MDT.

Adding the Setup Files

After creating the deployment share, you are ready to add the setup files to the Deployment Workbench, in this case the Windows 10 Enterprise x64 operating system.

Add Windows 10 Enterprise x64 (Full Source)

It is slightly complicated to create a useful reference image without an operating system, so you need to import that. In this guide, we assume that you have a Windows 10 ISO named Windows 10 Enterprise x64.iso in the C:\Setup\ISO folder on MDT01.

1. On **MDT01**, open an elevated **PowerShell prompt**.

2. Import the **Windows 10 Enterprise x64** operating system to the deployment share by running the following command (the command is wrapped and should be one line):

```
C:\Setup\Scripts\Import-VIAMDTOS.ps1 -Path "E:\MDTBuildlab"
-ISO 'C:\Setup\ISO\Windows 10 Enterprise x64.iso'
-MDTDestinationPath "Operating Systems\Windows 10"
-MDTDestinationFolderName W10X64
```

3. Using the **Deployment Workbench**, in the **MDT Build Lab** deployment share, review the **Operating Systems** node.

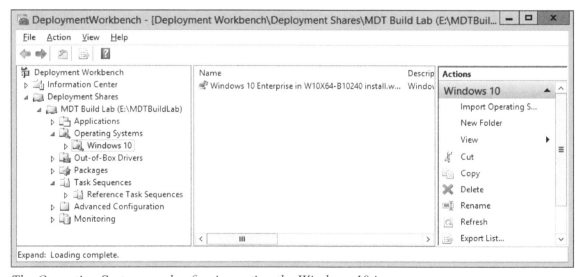

The Operating Systems node after importing the Windows 10 image.

Adding the Applications

Before you can start creating your task sequence, you need to add all the applications and other sample scripts to the MDT Build Lab share.

In this book, you learn to use a strict naming standard for your MDT applications. You add the "Install - " prefix for typical application installations that run a setup installer of some kind, and you use the "Configure - " prefix when an application configures a setting in the operating system. You also add an " - x86", " - x64", or " - x86-x64" suffix to indicate the application's architecture (some applications have installers for both architectures).

By storing configuration items as MDT applications, it is easy to move these objects between various solutions, or between test and production environments.

> **Real World Note:** In this book, we provide you with VBScript wrappers for all applications. This is not because you need to use VBScript wrappers to install applications in MDT (it supports running any type of Windows executable file as an application), but so you have a consistent way of working with applications, for supporting applications that require both x86 and x64 components without your having to create an application bundle, and for getting additional logging and installation options.

In this section's step-by-step guides, you create the following applications:

- Install - Microsoft Office 365 Click-to-Run - x86

- Install - Microsoft Visual C++ - x86-x64

- Install - BGInfo - x86

> **Note:** All the Microsoft Visual C++ downloads can be found on the following page: http://support.microsoft.com/kb/2019667.

Preparing for Microsoft Office 2016 Click-to-Run Deployment

As you learned in Chapter 5, before you can deploy Microsoft Office 2016, a.k.a. Office 365, you need to download the Office 2016 Deployment Tool and modify the configuration XML file. For this guide, we have created two configuration XML files to make it easier for you. One file is download.xml and is used to download Office 365 in the correct folder, and the other is configuration.xml and is used at the deployment time to install and configure Office.

Download Microsoft Office 2016 Click-to-Run

In this guide, you download the Office 2016 Deployment Tool, modify the XML file and download the core Office 2016 Click-to-Run package:

1. On **MDT01**, download the **Office 2016 Deployment Tool** (http://www.microsoft.com/en-us/download/details.aspx?id=49117) and save the file in **C:\Setup\DL\Microsoft_Office_2016**.

2. Run the **OfficeDeploymentTool.exe** and select **C:\Setup\DL\Microsoft_Office_2016** as your destination folder.

3. Using **File Explorer**, navigate to **C:\Setup\DL\Microsoft_Office_2016**, and delete the **configuration.xml** file.

4. Navigate to **C:\Setup\MDTBuildLab\Applications\Install - Microsoft Office 365 - x86** and copy the **download.xml** file to **C:\Setup\DL\Microsoft_Office_2016** (replace the existing file).

5. Review **download.xml**. It should look like this:

```
                                    download.xml - Notepad                          _  □  X
File  Edit  Format  View  Help
<Configuration>
 <Add SourcePath="C:\Setup\DL\Microsoft_Office_2016" OfficeClientEdition="32" Branch="Current" >
   <Product ID="O365ProPlusRetail">
     <Language ID="en-us" />
   </Product>
   <Product ID="VisioProRetail">
     <Language ID="en-us" />
   </Product>
 </Add>
</Configuration>
```

Reviewing the download.xml file.

6. Open an elevated **PowerShell prompt** and download **Office 2016** by running the following command, and then waiting until the download finishes (the command is wrapped and should be one line):

```
C:\Setup\DL\Microsoft_Office_2016\setup.exe /download
C:\Setup\DL\Microsoft_Office_2016\download.xml
```

7. Using **File Explorer**, examine the **C:\Setup\DL\ Microsoft_Office_2016** folder. It should have a folder named **Office** with a size of approximately 1 GB.

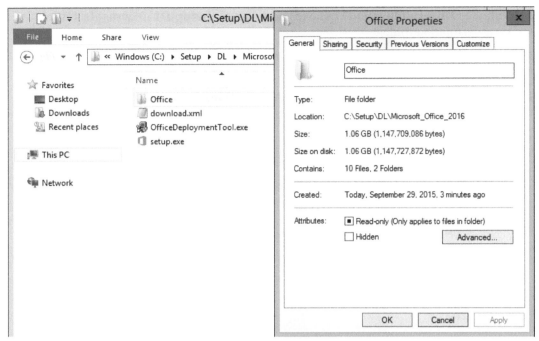

The downloaded Microsoft Office files is approximately 1 GB in size.

8. Review the **C:\Setup\MDTBuildLab\Applications\Install - Microsoft Office 365 - x86\Source\configuration.xml** file. It should look like this:

```
<Configuration>
 <Add SourcePath="C:\Minint\O365Inst" OfficeClientEdition="32" Branch="Current" >
  <Product ID="O365ProPlusRetail">
    <Language ID="en-us" />
  </Product>
  <Product ID="VisioProRetail">
    <Language ID="en-us" />
  </Product>
 </Add>
 <Updates Enabled="TRUE" Branch="Current" />
 <Display Level="None" AcceptEULA="TRUE" />
 <Logging Level="Standard" Path="%temp%" />
</Configuration>
```

Reviewing the configuration.xml file used at deployment time.

Import the Applications

In this guide, you copy all the downloaded applications to a folder structure and import the applications. We assume you have copied the downloaded C++ runtime and BGInfo files to C:\Setup\DL on MDT01. (You downloaded the files in Appendix A.)

1. On **MDT01**, using **File Explorer**, perform the following:

    a. Copy the following folders to **C:\Setup\MDTBuildLab\Applications\Install - Microsoft Visual C++ - x86-x64\source**.

    - **C:\Setup\DL\VC2005**
    - **C:\Setup\DL\VC2008**
    - **C:\Setup\DL\VC2010**
    - **C:\Setup\DL\VC2012**
    - **C:\Setup\DL\VC2013**
    - **C:\Setup\DL\VC2015**

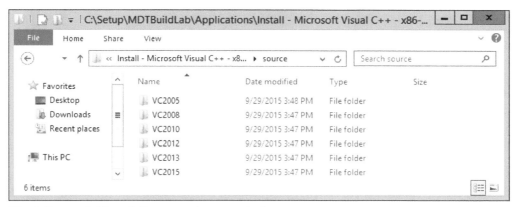

The Microsoft Visual C++ runtimes copied.

    b. Copy the content of the following folder to **C:\Setup\MDTBuildLab\Applications\Install - BGInfo - x86\Source**:

    C:\Setup\DL\BGInfo

    c. Copy the content of the following folder to **C:\Setup\MDTBuildLab\Applications\Install - Microsoft Office 365 - x86\Source**:

    C:\Setup\DL\Microsoft_Office_2016

2. On **MDT01**, open an elevated **PowerShell prompt** and execute the following command (the command is wrapped and should be one line):

```
C:\setup\Scripts\Import-VIAMDTApps.ps1 -Path
"E:\MDTBuildLab" -ImportFolder
"C:\Setup\MDTBuildLab\Applications"
```

3. On **MDT01**, open the **Deployment Workbench** and verify that your applications have been imported.

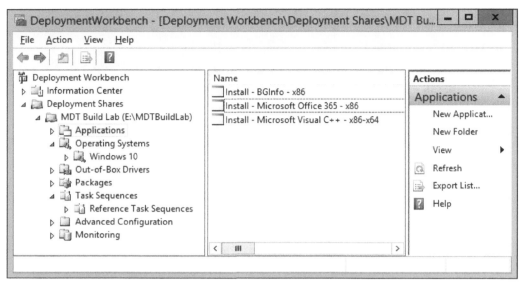

Applications have been imported to the Deployment Workbench.

Drivers and the Reference Image

Because we use modern virtual platforms for creating our reference images, we don't need to worry about drivers when creating reference images for Windows 10. It does not matter whether you use Hyper-V or VMware as your virtualization platform, either of them works. For Hyper-V, use Generation 1 VMs, and for VMware, use the default settings when creating a VM. To keep the image as clean as possible, we don't recommend installing the VMware Tools in the reference image.

Real World Note: In VMware, if you don't install the VMware Tools and open Device Manager in your virtual machine, you may see that the virtual machine is missing the driver for the VMware VMCI Bus. This is nothing to be alarmed about; the Sysprep process in Windows 10 is very good at cleaning out even undetected devices.

Creating the Reference Image Task Sequence

It is now time to create the build and capture task sequence for your reference image. You create one reference image based on Windows 10 Enterprise x64.

After creating the task sequence, you configure it to enable patching against the WSUS server. The Task Sequence Windows Update action supports getting updates directly from Microsoft Windows Update, but you get a more stable patching if you use a local WSUS server. WSUS also allows for an easy process of approving the patches that you are deploying.

Create a Task Sequence for Windows 10 Enterprise x64

1. On **MDT01**, using the **Deployment Workbench**, navigate to **MDT Build Lab / Task Sequences**.

2. Right-click the **Reference Task Sequences** folder and select **New Task Sequence**. Use the following settings for the **New Task Sequence Wizard**:

    a. Task sequence ID: **REFW10X64-001**

    b. Task sequence name: **Ref Windows 10 Enterprise x64**

    c. Task sequence comments: **Reference Build**

    d. Template: **Standard Client Task Sequence**

    e. Select OS: **Windows 10 Enterprise in W10X64 install.wim**

Note: The actual OS name may change for Windows 10 versions over time.

---

    f. Specify Product Key: **Do not specify a product key at this time**

    g. Full Name: **ViaMonstra**

    h. Organization: **ViaMonstra**

    i. Internet Explorer home page: **http://viamonstra.com**

    j. Select **Do not specify an Administrator password at this time**.

Edit the Windows 10 Task Sequence

1. In the **Task Sequences / Reference Task Sequences** folder, right-click the **Ref Windows 10 Enterprise x64** task sequence and select **Properties**.

2. On the **Task Sequence** tab, configure the **Ref Windows 10 Enterprise x64 Image** task sequence with the following settings:

    a. Preinstall: Select the **Apply Patches** action and change the **Selection Profile** to **Windows 10 x64 Packages**.

    b. State Restore: Enable the **Windows Update (Pre-Application Installation)** action.

Note: Enabling an action is done by going to the Options tab and clearing the Disable this step check box.

---

    c. State Restore. Enable the **Windows Update (Post-Application Installation)** action.

    d. State Restore: Rename the **Custom Tasks** group to **Custom Tasks (Post WU)**.

    e.   State Restore: After the **Tattoo** action, add a **New Group** action with the following setting:

             Name: **Custom Tasks (Pre WU)**

Real World Note: The reason for adding the applications after the Tattoo action but before Windows update is simply to save time during the deployment. This way we can add all applications that will upgrade some of the built-in components and therefore avoiding unnecessary "Windows Updating."

---

    f.   State Restore / Custom Tasks (Pre WU): Add a new **Install Roles and Features** action with the following settings:

-   Name: **Install - Microsoft NET Framework 3.5.1**

-   Select the operating system for which roles are to be installed: **Windows 10**.

-   Select the roles and features that should be installed: **.NET Framework 3.5 (includes .NET 2.0 and 3.0)** .

Real World Note: Of all things that you do when creating a reference image, this step is probably the most important one. Many applications need the .NET Framework, and we strongly recommend having it available in the image. The one thing that makes this different from other components is that .NET Framework 3.5.1 is not included in the WIM file; it is installed from the Sources\SxS folder on the media, and that makes it more difficult to add after the image has been deployed.

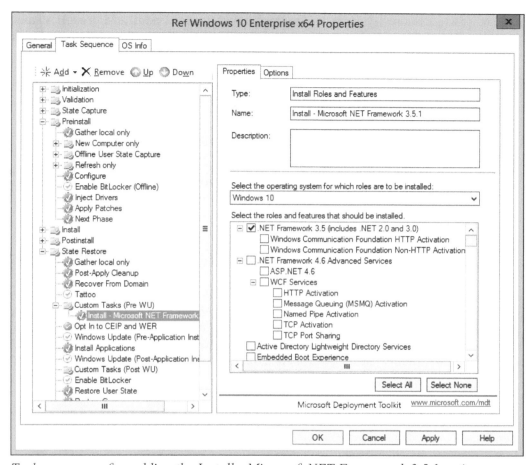

Task sequence after adding the Install - Microsoft NET Framework 3.5.1 action.

g. State Restore / Custom Tasks (Pre WU): After the **Install - Microsoft NET Framework 3.5.1** action, add a new **Install Application** action with the following settings:

  ▪ Name: **Install - Microsoft Visual C++ - x86-x64**

  ▪ Install a Single Application:
    Install - Microsoft Visual C++ - x86-x64

h. State Restore / Custom Tasks (Pre WU): After the **Install - Microsoft Visual C++ - x86-x64** action, add a new **Install Application** action with the following settings:

- Name: **Install - Microsoft Office 365 - x86**

- Install a Single Application:
  Install - Microsoft Office 365 -x86

i. After **the Install - Microsoft Office 365 - x86** action, add a new **Restart computer** action.

j. State Restore / Imaging / Sysprep Only: Before the **Execute Sysprep** action, add a new **Run Command Line** with the following settings:

- Name: **Delete unattend.xml**

- Command line:
  cmd.exe /c del C:\Windows\Panther\unattend.xml

Real World Note: If using the Sysprep Only feature in the deployment wizard (for example to build a reference image for System Center 2012 R2 Virtual Machine Manager, or the Windows Server 2012 R2 VDI solution), you need to make sure MDT deletes the Unattend.xml file in the image before turning of the machine. Another option is to create a WIM file, which automatically skips this file, and then simply use a PowerShell script to apply the WIM to a VHD or VHDX file.

---

3. Click **OK**.

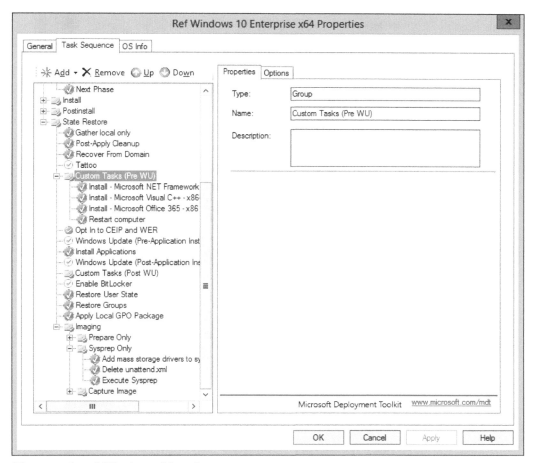

The completed Windows 10 task sequence.

Optional Configuration – Adding a Suspend Action

The goal when creating a reference image is, of course, to automate everything. But sometimes you have that special configuration, an application setup that is just too time-consuming to automate, or you just haven't had to figure out how to automate it yet. If you need to do some manual configuration, you can add a little-known feature called LTI Suspend.

If you add the LTISuspend.wsf script as a custom action in the task sequence, it suspends the task sequence until you click the Resume Task Sequence shortcut on the desktop. In addition to using the Suspend feature for manual configuration or installation, you also can use it for simply verifying a reference image before you allow the task sequence to continue and sysprep and capture the virtual machine.

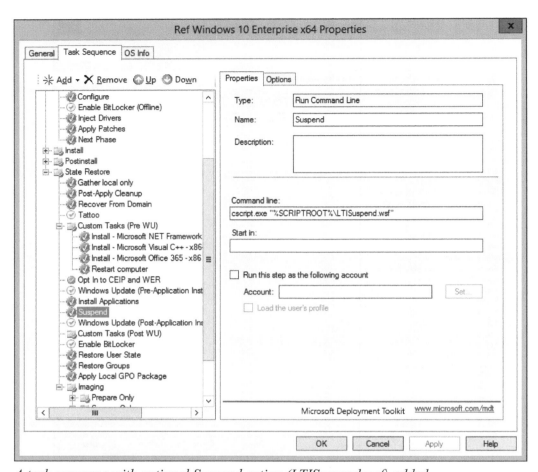

A task sequence with optional Suspend action (LTISuspend.wsf) added.

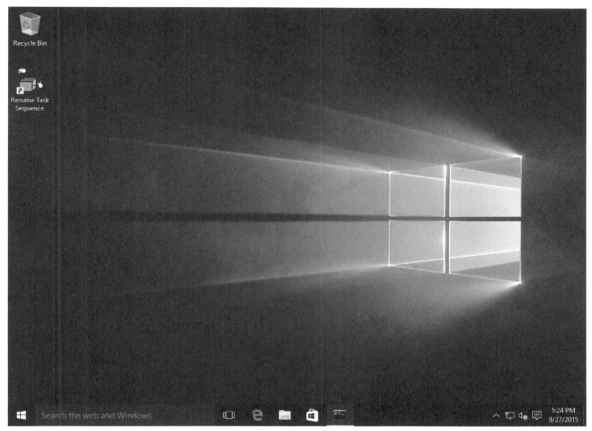

The Windows 10 desktop with the Resume Task Sequence shortcut.

Edit the Unattend.xml File for Windows 10 Enterprise

When using MDT, you don't need to edit the Unattend.xml file very often because most configurations are taken care of by MDT. But, for example, if you want to configure Internet Explorer 11 behavior, then you can edit Unattend.xml for this. Editing Unattend.xml for basic Internet Explorer settings is easy, but if you want to do more advanced settings, you probably want to use the Internet Explorer Administrator Kit.

Real World Note: You also can use Unattend.xml to enable components in Windows, like the Telnet Client or client Hyper-V. Normally we prefer to do this via the Install Roles and Features action, or by using DISM command-line tools, because then we can enable the component as an application, being dynamic, having conditions, and so forth. Also, if you are adding packages via Unattend.xml, it's version-specific, meaning Unattend.xml must match the exact version of the operating system you are servicing.

Follow these steps to configure Internet Explorer 11 settings in Unattend.xml for the Ref
Windows 10 Enterprise x64 task sequence:

1. Using the **Deployment Workbench**, right-click the **Ref Windows 10 Enterprise x64**
    task sequence and select **Properties**.

2. In the **OS Info** tab, click **Edit Unattend.xml**. MDT now generates a catalog file, which
    takes a few minutes, and then **Windows System Image Manager (WSIM)** starts.

3. In **Windows System Image Manager (WSIM)**, in the **Answer File** pane, expand the **4
    specialize** node and select the **amd64_Microsoft-Windows-IE-
    InternetExplorer_neutral** entry.

4. In the **amd64_Microsoft-Windows-IE-InternetExplorer_neutral** properties window
    (the right-side window), set the following value:

    DisableDevTools: **true**

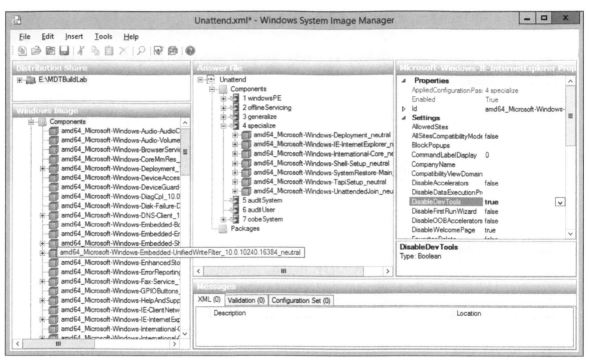

Editing the Unattend.xml file.

Real World Note: As fun as it ever is to debug web pages, the ViaMonstra users really don't have
to do that. ☺

5.   Save the **Unattend.xml** file, and close **Windows System Image Manager** (ignore the validation errors).

6.   In the **Ref Windows 10 Enterprise x64 Properties** window, click **OK**.

Real World Note: Windows System Image Manager validates the XML differently from the previous version. It doesn't like empty values. However, the Unattend.xml file is never used directly. It is used as a template, so the task sequence updates the Unattand.xml file before it is used, and you can ignore the error message "There are validation errors in this answer file. Do you want to continue?"

Review Deployment Share Rules

In MDT, there are always two rule files, the CustomSettings.ini file and the Bootstrap.ini file. You can add almost any rule to either; however, the Bootstrap.ini file is copied from the control folder to the boot image, so the boot image needs to be updated every time you change that file.

For that reason, we recommend adding only a minimal set of rules to Bootstrap.ini, such as which deployment server and share to connect to, the DEPLOYROOT value. Put the other rules in CustomSettings.ini because that file is updated immediately when you click OK (which saves the file). In the following steps, you review the rules that were configured for the MDT Build Lab deployment share:

1.   Using the **Deployment Workbench**, right-click the **MDT Build Lab** deployment share and select **Properties**.

2.   In the **Rules** tab, review the information.

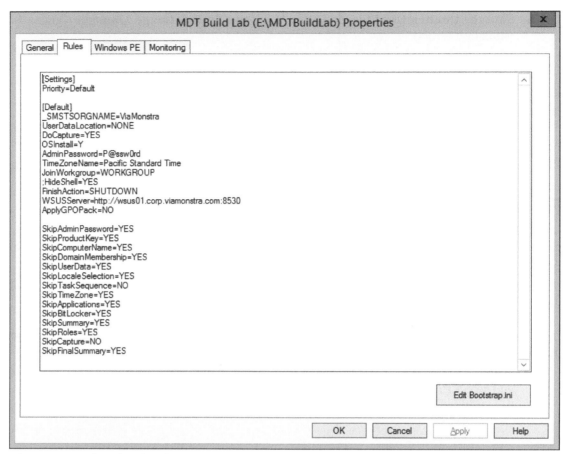

The server-side rules for the MDT Build Lab deployment share.

3. Click **Edit Bootstrap.ini** and review the information in the file.

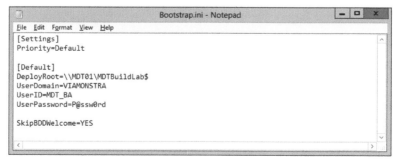

The boot image rules for the MDT Build Lab deployment share.

> **Real World Note:** For security reasons, you normally don't add the password to the Bootstrap.ini file; however, because this deployment share is for creating reference image builds only and should not be published to the production network, we think it is okay to do it here.

4. In the **Windows PE** tab, in the **Platform** drop-down list, make sure **x86** is selected and then review the current settings. Then click **Cancel**.

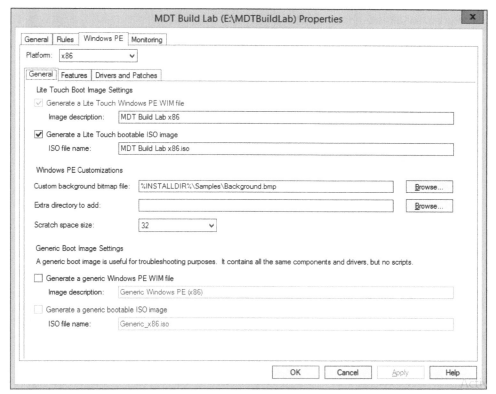

The MDT Build Lab settings created by the PowerShell script used to create the deployment share.

> **Real World Note:** One of MDT's features is that the x86 boot image can deploy both x86 and x64 operating systems (except for UEFI hardware). However, you still need to have both architectures available because the x64 boot image is still being used during computer refresh and other scenarios that are staging WinPE on the hard drive.

Update the Deployment Share

To create the WinPE boot images, the deployment share needs to be updated:

1. Using the **Deployment Workbench**, right-click the **MDT Build Lab** deployment share and select **Update Deployment Share**.

2. Use the default options for the **Update Deployment Share** wizard.

Note: The update process takes 5–10 minutes.

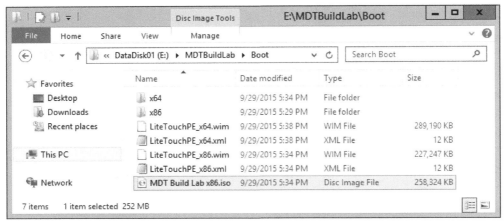

The WinPE boot images created, with the MDT Build Lab x86 ISO file.

Real World Note: Because you can use an x86 boot image for both x86 and x64 operating systems (reference images only), the MDT Build Lab deployment was configured not to create an ISO file for the x64 architecture.

The Rules Explained

Now that the MDT Build Lab deployment share (the share used to create the reference images) has been updated, and the WinPE boot images created, it is time to explain the various settings used in the Bootstrap.ini and CustomSettings.ini files.

The Bootstrap.ini and CustomSettings.ini files work together. The Bootstrap.ini file is always present on the boot image and is read first. The basic purpose for Bootstrap.ini is to provide just enough information for MDT to find the CustomSettings.ini on the deployment server.

The CustomSettings.ini file is normally stored on the server, in the deployment share\control folder, but also can be stored on the media (when using offline media).

The Bootstrap.ini File

Let's start with the easy one. The Bootstrap.ini file is available via the deployment share's Properties windows, or via the E:\MDTBuildLab\Control folder on MDT01.

```
[Settings]
Priority=Default

[Default]
DeployRoot=\\MDT01\MDTBuildLab$
UserDomain=VIAMONSTRA
UserID=MDT_BA
UserPassword=P@ssw0rd

SkipBDDWelcome=YES
```

So, what are these settings?

- **Priority.** This determines in what order different sections are read. This Bootstrap.ini has only one section, named [Default].

- **DeployRoot.** This is the location of the deployment share. Normally, this value is set by MDT, but you need to update the DeployRoot value if you move to another server or other share. If you don't specify a value, the Windows Deployment Wizard prompts you for a location.

- **UserDomain, UserID, and UserPassword.** These values are used for automatic logon to the deployment share. Again, if they are not specified, the wizard prompts you.

Real World Note: Caution is advised. These values are stored in clear text on the boot image. Use them only for the MDT Build Lab deployment share and not for the MDT Production deployment share.

- **SkipBDDWelcome.** Even though it is nice to be welcomed every time we start a deployment, we prefer to skip the initial welcome page of the Windows Deployment Wizard.

Real World Note: All properties beginning with "Skip" control only whether to display that pane in the Windows Deployment Wizard. Most of the panes also require you to actually set one or more values.

The CustomSettings.ini File

Now it is time for the heavy lifting. The CustomSettings.ini file, whose content you see on the Rules tab of the deployment share Properties window, contains most of the properties used in the configuration.

```
[Settings]
Priority=Default

[Default]
_SMSTSORGNAME=ViaMonstra
UserDataLocation=NONE
DoCapture=YES
OSInstall=Y
AdminPassword=P@ssw0rd
TimeZoneName=Pacific Standard Time
JoinWorkgroup=WORKGROUP
;HideShell=YES
FinishAction=SHUTDOWN
WSUSServer=http://wsus01.corp.viamonstra.com:8530
ApplyGPOPack=NO

SkipAdminPassword=YES
SkipProductKey=YES
SkipComputerName=YES
SkipDomainMembership=YES
SkipUserData=YES
SkipLocaleSelection=YES
SkipTaskSequence=NO
SkipTimeZone=YES
SkipApplications=YES
SkipBitLocker=YES
SkipSummary=YES
SkipRoles=YES
SkipCapture=NO
SkipFinalSummary=YES
```

The following list explains the CustomSettings.ini properties:

- **Priority.** Has the same function here as it does in Bootstrap.ini. Priority determines the order in which different sections are read. This CustomSettings.ini has only one section, named [Default]. In general, if you have multiple sections that set the same value, the value from the first section (higher priority) wins. The rare exceptions are listed in the ZTIGather.xml file.

- **_SMSTSORGNAME.** The organization name displayed in the task sequence progress bar window during deployment.

- **UserDataLocation.** Controls the settings for user state backup. You do not need to use any when building and capturing a reference image.

- **DoCapture.** Configures the task sequence to run Sysprep and capture the image to a file when the operating system is installed.

- **OSInstall.** Must be set to Y or YES (the code actually just looks for the Y character) for the setup to proceed.

- **AdminPassword.** Sets the local Administrator account password.

- **TimeZoneName.** The time zone to use. Don't confuse this value with TimeZone, which is only for legacy operating systems (Windows 7 and Windows Server 2003).

- **JoinWorkgroup.** Configures Windows to join a workgroup during deployment.

- **HideShell.** Hides the Windows shell during deployment. This is especially useful for Windows 8 and Windows 8.1 deployments where the deployment wizard otherwise appears behind the tiles. This setting is not used for Windows 10 deployments.

Real World Note: If you want to learn more about the HideShell behavior in Windows 10 deployments, please read this post by Michael Niehaus: http://blogs.technet.com/b/mniehaus/archive/2015/08/24/windows-10-mdt-2013-update-1-and-hideshell.aspx

---

- **FinishAction.** Instructs MDT what to do when the task sequence is complete.

Real World Note: The easiest way to find out the current time zone name on a Windows 10 machine is to run tzutil /g in a PowerShell prompt (or command prompt). You can also run tzutil /l to get a listing of all available time zone names.

- **WSUSServer.** Specifies which WSUS server (and port if needed) to use during the deployment.

- **SLSHARE.** Instructs MDT to copy the log files to a server share if something goes wrong during deployment, or when a deployment is successfully completed.

- **SkipAdminPassword.** Skips the wizard pane that asks for the Administrator password.

- **SkipProductKey.** Skips the pane that asks for the product key.

- **SkipComputerName.** Skips the Computer Name pane.

- **SkipDomainMemberShip.** Skips the Domain Membership pane. If set to Yes, you need to configure either the JoinWorkgroup value or the JoinDomain, DomainAdmin, DomainAdminDomain, and DomainAdminPassword properties.

- **SkipUserData.** Skips the pane for user state migration.

- **SkipLocaleSelection.** Skips the pane for selecting language and keyboard settings.

- **SkipTimeZone.** Skips the pane for setting the time zone.

- **SkipApplications.** Skips the Application pane.

- **SkipBitLocker.** Skips the BitLocker pane.

- **SkipSummary.** Skips the initial Windows Deployment Wizard summary pane.

- **SkipRoles.** Skips the Install Roles and Features pane.

- **SkipCapture.** Skips the Capture pane.

- **SkipFinalSummary.** Skips the final Windows Deployment Wizard summary. Because you use FinishAction=Shutdown, you don't want the wizard to stop in the end so that you need to click OK before the machine shuts down.

Chapter 9

Creating Reference Images

In this chapter, you use the previously created task sequence to create the reference image through a fully automated process.

Step-by-Step Guide Requirements

If you want to run the step-by-step guides in this chapter, you need a lab environment configured as outlined in Chapter 1 and Appendix A. In this chapter, you use the following virtual machines:

DC01   MDT01   WSUS01   REFW10X64-001

The VMs used in this chapter (the REFW10X64-001 VM is created in this chapter).

Build a Windows 10 Reference Image

1. Copy the **E:\MDTBuildLab\Boot\MDT Build Lab x86.iso** on **MDT01** to **C:\Setup\ISO** on the host PC.

Real World Note: In MDT, when building reference images, you can use the x86 boot image to deploy both x86 and x64 operating system images. That's why you use the x86 boot image in this guide instead of the x64 boot image.

---

2. Create a virtual machine with the following settings:

    a. Name: **REFW10X64-001**

    b. CPUs: **2** vCPUs

    c. Location: **C:\VMs** (or any location where you have space)

    d. Memory: **2048 MB** (if you have lots of memory, use 4 GB or more instead)

Note: Avoid using dynamic memory.

---

    e. Network: **Internal**

    f.   Hard disk: **60 GB** (dynamic disk)

    g.   Image file: **C:\Setup\ISO\MDT Build Lab x86.iso**

3. Create a checkpoint (snapshot) of the **REFW10X64-001** virtual machine, and name it **Clean with MDT Build Lab x86 ISO**.

Real World Note: Taking a checkpoint is really useful if you need to restart the process and want to make sure you can start clean.

---

4. Start the **REFW10X64-001** virtual machine, and after booting into WinPE, complete the **Windows Deployment Wizard** using the following setting:

    a.   Select a task sequence to execute on this computer: **Ref Windows 10 Enterprise x64**

    b.   Specify whether to capture an image: **Capture an image of this reference computer**

           Location: **\\MDT01\MDTBuildLab$\Captures**

    c.   File name: **REFW10X64-001.wim**

The setup now starts and does the following:

    a.   Installs the Windows 10 Enterprise operating system

    b.   Installs the added applications, roles, and features

    c.   Updates the operating system via your local WSUS server

    d.   Stages WinPE on the local disk

    e.   Runs Sysprep and reboots into WinPE

    f.   Captures the installation to a WIM file

    g.   Turns off the virtual machine

After some time, you will have a fully patched, sysprepped image of Windows 10 Enterprise x64 in the E:\MDTBuildLab\Captures folder on your deployment server. The filename is REFW10X64-001.wim.

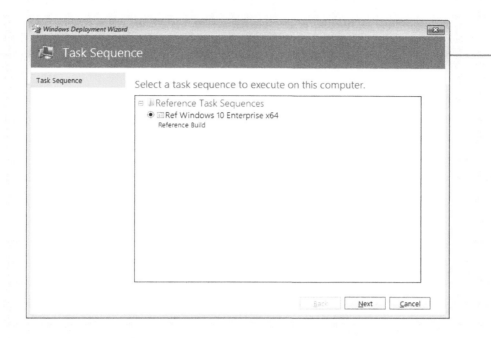

The Windows Deployment Wizard – Selecting the Windows 10 task sequence.

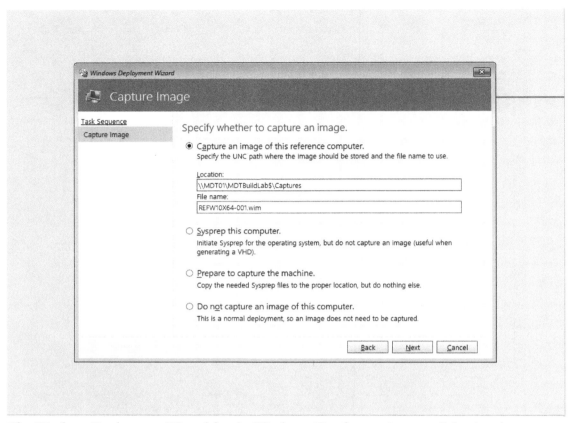

The Windows Deployment Wizard for the Windows 10 reference image – Selecting the capture location.

Chapter 10

Setting Up MDT for Production Deployment

In the preceding chapter, you created the reference image for Windows 10 Enterprise x64. It's now time to deploy that image. For production deployment, you create a separate MDT Production deployment share, a new task sequence, and additional applications. You also add drivers and different rules. The main reason for having multiple deployment shares is to make it easy to have different deployment settings. It is easier to separate the processes of creating reference images from the processes that are used to deploy them in production.

Step-by-Step Guide Requirements

If you want to run the step-by-step guides in this chapter, you need a lab environment configured as outlined in Chapter 1 and Appendix A. In this chapter, you use the following virtual machines:

DC01   MDT01   WSUS01

The VMs used in this chapter.

Setting Up the MDT Production Deployment Share

For production deployment, you just create another deployment share. However, for the MDT Production deployment share, you import the custom Windows 10 image you created (including Office, updates, and so forth) instead of the default Windows 10 image. You actually will have both types of images. The custom image is used for bare metal deployment, refresh, and replace scenarios, and the default image is used for the in-place upgrade scenario.

In the MDT Production deployment share, you also add drivers for your hardware models, as well as configure the deployment share to join the machines into the corp.viamonstra.com domain rather than a workgroup.

Create the MDT Production Deployment Share

1. On **MDT01**, open an elevated **PowerShell prompt**.

2. Create the deployment share by running the following command (the command is wrapped and should be one line):

    ```
    C:\Setup\Scripts\New-VIAMDTProductionDS.ps1 -Path
    "E:\MDTProduction" -Description "MDT Production"
    ```

3. From the **Start screen**, start the **Deployment Workbench** and review the **MDT Production** deployment share. You should find folders in the **Operating Systems**, **Out-of-Box Drivers**, and **Task Sequences** folders. Close the **Deployment Workbench** after reviewing the configuration.

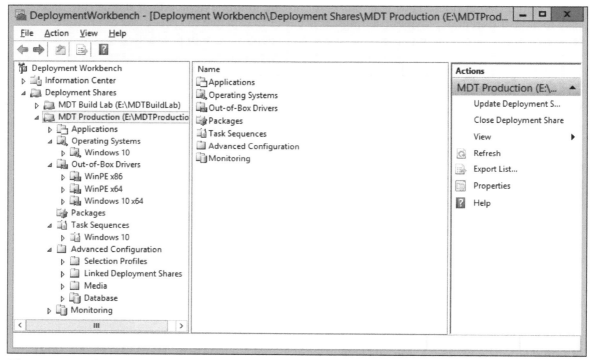

The MDT Production deployment share showing the folders created.

Configure the MDT Production Deployment Share

The newly created deployment share needs to be configured. Items that need to be configured are Bootstrap.ini, CustomSettings.ini, and the boot image names and settings; and, of course, the ViaMonstra logo needs to be injected into the boot images.

1. On **MDT01**, open an elevated **PowerShell prompt**.

2. Configure the deployment share by running the following command (the command is wrapped and should be one line):

```
C:\setup\Scripts\Set-VIAMDTProductionDS.ps1 -Path
"E:\MDTProduction"
```

Configure the MDT Production Deployment Share for Updates

The Set-VIAMDTProductionDS.ps1 script also copies a sample set of deployment rules (Bootstrap.ini and CustomSettings.ini); however, to get the updates during OS deployment, you should configure the rules to use your local WSUS server (unless you are using WSUS01 as your WSUS server). It also is possible to use the same server that you use for the MDT Build Lab deployment share.

If you have a WSUS server in your environment, use these steps to configure MDT to use it; otherwise, simply skip these steps, and MDT will use Microsoft Update directly.

1. On **MDT01**, using the **Deployment Workbench**, right-click the **MDT Production** deployment share and select **Properties**.

2. In the **Rules** tab, remove the comment (;) from the WSUSServer line and type in your WSUS server (WSUS01):

```
WSUSServer=http://wsus01.corp.viamonstra.com:8530
```

3. Click **OK** to save the changes.

Adding the Setup Files

After creating and configuring the deployment share, you are ready to add the custom image you created in Chapter 9 to the Deployment Workbench.

Add Windows 10 Enterprise x64 (Custom)

In this guide, you import the previously captured WIM file plus the setup files from the MDT Build Lab deployment share into the MDT Production deployment share:

1. On **MDT01**, open an elevated **PowerShell prompt**.

2. Import the **Windows 10 Enterprise X64** operating system to the deployment share by running the following command (the command is wrapped and should be one line):

```
C:\Setup\Scripts\Import-VIAMDTCOS.ps1 -Path
"E:\MDTProduction" -WIM "E:\MDTBuildlab\Captures\
REFW10X64-001.wim" -SetupFiles "E:\MDTBuildlab\Operating
Systems\W10X64" -MDTDestinationPath "Operating
Systems\Windows 10" -MDTDestinationFolderName
"CW10X64"
```

Adding the Applications

For various reasons, not all applications are suitable to have in the reference image. In ViaMonstra, a decision has been made to install two applications at deployment time for some users. The first step is to download the applications from the correct locations and then import them into the Deployment Workbench. It is not necessary to use application wrappers, but we created them for you because it is so much easier. The wrappers are very simple and can be used for more or less any application that understands command-line switches, which most of them do. Here is the list of application that will be installed during deployment:

- Adobe Acrobat Reader DC

- Oracle Java 8

Download the Applications

In the next guide, you download the applications to MDT01. If you are downloading any other version than the ones we are using, you might need to modify the scripts to match the current names of the files.

Adobe Acrobat Reader DC

Acrobat Reader is a free PDF reader, but you need a license to distribute it internally. Go to https://distribute.adobe.com/mmform/index.cfm?name=distribution_form&pv=rdr and fill out the form. It takes some time to get a reply with links for download.

> **Real World Note:** There also are MSI versions of Adobe Reader DC available, but they are typically one version behind, at least for a while.

Oracle Java 8

Oracle Java 8 is a Java runtime used for Java-based applications. You can download Java from http://www.java.com/en/download/windows_offline.jsp.

Import the Applications

In this guide, you copy all the downloaded applications to a folder structure and then use a PowerShell script to import the applications:

1. On **MDT01**, download **Adobe Acrobat Reader DC** (AcroRdrDC1500820082_en_US.exe) and copy it to the following folder:

   **C:\Setup\MDTProduction\Applications\\
   Install - Adobe Acrobat Reader DC\Source**

2. Download **Oracle Java 8** (jre-8u60-windows-i586.exe) and copy it to the following folder:

   C:\Setup\MDTProduction\Applications\Install - Oracle Java 8\Source

> **Note:** If you are using a newer version of Java (very likely), you also need to update the Install-OracleJava8.wsf script with the new file name.

3. Import the applications by opening an elevated **PowerShell prompt** and running the following command (the command is wrapped and should be one line):

```
C:\Setup\Scripts\Import-MDTApps.ps1 -Path "E:\MDTProduction"
-ImportFolder "C:\Setup\MDTProduction\Applications"
```

4. On **MDT01**, open the **Deployment Workbench** and verify that your applications has been imported.

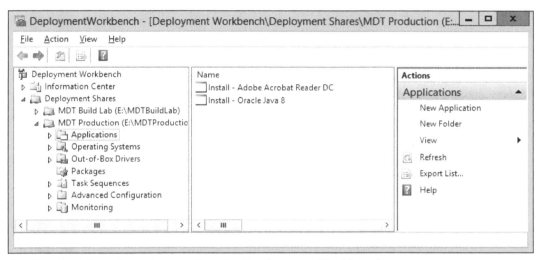

Applications have been imported to the Deployment Workbench.

Preparing the Drivers Repository

As you learned in Chapter 3, you need drivers both for the boot images and for the actual operating system. In this section, you add drivers for the boot image and the operating system for the following hardware models:

- Dell XPS 13

- Intel NUC D54250WYK

- Microsoft Surface 3 Pro

For boot images, you need to have storage and network drivers, and for the operating system, you need to have the full suite of drivers. In addition to downloading and extracting the drivers, you also need to clean up some unneeded drivers to save space on the file server and avoid conflicts with drivers not matching Windows 8 x64.

Real World Note: Most of the drivers will be downloaded and extracted using each vendor's tool, but some of the drivers have to be installed on a machine with matching hardware. Then you get the actual driver from that installation directory. But don't worry, as you will learn all the gory details shortly. ☺

Create the Driver Source Structure in the File System

The key to successful management of drivers for MDT, as well as any other deployment solution, is to have a really good drivers repository. From this repository, you import drivers into MDT for deployment, but you should always maintain the repository for future use.

1. On **MDT01**, using **File Explorer**, create the **E:\Drivers** folder.

2. In the **Drivers** folder, create the following folder structure:

    WinPE x86

    WinPE x64

    Windows 10 x64

3. In the new **Windows 10 x64** folder, create the following folders:

    NUC D54250WYK

    Surface 3 Pro

    XPS 13 9343

Real World Note: Even if you are not going to use both the x86 and x64 boot images in this book, we still recommend that you add the support structure for it because you might need it in the future.

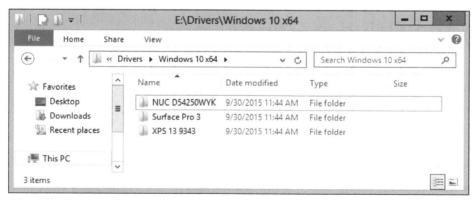

The E:\Drivers structure on MDT01.

The Logical Driver Structure in MDT

When importing drivers to the MDT driver repository, MDT creates a single instance folder structure based on driver class names. However, you can, and should, mimic the driver structure of your driver source repository in the Deployment Workbench. This is done by creating logical folders in the Deployment Workbench. When you created the MDT Production deployment share earlier in this chapter, the needed folders were automatically created for you.

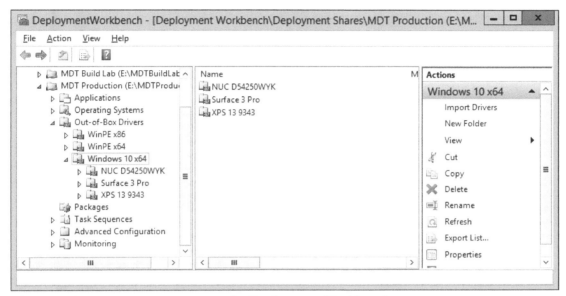

The Out-of-Box Drivers structure in the Deployment Workbench.

Selection Profiles for Boot Image Drivers

By default, MDT adds any storage and network driver that you import to the boot images. You want to have more control than that. You should add only the drivers that are actually needed to the boot image, and the way you control that is by using selection profiles.

When you created the MDT Production deployment share earlier in this chapter, two additional selection profiles were created for boot image drivers. In this guide, you review the setup that was created by the New-VIAMDTProductionDS.ps1 script.

1. On **MDT01**, using the **Deployment Workbench**, navigate to **MDT Production / Advanced Configuration / Selection Profiles**.

    You should now see the **WinPE x86** and **WinPE x64** selection profiles.

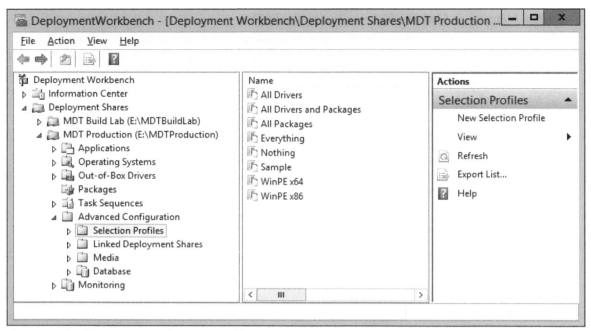

Creating the WinPE x64 selection profile.

2. Double-click the **WinPE x64** selection profile and review the properties.

    You should see that the **WinPE x64** folder in **Out-of-Box Drivers** is selected.

3. Click **Cancel**.

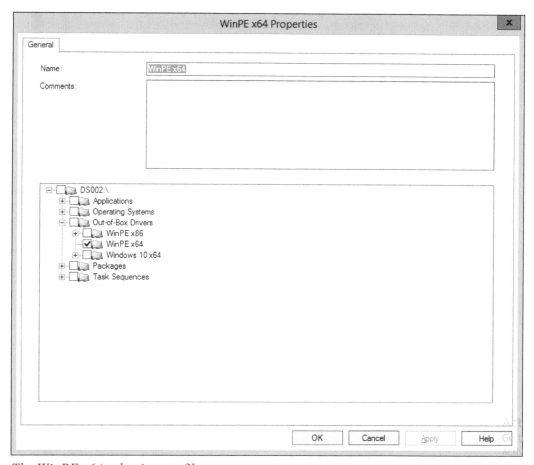

The WinPE x64 selection profile.

4. Using the **Deployment Workbench**, right-click the **MDT Production** deployment share and select **Properties**.

5. In the **Windows PE** tab, select the **x64** platform, and then click the **Driver and Patches** tab.

You should now see that the **WinPE x64** selection profile is already selected and the deployment share is configured to include only drivers from that selection profile.

> **Note:** If you had Deployment Workbench open when running the Set-VIAMDTProductionDS.ps1 script, you won't see the changes until you close and reopen Deployment Workbench.

6. Click **Cancel**.

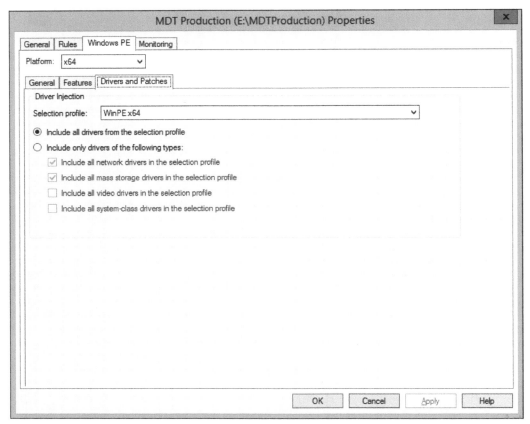

The MDT Production deployment share.

Extract and Import Drivers for the x64 Boot Image

WinPE supports all the hardware models that we have, but here you learn to add boot image drivers, anyway. Who knows, you might buy new hardware in the future and need additional drivers. In this example, you add some Intel network drivers to the x64 boot image.

In these steps, we assume you have downloaded a somewhat new version PROWinx64.exe from Intel.com and saved it to a temporary folder. We used version 20.3 in this example

1. Extract the **PROWinx64.exe** to a temporary folder—in this example to **C:\Tmp\ProWinx64**.

> **Real World Note:** Use WinRAR or any other extractor. Even if the PROWinx64.exe file supports a switch for silent extraction (/s), it will fail unless you run it on an operating system with the same architecture. Our favorite extractors are WinRAR and 7-Zip.

2. Using **File Explorer**, create the **E:\Drivers\WinPE x64\Intel PRO1000** folder.

3. Copy the content of the **C:\Tmp\PROWinx64\PRO1000\Winx64\NDIS65** folder to **E:\Drivers\WinPE x64\Intel PRO1000**.

Real World Note: Even if it is possible to import the entire folder, it is a very bad idea. You will end up with hundreds of drivers that you never use, every deployment will copy all drivers in the folder down to the machine, and you will have a massive number of drivers to deal with for a long time. The saying "less is more" really applies here.

---

4. Using the **Deployment Workbench**, navigate to **MDT Production / Out-of-Box Drivers**, right-click **WinPE x64**, and select **Import Drivers**.

5. Use the following setting for the **Import Drivers Wizard**:

> Driver source directory: **E:\Drivers\WinPE x64\Intel PRO1000**

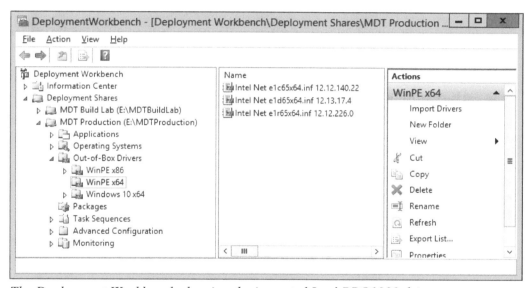

The Deployment Workbench showing the imported Intel PRO1000 drivers.

Download, Extract, and Import Drivers for Intel NUC D54250WYK

For the Intel NUC D54250WYK model, you use the Windows 10 drivers from Intel's website. In these steps, we assume you have downloaded the following files from Intel (https://downloadcenter.intel.com/product/76977/Intel-NUC-Kit-D54250WYK) to a temporary location:

*   AUD_Win7_8_8.1_10_6.0.1.7581.zip
*   Chipset_Win7_8_8.1_10_10.1.1.9.zip
*   GFX_Win7_8.1_10_64_15.40.3.4248.zip
*   ME_Win10_1.5M_11.0.0.1158.zip
*   PROWin10_64_20.2.exe

After these files are downloaded, you are ready to extract the drivers and copy them to your drivers folder on your deployment server (MDT01):

1. On **MDT01**, extract the preceding list of files to a temporary location, for example **C:\Windows\Temp**.

2. In the **AUD_Win7_8_8.1_10_6.0.1.7581\ 7581_PG433_Win10_Win8.1_Win8_Win7_WHQL** folder, delete the **Vista** folder. (You really don't need 300 MB of x86 drivers for an x64 deployment.)

3. Copy the **AUD_Win7_8_8.1_10_6.0.1.7581** folder to **E:\Drivers\Windows 10 x64\ NUC D54250WYK**.

4. From the **Chipset_Win7_8_8.1_10_10.1.1.9** folder, run the following command to extract the chipset drivers:

   ```
   SetupChipset.exe -extract C:\IntelChipset
   ```

5. Move the **C:\IntelChipset** folder to **E:\Drivers\Windows 10 x64\NUC D54250WYK**.

6. Copy the **GFX_Win7_8.1_10_64_15.40.3.4248** folder to **E:\Drivers\Windows 10 x64\NUC D54250WYK**.

7. In the **ME_Win10_1.5M_11.0.0.1158\ Intel(R)_ME_11.0_Consumer_11.0.0.1158_SW_Only** folder, delete the following folders:

   o **ME_SW_MSI**

   o **MEI-Only Installer MSI**

8. Copy the **ME_Win10_1.5M_11.0.0.1158** folder to **E:\Drivers\Windows 10 x64\NUC D54250WYK**.

9. From the **PROWin10_64_20.2\PRO1000\Winx64** folder, copy the **NDIS65** folder to **E:\Drivers\Windows 10 x64\NUC D54250WYK**.

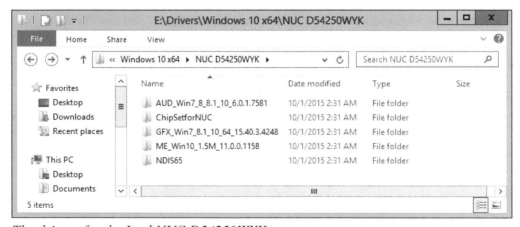

The drivers for the Intel NUC D54250WYK.

10. Using the **Deployment Workbench**, navigate to **MDT Production / Out-Of-Box Drivers / Windows 10 x64**.

11. Right-click **NUC D54250WYK**, select **Import Drivers**, and use the following setting for the **Import Driver** wizard:

> Driver source directory: **E:\Drivers\Windows 10 x64\NUC D54250WYK**

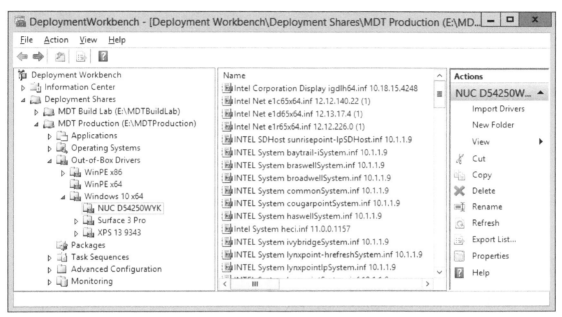

The imported drivers for Intel NUC D54250WYK.

Download, Extract, and Import Drivers for Surface Pro 3

For the Surface Pro 3 machine, you download the drivers from Microsoft's website (https://www.microsoft.com/en-us/download/details.aspx?id=38826) and import them into MDT:

1. On **MDT01**, download the Windows 10 driver ZIP file (**SurfacePro3_Win10_150915_0.zip**), and extract it to **E:\Drivers\Windows 10 x64\Surface Pro 3**.

2. Using the **Deployment Workbench**, navigate to **MDT Production / Out-Of-Box Drivers / Windows 10 x64**.

3. Right-click **Surface Pro 3**, select **Import Drivers**, and use the following setting for the **Import Driver** wizard:

> Driver source directory: **E:\Drivers\Windows 10 x64\Surface Pro 3**

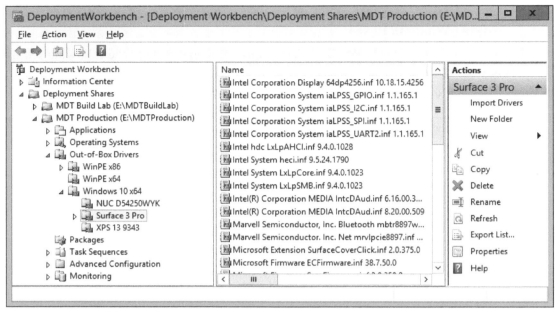

Drivers imported for Surface Pro 3.

Download, Extract, and Import Drivers for Dell XPS 13 (9343)

For the Dell XPS 13 (9343) machine, you download the Windows 10 CAB file from Dell's website (http://en.community.dell.com/techcenter/enterprise-client/w/wiki/11514.xps-13-9343-windows-10-driver-pack) and import them into MDT:

1. On **MDT01**, download the Windows 10 driver CAB file for Dell XPS 13 (**9343**), and extract it to **E:\Drivers\Windows 10 x64\XPS 13 9343**.

Note: It's not required to extract the CAB file. MDT actually knows how to import the CAB file content as it is, but extracting it makes it easier to review the content and do some house-cleaning if needed.

---

2. Using the **Deployment Workbench**, navigate to **MDT Production / Out-Of-Box Drivers / Windows 10 x64**.

3. Right-click **XPS 13 9343**, select **Import Drivers**, and use the following setting for the **Import Driver** wizard:

   Driver source directory: **E:\Drivers\Windows 10 x64\XPS 13 9343**

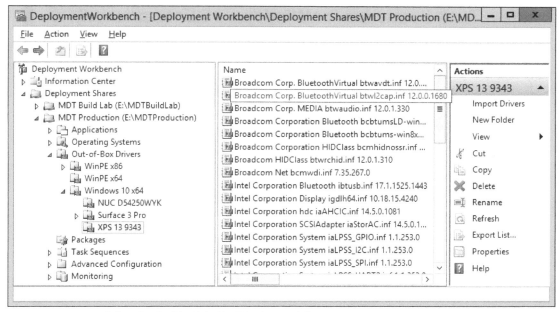

Drivers imported for the Dell XPS 13 (9343) model.

Creating the Deployment Task Sequence

It is now time to create the task sequence for your production image. After creating the task sequence, you configure it for driver injection and to enable patching against a WSUS server (WSUS01).

Create a Task Sequence for Windows 10 Enterprise x64

1. Using the **Deployment Workbench**, navigate to **MDT Production / Task Sequences / Windows 10**.

2. Right-click **Windows 10** and select **New Task Sequence**. Use the following settings for the **New Task Sequence Wizard**:

    a. Task sequence ID: **CW10X64-001**

    b. Task sequence name: **Custom Windows 10 Enterprise x64**

    c. Task sequence comments: **Production Image with Office 2016**

    d. Template: **Standard Client Task Sequence**

    e. Select OS:
        REFW10X64-001DDrive in CW10x64 REFW10X64-001.wim

    f. Specify Product Key**: Do not specify a product key at this time**

    g. Full Name: **ViaMonstra**

    h. Organization: **ViaMonstra**

    i. Internet Explorer home page: **http://viamonstra.com**

    j. Select **Do not specify an Administrator password at this time**

Edit the Windows 10 Enterprise x64 Task Sequence

1. Right-click the **Custom Windows 10 Enterprise x64** task sequence and select **Properties**.

2. On the **Task Sequence** tab, configure the **Custom Windows 10 Enterprise x64** task sequence with the following settings:

    a. Preinstall. After the **Enable BitLocker (Offline)** action, add a **Set Task Sequence Variable** action with the following settings:

        ▪ Name: **Set DriverGroup001**

        ▪ Task Sequence Variable: **DriverGroup001**

        ▪ Value: **Windows 10 x64\%ModelAlias%**

    b. Preinstall. Configure the **Inject Drivers** action with the following settings:

        ▪ Choose a selection profile: **Nothing**

        ▪ **Install all drivers from the selection profile**

Real World Note: The labels "Choose a selection profile" and "Install all drivers from the selection profile" are not worded very well. What the preceding configuration really means is that MDT should use only drivers from the folder specified by the DriverGroup001 property (which is what "Choose a selection profile = Nothing" does), and that MDT should not use plug and play to determine what drivers to copy (which is what the "Install all drivers from the selection profile" setting does).

Why not plug and play? The main reason not to rely on plug and play for driver detection is its limitations. The first limitation is that it can detect only drivers for devices that are activated in the BIOS. As an example, if Bluetooth is disabled, plug and play might not detect the Bluetooth device. Another issue is multi-tier drivers. Because plug-and-play scanning might detect only the first level of drivers, it may copy only half the drivers needed. That means it will copy only the bus driver because that was detected, but the other drivers for that device are never copied, which results in a yellow exclamation mark on the device in Device Manager and possibly a sad user.

---

      c. State Restore. Enable the **Windows Update (Pre-Application Installation)** action.

      d. State Restore. Enable the **Windows Update (Post-Application Installation)** action.

3. Click **OK**.

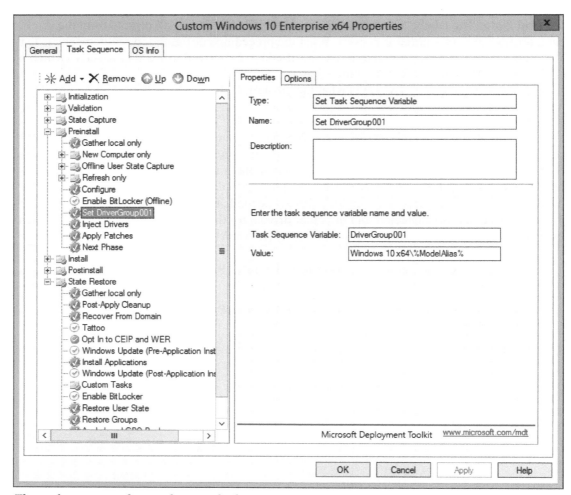

The task sequence for production deployment.

Configuring the MDT Production Deployment Share

As with the MDT Build Lab deployment share, the script that created the deployment share also prepared the MDT Production rules, and some basic configuration. In this section, you enable monitoring, review the settings provided by the setup script, and then update the deployment share to create the boot images.

Enable Monitoring

In these steps, you enable monitoring on the MDT Production deployment share:

1. On **MDT01**, right-click the **MDT Production** deployment share and select **Properties**.

2. In the **Monitoring** tab, select the **Enable monitoring for this deployment share** check box.

3. Click **OK**.

Real World Note: You can have only one deployment share configured for monitoring; however, it is possible to add a property manually to all other deployment shares. If you want to have monitoring enabled for, let's say, the MDT Build Share deployment share, just add the following to the rules: EventService=http://MDT01:9800.

Review the Rules and Add Sample Scripts

In these steps, you verify the rules and boot image settings:

1. On **MDT01**, right-click the **MDT Production** deployment share and select **Properties**.

2. In the **Windows PE** tab, in the **Platform** drop-down list, make sure **x86** is selected.

3. In the **General** sub-tab, verify the following settings:

   o Image description: **MDT Production x86**

   o Generate a Lite Touch bootable ISO image: **Selected**

   o ISO file name: **MDT Production x86.iso**

   o Custom background bitmap file:
   %DEPLOYROOT%\Branding\ViaMonstraLogo.bmp

4. In the **Windows PE** tab, in the **Platform** drop-down list, make sure **x64** is selected.

5. In the **General** sub-tab, verify the following settings:

   o Image description: **MDT Production x64**

   o Generate a Lite Touch bootable ISO image: **Selected**

   o ISO file name: **MDT Production x64.iso**

   o Custom background bitmap file:
   %DEPLOYROOT%\Branding\ViaMonstraLogo.bmp

Real World Note: Because you are going to use PXE later to deploy the machines, you don't really need the ISO file; however, we recommend creating ISO files because they are very useful when troubleshooting deployments and for quick tests.

6. In the **Drivers and Patches** sub-tab, select the **WinPE x86** selection profile and verify the following settings.

   o   Selection Profile: **WinPE x86**

   o   Include all drivers from the selection profile: **Selected**

7. In the **Drivers and Patches** sub-tab, select the **WinPE x64** selection profile and verify the following settings.

   o   Selection Profile: **WinPE x64**

   o   Include all drivers from the selection profile: **Selected**

8. Click **Cancel**.

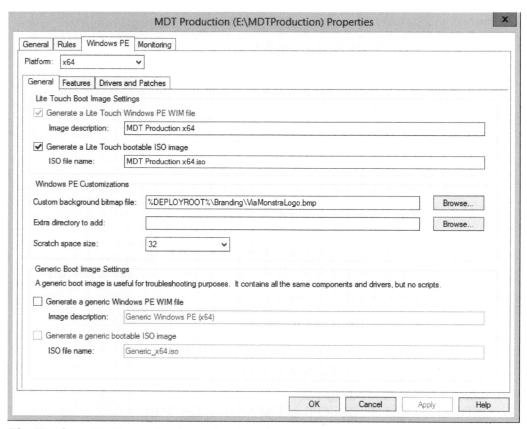

The Windows PE General sub-tab for the x64 boot image.

Update the Deployment Share

To create the WinPE boot images, the deployment share needs to be updated:

1. Using the **Deployment Workbench**, right-click the **MDT Production** deployment share and select **Update Deployment Share**.

2. Use the default options for the **Update Deployment Share** wizard.

> **Note:** The update process takes 5–10 minutes.

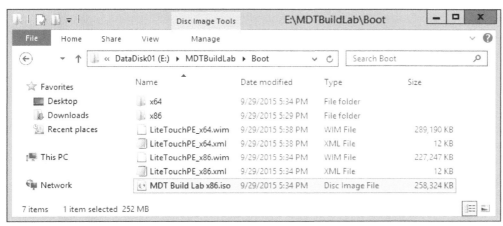

The WinPE boot images for MDT Production created.

The Rules Explained

The rules for the MDT Production deployment share are slightly different from the ones you used for the MDT Build Lab deployment share. The biggest changes are that you are now deploying the machines into a domain instead of a workgroup and you did not automate the login.

The Bootstrap.ini File

This is the MDT Production Bootstrap.ini, without the user credentials (except domain information):

```
[Settings]
Priority=Default

[Default]
DeployRoot=\\MDT01\MDTProduction$

UserDomain=VIAMONSTRA
UserID=MDT_BA

SkipBDDWelcome=YES
```

The CustomSettings.ini File

This is the CustomSettings.ini file, with the new join domain information:

```
[Settings]
Priority=ByIsOnBattery, HardwareInfo, Default
Properties=ModelAlias,StagingOU

[ByIsOnBattery]
SubSection=ByIsOnBattery-%IsOnBattery%

[ByIsOnBattery-True]
OSInstall=NO

[HardwareInfo]
UserExit=AliasUserExit.vbs
ModelAlias=#SetModelAlias()#

[Default]
_SMSTSORGNAME=ViaMonstra
OSInstall=Y
UserDataLocation=AUTO
TimeZoneName=Pacific Standard Time
AdminPassword=P@ssw0rd
JoinDomain=corp.viamonstra.com
DomainAdmin=MDT_JD
DomainAdminDomain=VIAMONSTRA
StagingOU=ou=Staging,ou=Internal IT,ou=ViaMonstra,dc=corp,
dc=viamonstra,dc=com
MachineObjectOU=ou=Workstations,ou=viamonstra,dc=corp,
dc=viamonstra,dc=com
SLShare=\\MDT01\Logs$
ScanStateArgs=/ue:*\* /ui:VIAMONSTRA\*
USMTMigFiles001=MigApp.xml
USMTMigFiles002=MigUser.xml
HideShell=NO
ApplyGPOPack=NO
FinishAction=REBOOT
;WSUSServer=http://wsus01.corp.viamonstra.com:8530

SkipAppsOnUpgrade=NO
SkipAdminPassword=YES
SkipProductKey=YES
SkipComputerName=NO
SkipDomainMembership=YES
SkipUserData=YES
SkipLocaleSelection=YES
```

```
SkipTaskSequence=NO
SkipTimeZone=YES

SkipApplications=NO
SkipBitLocker=YES
SkipSummary=YES
SkipCapture=YES
SkipFinalSummary=YES


[MoveComputerToOU]
WebService=http://MDT01/DeploymentWebService/ad.asmx/MoveComputerToOU
Parameters=OSDComputerName,MachineObjectOU
OSDComputerName=ComputerName
MachineObjectOU=OUPath
```

In Chapter 8, you learned the basics about the CustomSettings.ini properties. Here is a list the additional properties that we use in the MDT Production rules file:

- **ByIsOnBattery.** This section is used to abort the deployment if running on battery.

- **HardwareInfo.** This section is used to call the AliasUserExit.vbs script that assigns friendly names to make and model alias. These values are in turn being used to assign drivers from the driver repository.

- **JoinDomain**. This indicates which domain to join.

- **DomainAdmin**. This identifies which account to use when joining the machine to the domain.

- **DomainAdminDomain.** This is the domain for the join domain account.

- **DomainAdminPassword**. This is the password for the join domain account.

- **MachineObjectOU.** This specifies into which OU to add the computer account.

- **StagingOU.** This custom property is used for the move computer scenario in Chapter 19.

- **ScanStateArgs.** These are the arguments for the USMT Scanstate command.

- **USMTMigFiles(*).** This is the list of USMT templates (controlling what to back up and restore).

- **MoveComputerToOU.** This custom section is used for the move computer scenario in Chapter 19.

Creating the Logs Folder

When you deploy computers, it is possible to collect the log files after each machine has been deployed. Although it is not required, it is highly recommended. We have already configured CustomSettings.ini to save the log files to a share. In the following guide, you create, share, and set the correct permissions:

1. On **MDT01**, open an elevated **PowerShell prompt**.

2. Create the deployment share by running the following command (the command is wrapped and should be one line):

   ```
   C:\Setup\Scripts\New-VIAMDTLogShare.ps1 -Path "E:\Logs"
   -BuildAccount "MDT_BA"
   ```

Creating the MigData folder

For the computer replace scenario, you need to have a location to store the migration data, a MigData folder. In the following guide, you create, share, and set the correct permissions:

1. On **MDT01**, open an elevated **PowerShell prompt**.

2. Create the deployment share by running the following command (the command is wrapped and should be one line):

   ```
   C:\Setup\Scripts\New-VIAMDTMigDataShare.ps1
   -Path "E:\MigData" -BuildAccount "MDT_BA"
   ```

Configure Windows Deployment Services (WDS)

You need to add the MDT Production Lite Touch x64 Boot image to WDS in preparation for the deployment. For the following steps, we assume that Windows Deployment Services has already been installed on MDT01 according to the instructions in Appendix A and Chapter 7.

1. Using the **WDS console**, right-click **Boot Images** and select **Add Boot Image**.

2. Browse to the **E:\MDTProduction\Boot\LiteTouchPE_x64.wim** file and add the image with the default settings.

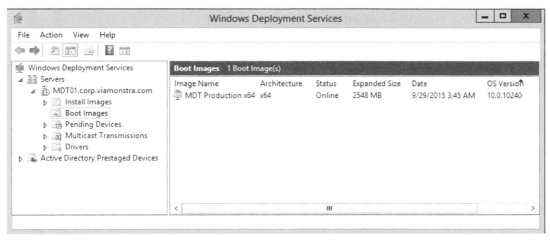

The boot image added to the WDS console.

Set Default Boot Image

1. In the **WDS console**, right-click the **MDT01.corp.viamonstra.com** server and select **Properties**.

2. In the **Boot** tab, in the **Default boot image (optional)** area, select the **MDT Production x64** boot image as default for the following architectures:

    o   **x64 architecture**

    o   **x64 (UEFI) architecture**

3. Click **OK**.

Real World Note: You can also automate "Press Enter" or "Press F12" (depending on BIOS or UEFI) during deployment by changing the boot properties to always continue the PXE boot. However, that PXE setting might increase the chance for an "Oops, I reloaded my machine" situation because it will force a machine that is configured to PXE boot first in the BIOS boot order to start the deployment. Setting boot properties to always continue the PXE boot works best when you don't have machines that are configured to boot on the network device in the first place and should be used with caution. It also is possible to prestage the machines in Active Directory using the WDS console or wdsutil.exe.

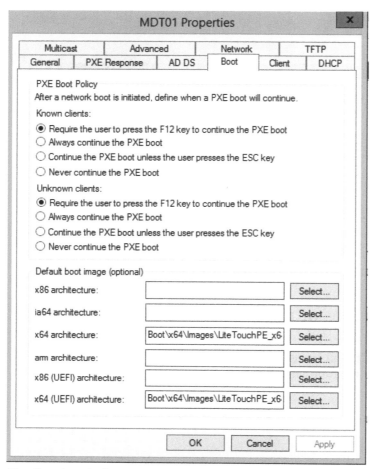

Configuring the boot options in WDS.

TFTP Configuration

In some cases, you need to modify TFTP Maximum Block Size settings for performance tuning reasons, especially when PXE traffic travels through routers and such. In the previous version of WDS, it was possible to change that, but the method of doing it was far from friendly (editing the registry). Changes in Windows Server 2012 and Windows Server 2012 R2 make it easy—just click the TFTP tab in the WDS UI and modify the settings for Maximum Block Size, and you are done.

Real World Note: Normally you start by setting the block size to 16384 (decimal) and then test whether it works on your hardware. If it doesn't, try 8192 first, then 4096, and so forth.

If you are running your PXE server in a VMware environment, this setting might make the deployment process slower, test and verify before using this setting in production.

Also, there are a few new features related to TFTP performance:

- **Scalable buffer management.** Allows buffering an entire file instead of a fixed size buffer for each client, allowing different sessions to read from the same shared buffer.

- **Scalable port management.** Provides the ability to service clients with shared UDP port allocation, increasing scalability.

- **Variable-size transmission window (Variable Windows Extension).** Improves TFTP performance by allowing the client and server to determine the largest workable window size.

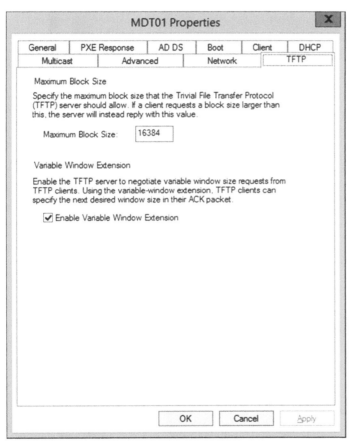

TFTP changes are now easy to perform.

Chapter 11

New Computer Scenario

In this chapter, you use the previously created task sequences to deploy the images through a fully automated process. First, you need to add the boot image to Windows Deployment Services (WDS) and then start the deployment. In contrast with deploying images from the MDT Build Lab deployment share, we recommend using PXE to start the full deployments, even though you technically can use USB or ISO/CD media to start the process, as well.

Step-by-Step Guide Requirements

If you want to run the step-by-step guides in this chapter, you need a lab environment configured as outlined in Chapter 1 and Appendix A. In this chapter, you use the following virtual machines:

DC01   MDT01   WSUS01   PC0003

The VMs used in this chapter (the PC0003 VM is created in this chapter).

Deploying the Windows 10 Client

Great work! At this point, you should have a deployment solution ready for deploying Windows. We do recommend starting slowly, trying a few deployments at the time, until you are confident that your configuration works as expected.

Create a Virtual Machine and Start the Deployment

We find it very useful to try some initial tests on virtual machines before testing on real physical hardware. This is simply because you can always rule out hardware issues when testing (or troubleshooting). The following guide includes the steps to deploy your Windows 10 image to a virtual machine:

1. Create a virtual machine with the following settings:

   o Name: **PC0003**

   o Location: **C:\VMs**

   o Memory: **2048 MB**

   o Network: **Internal**

o   Hard disk: **60 GB** (dynamic disk)

o   Installation options: Install an operating system from a network-based installation server.

2.   Start the **PC0003** virtual machine, and press **Enter** (or F12 if using a BIOS-based virtual machine) to start the PXE boot.

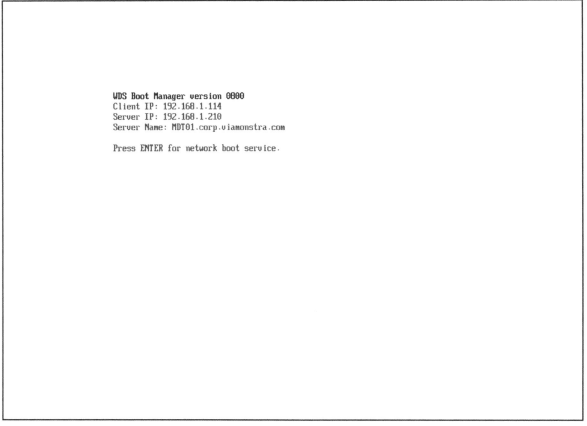

```
WDS Boot Manager version 0000
Client IP: 192.168.1.114
Server IP: 192.168.1.210
Server Name: MDT01.corp.viamonstra.com

Press ENTER for network boot service.
```

The initial PXE boot process of PC0003.

3.   After WinPE has booted, complete the **Windows Deployment Wizard** using the following settings. Note that many values are preselected, so you don't need to change them.

a.   Password: **P@ssw0rd**

b.   Select a task sequence to execute on this computer: **Custom Windows 10 Enterprise x64**

c.   Computer Name: **PC0003**

d.   Domain to Join (preselected): ***corp.viamonstra.com***

e. Organizational Unit (preselected):
    OU=Workstations,OU=viamonstra,DC=corp,DC=viamonstra,DC=com

f. User Name (preselected): **MDT_JD**

g. Password (preselected): **P@ssw0rd**

h. Domain (preselected): **VIAMONSTRA**

i. Do not move user data and settings: **Selected**

j. Do not restore user data and settings: **Selected**

k. Applications: Select the following applications:

    ▪ **Install - Adobe Acrobat Reader DC**

    ▪ **Install - Oracle Java 8**

l. Do not enable BitLocker for this computer: **Selected**

m. Click **Next** to start the deployment.

The setup now starts and does the following:

a. Installs the Custom Windows 10 Enterprise x64 operating system

b. Updates the operating system via your local WSUS server

c. Installs the added applications

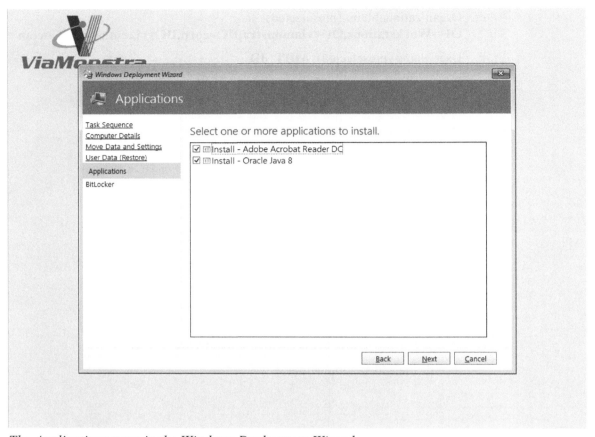

The Applications page in the Windows Deployment Wizard.

Use the MDT Monitoring Feature

Because you enabled monitoring on the MDT Production deployment share, you can now follow your deployment of PC0003 via the monitoring node:

1. On **MDT01**, using the **Deployment Workbench**, navigate to **MDT Production / Monitoring** node and wait until you see **PC0003**.

2. Double-click **PC0003**, and review the information.

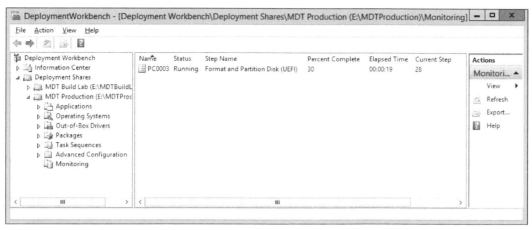

The Monitoring node, showing the deployment progress of PC0003.

Use Information in the Event Viewer

When monitoring is enabled, MDT also writes information to the event viewer on MDT01. This information also can be used to trigger notifications, via scheduled tasks, when deployment is completed. For example, you can configure scheduled tasks to send an email when a certain event is created in the event log.

1. On **MDT01**, start the **Event Viewer**.

2. In **Event Viewer**, right-click **Custom Views** and select **Create Custom View**.

3. In the **Create Custom View** window, configure the following:

   a. Event level:

      Select the **Warning, Error** and **Information** check boxes.

   b. By log:

      Event logs: **Windows Logs / Application**

   c. By source:

      Event sources: **MDT_Monitor**

4. Click **OK**.

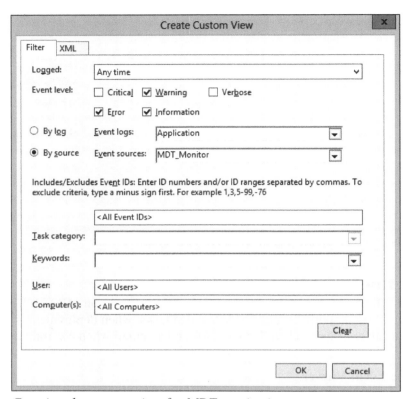

Creating the custom view for MDT monitoring events.

5. Name the custom view **MDT Monitoring**, and click **OK**.

6. Select the **MDT Monitoring** custom view and review the information in the events pane.

Real World Note: The MDT Monitoring feature can be extended even more. Because the Event viewer and Task Scheduler work together, you can, for example, configure the deployment server to send you an email after a successful deployment or event, and even better, if a deployment fails.

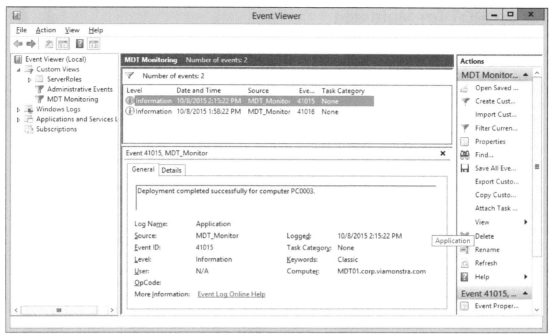

The Event Viewer showing a successful deployment of PC0003.

Multicast Deployments

Multicast deployment allows for image deployment with reduced network load during simultaneous deployments. Although multicast is a nice OS deployment feature in MDT deployments, it requires that your network supports it and also is designed for it.

Requirements

Multicast requires that Windows Deployment Services (WDS) is running on Windows Server 2008 or later. In addition to the core MDT setup for multicast, the network needs to be configured to support multicast. In general, this means involving the organization networking team to make sure that Internet Group Management Protocol (IGMP) snooping is turned on and that the network is designed for multicast traffic. The multicast solution uses IGMPv3.

Set Up MDT for Multicast

Setting up MDT for multicast is very easy. You just enable multicast on the deployment share, and MDT takes care of the rest.

1. On **MDT01**, right-click the **MDT Production** deployment share and select **Properties**.

2. In the **General** tab, select the **Enable multicast for this deployment share (requires Windows Server 2008 Windows Deployment Services)** check box, and click **OK**.

3. Right-click the **MDT Production** deployment share and select **Update Deployment Share**.

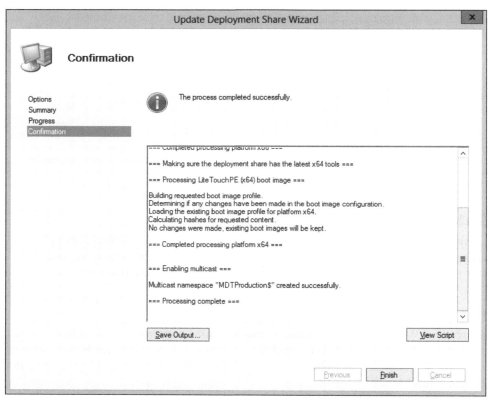

The Update Deployment Share Wizard showing the Multicast namespace.

Start the Multicast Deployment

After enabling multicast on the deployment share, you can start deploying clients. The difference compared with the deployments you've done previously is that MDT now uses multicast to download the image to the drive.

1. Create a virtual machine with the following settings:

   a. Name: **PC0004**

   b. Location: **C:\VMs**

   c. Memory: **2048 MB**

   d. Network: **Internal**

   e. Hard disk: **60 GB** (dynamic disk)

   f. Installation options: Install an operating system from a network-based installation server.

2. Take a snapshot of the **PC0004** virtual machine, and name it **Clean with PXE**.

3. Start the **PC0004** virtual machine, and allow it to PXE boot.

4. After WinPE has booted, complete the **Windows Deployment Wizard** using the following setting. (Note that many values are preselected so you don't need to change them.)

   a. Password: **P@ssw0rd**

   b. Select a task sequence to execute on this computer: **Custom Windows 10 Enterprise x64**

   c. Computer Name: **PC0004**

   d. Domain to Join (preselected): **corp.viamonstra.com**

   e. Organizational Unit (pre-selected): **OU=Workstations,OU=viamonstra,DC=corp,DC=viamonstra,DC=com**

   f. User Name (preselected): **MDT_JD**

   g. Password (preselected): **P@ssw0rd**

   h. Domain (preselected): **VIAMONSTRA**

   i. Do not move user data and settings: **Selected**

   j. Do not restore user data and settings: **Selected**

   k. Applications: Select the following applications:

      - **Install - Adobe Acrobat Reader DC**

      - **Install - Oracle Java 8**

   l. Do not enable BitLocker for this computer: **Selected**

   m. Click **Next** to start the deployment.

163

The setup now starts and does the following:

a. Installs the Custom Windows 10 Enterprise x64 operating system

b. Updates the operating system via your local WSUS server

c. Installs the added applications

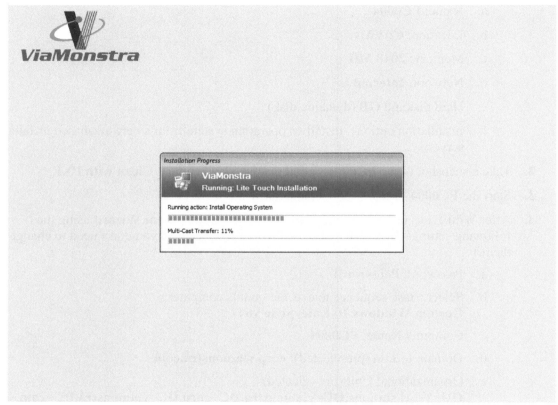

Multicast deployment in progress.

Using Boot Media

Booting with PXE is very convenient, but sometimes not practical for various reasons. For example, you may not be allowed to set up a PXE server on that network, or the computer may not have PXE support unless you have a specific network adapter in the computer. Or, it may be that you are replacing a current PXE-based deployment solution and simply want to verify all models, drivers, and task sequences before your shift from the old solution. In such cases, using boot media is a useful scenario.

Creating a Bootable USB Stick

If you followed all the steps to create and configure the MDT Production share, you already have configured a bootable ISO image. When you update the deployment share, it also generates a boot media. You can use it directly as an .iso file to deploy virtual machines, burn it to CD/DVD, or use a USB stick. We prefer to use USB sticks, rather than CD/DVD media, because it is faster, and also because not all machines have CD/DVD these days.

Follow these steps to create a bootable USB stick from the boot media content:

1. On the machine you use to manage Hyper-V or VMware, insert the USB stick you want to use and open an elevated **PowerShell prompt**.

2. Get the USB stick information, and assign it to the **$Disk** variable by running the following command (the command is wrapped and should be one line):

    ```
    $Disk = Get-Disk | Where-Object {$_.Path -match "USBSTOR"
    -and $_.Size -gt 7Gb -and -not $_.IsBoot}
    ```

3. Verify that you are going to work on the correct USB stick by running the following command:

    ```
    $Disk
    ```

Verifying that you are working with the correct USB stick.

4. Continue if you see the correct disk in the list; otherwise, remove/replace the USB stick.

5. Clear the disk from any existing volume by running the following command:

    ```
    Clear-Disk -InputObject $Disk -RemoveData -confirm:$False
    ```

6. Create a partition on the USB stick by running the following command (the command is wrapped and should be one line):

    ```
    $Partition = New-Partition -InputObject $Disk
    -UseMaximumSize
    ```

7. Format the USB stick by running the following command (the command is wrapped and should be one line):

    ```
    Format-Volume -NewFileSystemLabel "BOOT" -FileSystem NTFS
    -Partition $Partition -Confirm:$False
    ```

8. Assign a drive letter by running the following command (the command is wrapped and should be one line):

```
Add-PartitionAccessPath -DiskNumber $Disk.Number
-PartitionNumber 1 -AssignDriveLetter
```

9. Get the assigned drive letter, and assign it to the **$Volume** variable by running the following command:

```
$Volume = Get-Volume -FileSystemLabel "BOOT"
```

10. Review the assigned drive letter by running the following command:

```
$Volume
```

11. Make the USB stick active by running the following command (the command is wrapped and should be one line):

```
Set-Partition -DriveLetter $Volume.DriveLetter -IsActive
$True
```

12. Verify the configuration by running the following command (the command is wrapped and should be one line):

```
Get-Partition -DriveLetter $Volume.DriveLetter |
Select-Object *
```

Verifying the configuration.

13. Using **File Explorer**, copy the **\\MDT01\MDTProduction$\Boot\ MDT Production x64.iso** file to **C:\Setup\ISO**.

14. Mount the **C:\Setup\ISO\MDT Production x64.iso** file by double-clicking on it.

15. Copy the content from the mounted ISO to the root of the USB stick.

Congrats! Now you have a bootable USB stick!

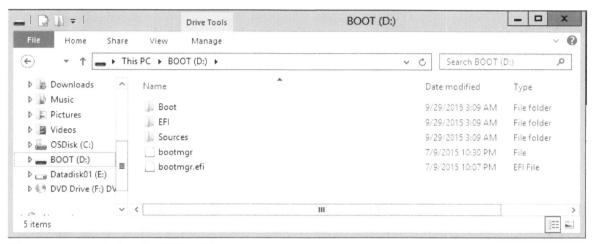

The content copied to the USB stick.

Using Offline Media

In addition to network-based deployments, MDT also supports the use of offline media-based deployments. You can very easily generate an offline version of your deployment share, either the full deployment share or a subset of it by the use of selection profiles. The generated offline media can be burned to a DVD or copied to a USB stick for deployment.

Offline media is useful not only when you don't have network connectivity to the deployment share, but also when you have limited connection to the deployment share and don't want to copy 5 GB of data over the wire. Offline media can still join the domain, but you save the transfer of operating system images, drivers, and applications over the wire.

Real World Note: Please don't use USB hard drives for your offline media deployments. There are simply too many known issues with this. Use USB sticks instead. While you may get offline media deployment to work from a USB hard drive, we have seen too many cases where it fails because of the BIOS version/configuration or hard drive model being used. What can happen is that MDT tries to deploy the image to the external hard drive instead of using the internal drive, this because of how WinPE enumerates the drives. Don't say we didn't warn you. ☺

Create the Offline Media Selection Profile

To filter what is being added to the media, you create a selection profile. When creating selection profiles, you quickly realize the benefits of having created a good logical folder structure in the Deployment Workbench.

1. On **MDT01**, using the **Deployment Workbench**, navigate to **MDT Production / Advanced Configuration** node, right-click **Selection Profile**, and select **New Selection Profile**.

2. Use the following settings for the **New Selection Profile Wizard**:

   a. General Settings

      Selection profile name: **Windows 10 Offline Media**

   b. Folders

      - **Applications**

      - **Operating Systems / Windows 10**

      - **Out-Of-Box Drivers / WinPE x64**

      - **Out-Of-Box Drivers / Windows 10 x64**

      - **Task Sequences / Windows 10**

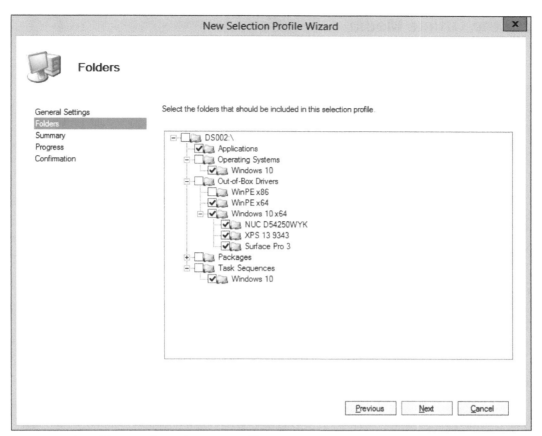

Creating the offline media selection profile.

Create the Offline Media

In these steps, you generate offline media from the MDT Production deployment share. To filter what is being added to the media, you use the previously created selection profile.

1. On **MDT01**, using the **Deployment Workbench**, navigate to **MDT Production / Advanced Configuration**, right-click **Media**, and select **New Media**.

2. Use the following settings for the **New Media Wizard**:

   General Settings

   - Media path: **E:\MDTOfflineMedia**

   - Selection profile: **Windows 10 Offline Media**

> **Real World Note:** When creating offline media, never, ever, create a subfolder inside the deployment share folder because that will break the offline media.

Configure the Offline Media

Offline media have their own rules, their own Bootstrap.ini and CustomSettings.ini files. They are stored in the Control folder of the offline media, but can also be accessed via properties of the offline media in the Deployment Workbench.

1. On **MDT01**, using **File Explorer**, copy the following files from **C:\Setup \MDTOfflineMedia\Control** folder to **E:\MDTOfflineMedia\Content\Deploy \Control**. Overwrite the existing files.

   o **Bootstrap.ini**

   o **CustomSettings.ini**

2. Using **File Explorer**, copy the **C:\Setup\MDTOfflineMedia\Branding** folder to **E:\MDTOfflineMedia\Content\Deploy**.

3. Using the **Deployment Workbench**, navigate to **MDT Production / Advanced Configuration / Media**, right-click **MEDIA001**, and select **Properties**.

4. In the **General** tab, configure the following:

   o Clear the **Generate x86 boot image** check box.

   o ISO file name: **Windows 10 Offline Media.iso**

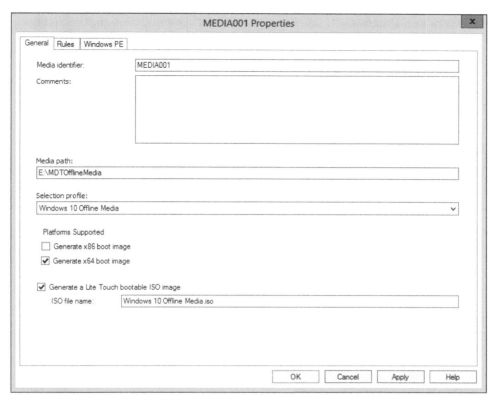

The offline media properties.

5. In the **Rules** tab, remove the comment (;) from the WSUSServer line and type in your WSUS server (WSUS01):

    ```
    WSUSServer=http://wsus01.corp.viamonstra.com:8530
    ```

6. In the **Windows PE** tab, in the **Platform** drop-down list, make sure **x64** is selected.

7. In the **General** sub-tab, configure the following setting:

    In the **Windows PE Customizations** area:

    Custom background bitmap file:
    %DEPLOYROOT%\Branding\ViaMonstraLogo.bmp

8. In the **Features** sub-tab, enable the following components:

    o **DISM Cmdlets**

    o **Microsoft Data Access Components (MDAC/ADO) support**

    o **.NET Framework**

    o **Windows PowerShell**

    o **Secure Boot Cmdlets**

    o **Storage Management Cmdlets**

9. In the **Drivers and Patches** sub-tab, select the **WinPE x64** selection profile and select the **Include all drivers from the selection profile** option.

10. Click **OK**.

Generate the Offline Media ISO and Deploy Folder

Now everything is set to generate, or build, the offline media ISO and Deploy folder:

1. On **MDT01**, using the **Deployment Workbench**, navigate to **MDT Production / Advanced Configuration / Media**.

2. Right-click **MEDIA001** and select **Update Media Content**. The Update Media Content process now generates the offline media in the **E:\MDTOfflineMedia** folder.

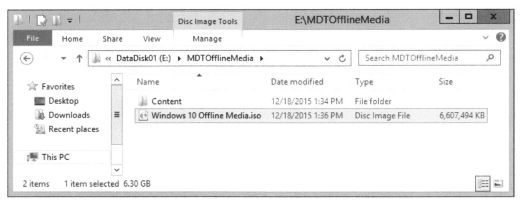

The MDTOfflineMedia folder after updating the media item.

> **Real World Note:** The full path in Windows cannot be longer than 260 characters, and it's often when you generate offline media that you run into that issue. This is because the offline media adds the Content/Deploy folder to the existing path, and sometimes that is all it takes to have the update fail. Fixing the problem is easy; just use a shorter path when importing the operating system.

Create a Bootable USB Stick

The ISO that you got when updating the offline media item can be burned to a DVD and used directly (it is bootable), but it's often more efficient to use USB sticks. They are both faster and can hold more data. (A dual-layer DVD is limited to 8.5 GB.)

Follow these steps to create a bootable USB stick from the offline media content:

1. On the machine you use to manage Hyper-V or VMware, insert the USB stick you want to use and open an elevated **PowerShell prompt**.

2. Get the USB stick information, and assign it to the **$Disk** variable by running the following command (the command is wrapped and should be one line):

    ```
    $Disk = Get-Disk | Where-Object {$_.Path -match "USBSTOR"
    -and $_.Size -gt 7Gb -and -not $_.IsBoot}
    ```

3. Verify that you are going to work on the correct USB stick by running the following command:

    ```
    $Disk
    ```

```
PS C:\Windows\System32> $Disk = Get-Disk | Where-Object {$_.Path -match "USBSTOR" -and $_.Size -gt 7
Gb -and -not $_.IsBoot}
PS C:\Windows\System32> $Disk

Number Friendly Name                         OperationalStatus      Total Size Partition Style
------ -------------                         -----------------      ---------- ---------------
1      Kingston DT Ultimate G2 USB Device    Online                  29.84 GB MBR


PS C:\Windows\System32> _
```

Verifying that you are working with the correct USB stick.

4. Continue if you see the correct disk in the list; otherwise, remove/replace the USB stick.

5. Clear the disk from any existing volume by running the following command:

    ```
    Clear-Disk -InputObject $Disk -RemoveData -confirm:$False
    ```

6. Partition the USB stick by running the following command (the command is wrapped and should be one line):

    ```
    $Partition = New-Partition -InputObject $Disk
    -UseMaximumSize
    ```

7. Format the USB stick by running the following command (the command is wrapped and should be one line):

    ```
    Format-Volume -NewFileSystemLabel "BOOT" -FileSystem NTFS
    -Partition $Partition -Confirm:$False
    ```

8. Assign a drive letter by running the following command (the command is wrapped and should be one line):

    ```
    Add-PartitionAccessPath -DiskNumber $Disk.Number
    -PartitionNumber 1 -AssignDriveLetter
    ```

9. Get the assigned drive letter, and assign it to the **$Volume** variable by running the following command:

```
$Volume = Get-Volume -FileSystemLabel "USBDISK01"
```

10. Review the assigned drive letter by running the following command:

```
$Volume
```

11. Make the USB stick active by running the following command (the command is wrapped and should be one line):

```
Set-Partition -DriveLetter $Volume.DriveLetter -IsActive
$True
```

12. Copy the content of the **MDTOfflineMedia\Content** folder to the root of the USB stick.

Congrats, now you have a bootable USB stick with a portable deployment solution!

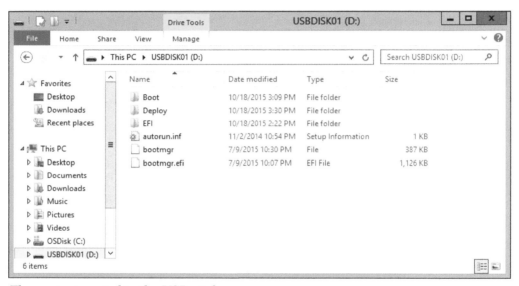

The content copied to the USB stick.

Real World Note: The USB stick can be formatted with either FAT32 or NTFS, as either works; however, we recommend using FAT32 to support UEFI deployment. There is a limitation on FAT32 filesystem: it only allows file sizes up to 4 GB, but in MDT, it is possible to overcome that limitation by using the split-WIM feature. The feature needs to be enabled, as it's disabled by default. To do that, open the Settings.xml file in the Control folder and change <SkipWimSplit>True</SkipWimSplit> to <SkipWimSplit>False</SkipWimSplit>. After this change, you need to update the media deployment share.

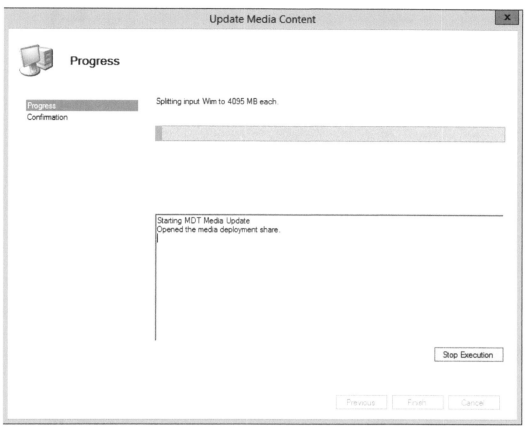

Splitting the WIM when creating the media.

Chapter 12

In-Place Upgrade Scenario

As you learned in chapter 2, the in-place upgrade scenario is a new scenario available for Windows 10 deployment only. In this scenario, you don't use a custom reference image. Instead, you use the default Windows 10 image that Microsoft provides.

In this chapter, you upgrade an existing Windows 7 SP1 client to Windows 10 using the in-place upgrade method.

Step-by-Step Guide Requirements

If you want to run the step-by-step guides in this chapter, you need a lab environment configured as outlined in Chapter 1 and Appendix A. In this chapter, you use the following virtual machines:

DC01   MDT01   WSUS01   PC0001

The VMs used in this chapter.

Upgrading PC0001 to Windows 10

Adding support in MDT for the in-place upgrade process involves importing a default Windows 10 image, creating an in-place upgrade task sequence, and then initiating the process on a machine running a previous version of Windows.

Start the Virtual Machines

1. Make sure the **DC01**, **MDT01** and **WSUS01** virtual machines are running.

2. Start the **PC0001** virtual machine.

Add the Windows 10 Default Image

1. On **MDT01**, log on as **Administrator** in the **VIAMONSTRA** domain using a password of **P@ssw0rd**.

2. Using the **Deployment Workbench**, navigate to **MDT Production / Operating Systems**.

3. Right-click the **Windows 10** folder and select **Import Operating System**. Use the following settings for the **Import Operating System Wizard**:

    a. **Full set of source files**

    b. Source directory: **E:\MDTBuildLab\Operating Systems\W10X64**

    c. Destination directory name: **W10X64**

> **Real World Note:** You also copy and paste the imported operating system from MDT Build Lab to MDT Production directly using the Deployment Workbench.

Create a Windows 10 Upgrade Task Sequence

1. On **MDT01**, using the **Deployment Workbench**, navigate to **MDT Production / Task Sequences**.

2. Right-click **Windows 10** and select **New Task Sequence**. Use the following settings for the **New Task Sequence Wizard**:

    a. Task sequence ID: **W10X64-001**

    b. Task sequence name: **Upgrade Windows 10 Enterprise x64**

    c. Task sequence comments: **In-place upgrade using Default Image**

    d. Template: **Standard Client Upgrade Task Sequence**

    e. Select OS: **Windows 10 Enterprise in W10X64 install.wim**

    f. Specify Product Key: **Do not specify a product key at this time**

    g. Full Name: **ViaMonstra**

    h. Organization: **ViaMonstra**

    i. Internet Explorer home page: **http://viamonstra.com**

    j. Select **Do not specify an Administrator password at this time**

Edit the Upgrade Windows 10 Enterprise x64 Task Sequence

1. In the **Task Sequences / Windows 10** node, double-click the **Upgrade Windows 10 Enterprise x64** task sequence, and click the **Task Sequence** tab.

2. Expand the **Upgrade the Operating System** group. After the **Copy scripts** action, add a new **Set Task Sequence Variable** action with the following settings:

    o Name: **Set DriverGroup001**

    o Task Sequence Variable: **DriverGroup001**

    o Value: **Windows 10 x64\%ModelAlias%**

3. Select the **Inject Drivers** action, and configure the following:

   o   Choose a selection profile: **Nothing**

   o   **Install all drivers from the selection profile**

4. Post-Processing: Enable the **Windows Update (Pre-Application Installation)** action.

5. Post-Processing: Enable the **Windows Update (Post-Application Installation)** action.

6. Review the other actions in the upgrade task sequence, and then click **OK.**

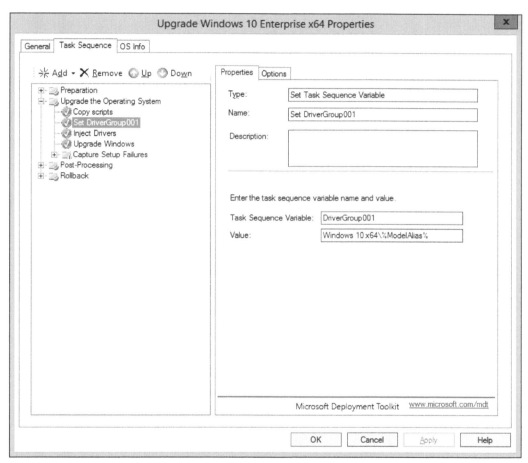

The upgrade task sequence configured for drivers, total control style.

Initiate the Windows 10 In-Place Upgrade

1. On **PC0001**, log on as **VIAMONSTRA\frank.sheep** and make some customizations like adding favorites to Internet Explorer, adding icons and documents to the desktop, creating your own custom background in Microsoft Paint, and so forth.

2. Log out and then log on as **VIAMONSTRA\Administrator**. Start the **Lite Touch Deploy Wizard** by running **MDT01\MDTProduction$\Scripts\Litetouch.vbs**. Complete the guide using the following settings:

   a. Select a task sequence to execute on this computer:

      Upgrade Windows 10 Enterprise x64

   b. Select one or more applications to install:

      ▪ **Install - Adobe Acrobat Reader DC**

      ▪ **Install - Oracle Java 8**

   c. Do not enable BitLocker for this computer: **Selected**

   d. Credentials / Password: **P@ssw0rd**

3. Relax while **PC0001** is upgraded to Windows 10.

4. When the upgrade is completed, log on as **VIAMONSTRA\frank.sheep** and verify that the customizations you did are still there.

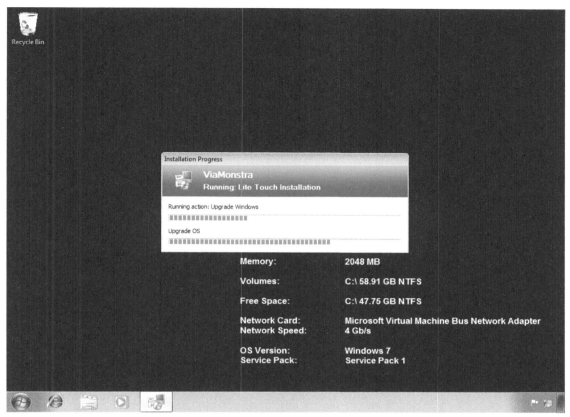

Windows 10 in-place upgrade is running.

Chapter 13

Computer Refresh Scenario

In this chapter, you use MDT Lite Touch to refresh a computer. Simply put, the refresh scenario, or *computer refresh* to use the official term, is a reinstallation of the same machine. The machine can be refreshed to the same operating system that it's currently running or to a later version.

Even though Windows 10 supports in-place upgrades, the refresh scenario is useful when the in-place upgrade cannot be used, such as when upgrading from an x86 platform to an x64 platform.

When refreshed to a later version, it appears as an upgrade to the end user, but technically it's not an in-place upgrade. A computer refresh also involves taking care of user data and settings from the old installation and making sure to restore those at the end of the installation.

Step-by-Step Guide Requirements

If you want to run the step-by-step guides in this chapter, you need a lab environment configured as outlined in Chapter 1 and Appendix A. In this chapter, you use the following virtual machines:

DC01   MDT01   WSUS01   PC0002

The VMs used in this chapter.

Preparing for Computer Refresh

In a computer refresh with MDT (with the ADK deployment tools in the background), the User State Migration Tool (USMT) is used to migrate user data and settings. A computer refresh involves the following steps:

1. Data and settings are backed up locally in a backup folder.

2. The partition is wiped, except for the backup folder.

3. The new operating system image is applied.

4. Other applications are installed.

5. Data and settings are restored.

You might think that a migration consumes a lot of space during the computer refresh, but it doesn't. USMT uses a feature called *hard-link migration store*. When you use this feature, the files are simply linked in the file system. This also means that the migration is very fast, even when there is a lot of data.

Real World Note: Data and settings that are migrated with USMT are often referred to as "user state," even though technically computer-specific data and settings also are stored in the backup. You also don't need to worry about getting junk migrated from the old installation. USMT only migrates what you configure it to migrate.

In addition to the USMT backup, you can enable an optional full WIM backup of the machine by configuring the MDT rules. If you do this, a .wim file is created in addition to the USMT backup. This .wim file contains the entire volume from the computer, and helpdesk personnel can extract content from it if needed.

Real World Note: Even though the optional backup is a .wim file, applying this image to restore a running operating system is not supported. The intention of the .wim file is to have a backup of data, not a computer backup that can be restored. We also have seen customers who back up the machine to a VHD file instead. It uses much more disk space, but the resulting VHD can then be used to create a virtual machine, which you then can run as a VDI machine if something does not work correctly. Creating a VHD file is done by running the disk2vhd.exe utility, which can be used as a command-line utility in a task sequence.

Multi-User Migration

By default, ScanState backs up all profiles on the machine, even the local computer profiles that you are normally not very interested in. Also, if you have a machine that has been in your environment for a while, the odds are that it has quite a few domain-based profiles on it, including those of users who no longer use the computer. This, of course, depends on the environment, but it's nice for you to know that you can limit which profiles are backed up by configuring command-line switches to ScanState (added as rules in MDT).

In ViaMonstra, each machine usually has a primary user, meaning there are not many domain user profiles on each machine. For this scenario, it makes sense to configure ScanState to capture only domain-based profiles. As you may remember from Chapter 10, the CustomSettings.ini file (the rules) has the following line:

```
ScanStateArgs=/ue:*\* /ui:VIAMONSTRA\*
```

This line configures ScanState to back up only domain-based profiles on your machines.

> **Real World Note:** If you have many user domain profiles on your machines, it probably makes more sense to use the /uel switch which excludes profiles that have not been accessed within a specific number of days. For example, adding /uel:60 configures ScanState (or LoadState) not to include profiles that haven't been accessed for more than 60 days.

Support for Additional Settings

In addition to the command-line switches that control which profiles to migrate, the XML templates control exactly what data is being migrated. You can control data both within and outside the user profiles.

Since the XML templates are structured text files, we recommend using Windows PowerShell ISE or any other XML editor when editing the templates.

Create a Custom USMT Template

In the ViaMonstra environment, we have decided to migrate two settings in addition to what the default templates migrate. In this section, you configure the environment to use a custom USMT XML template that does the following:

- Backs up the C:\Data folder (including all files and folders)

- Scans the local disk for PDF documents (*.pdf files) and restores them to the C:\Data\PDF Documents folder on the destination machine

The custom USMT template is named MigViaMonstraData.xml, and you can find it in the book sample files.

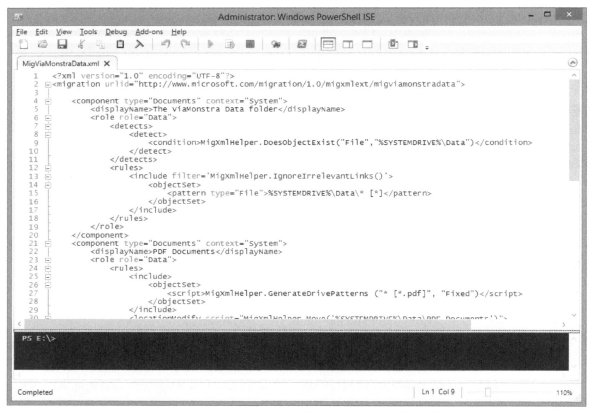

The MigViaMonstraData.xml template opened in Windows PowerShell ISE.

Add the ViaMonstra Custom XML Template

In order to use the custom MigViaMonstraData.xml USMT template, you need to copy it to the MDT Production deployment share and update the CustomSettings.ini file. In these steps, we assume you have copied the book sample files to C:\Setup on MDT01.

1. On **MDT01**, using **File Explorer**, copy the **C:\Setup\MDT Production\USMT\MigViaMonstraData.xml** file to the following folders:

   o   **E:\MDTProduction\Tools\x86\USMT5**

   o   **E:\MDTProduction\Tools\x64\USMT5**

Note: Yes, the folders are still named USMT5 even though you are using USMT from Windows ADK 10 in them.

---

2. Start **Notepad** from an elevated **PowerShell prompt**, and then edit the **E:\MDTProduction\Control\CustomSettings.ini** file. After the **USMTMigFiles002=MigUser.xml** line add the following line:

```
USMTMigFiles003=MigViaMonstraData.xml
```

3. Save the **CustomSettings.ini** file.

Note: If you want your offline media to use the new template, as well, you also need to update the CustomSettings.ini file belonging to that media.

Refreshing a Windows 7 Client

After adding the additional USMT template and configuring the CustomSettings.ini file to use it, you are now ready to refresh a Windows 7 SP1 client to Windows 10.

Upgrade (Refresh) a Windows 7 SP1 Client

In these steps, we assume you have a Windows 7 SP1 client named PC0002 in your environment.

1. Start the **PC0002** virtual machine.

2. On **PC0002**, log on as **VIAMONSTRA\frank.sheep** and make some customizations like adding favorites to Internet Explorer, adding icons and documents to the desktop, putting some documents in the C:\Data folder, creating your own custom background in Microsoft Paint, adding some PDF documents to a few folders, and so forth.

3. Log out and then log on as **VIAMONSTRA\Administrator**. Start the **Lite Touch Deploy Wizard** by running \\MDT01\MDTProduction$\Scripts\Litetouch.vbs. Complete the wizard using the following settings:

   a. Select a task sequence to execute on this computer: **Custom Windows 10 Enterprise x64**

   b. Computer name: **<default>**

   c. Specify where to save your data and settings: **<default>**

   d. Specify where to save a complete computer backup: **Do not back up the existing computer**.

Note: This is the optional full WIM backup you skip. The USMT backup will still run.

---

4. Select one or more applications to install:

   o **Install - Adobe Acrobat Reader DC**

   o **Install - Oracle Java 8**

   o Do not enable BitLocker for this computer: **Selected**

   o Credentials / Password: **P@ssw0rd**

The setup now starts and does the following:

    a.   Backs up user settings and data using USMT

    b.   Installs the Windows 10 Enterprise operating system

    c.   Updates the operating system via your local WSUS server

    d.   Installs the added applications

    e.   Restores user settings and data using USMT

5. When the computer refresh is completed, log on as **VIAMONSTRA\frank.sheep** and verify that the customizations you did have been restored.

Chapter 14
Computer Replace Scenario

In this chapter, you use the computer replace scenario. As you learned in Chapter 2, a computer replace is quite similar to a computer refresh. The difference is the location of the backup. Because we are replacing a machine, we cannot store the backup on the old computer, so we store the backup on the MDT server.

During a computer replace, these are the high-level steps that occur:

1. On the old machine (the computer you are replacing), a special replace task sequence runs the USMT backup and, if you configured it, runs the optional full WIM backup.

2. On the new machine, you perform a standard bare metal deployment. At the end of the bare metal deployment, the USMT backup from the old computer is restored.

> **Real World Note:** When a computer is being retired, there might be a lot of additional actions that should occur, such as disabling the computer account in Active Directory. If you need additional automation around removing/replacing a computer, consider adding Orchestrator Runbooks, web services, or scripts that perform other configuration actions. Such actions ensure the machine is removed from all systems.

Step-by-Step Guide Requirements

If you want to run the step-by-step guides in this chapter, you need a lab environment configured as outlined in Chapter 1 and Appendix A. In this chapter, you use the following virtual machines:

DC01   MDT01   WSUS01   PC0002   PC0005

The VMs used in this chapter (you create the PC0005 VM in this chapter).

Preparing for the Computer Replace

In this chapter, the scenario is to replace PC0002 (running Windows 10, previously upgraded from Windows 7 SP1 via the computer refresh scenario) with PC0005 (a new machine, not yet deployed). The high-level steps to do this are the following:

1. Create the replace task sequence.

2. Run the replace task sequence (the backup only task sequence) on the old computer (PC0002).

3. Perform a bare metal deployment of the new computer (PC0005).

Real World Note: With Windows 10, the replace computer scenario also can be used to change a machine configuration from BIOS to UEFI.

Depending of the size of your organization, you might need to do some storage calculations before starting to do computer replace deployments. We have seen customers underestimate the actual amount of data being copied over the network, forcing them to slow down the overall deployment project. You also might need to dedicate additional storage on the MDT server.

There are two things that could help you keep storage usage down a bit. If your server runs Windows Server 2012 or later (like you do if you are using the proof-of-concept environment for this book), you can enable the data deduplication feature. (data deduplication was enabled as part of preparing MDT01 in Chapter 7.) You also can use the File Server Managers automation functions to schedule a cleanup job for the MigData folder.

Create a Replace (Backup Only) Task Sequence

1. On **MDT01**, using the **Deployment Workbench**, navigate to **MDT Production / Task Sequences** and create a new folder named **Other**.

2. Right-click the **Other** folder and select **New Task Sequence**. Use the following settings for the **New Task Sequence Wizard**:

    a. Task sequence ID: **REPLACE-001**

    b. Task sequence name: **Backup Only Task Sequence**

    c. Task sequence comments: **Run USMT to backup user data and settings**

    d. Template: **Standard Client Replace Task Sequence**

Edit the Replace (Backup Only) Task Sequence

1. In the **Task Sequences / Other** node, double-click the **Backup Only Task Sequence** and click the **Task Sequence** tab.

2. In the **Initialization** group, after the **Gather local only** action, add a new **Set Task Sequence Variable** action with the following settings:

    o   Name: **Set FinishAction**

    o   Task Sequence Variable: **FinishAction**

    o   Value: **SHUTDOWN**

3. Review the sequence. Notice that it contains only a subset of the normal client task sequence actions. Then click **OK** to save the changes.

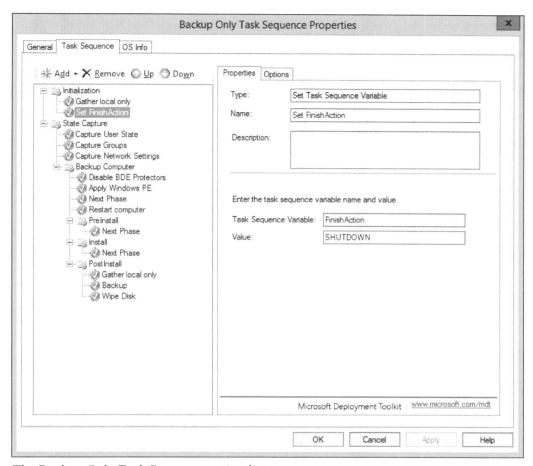

The Backup Only Task Sequence action list.

Start the Replace (Backup Only) Task Sequence

1. Start the **PC0002** virtual machine.

2. On **PC0002**, log on as **VIAMONSTRA\frank.sheep** and make some customizations like adding favorites to Internet Explorer, adding icons and documents to the desktop, creating your own custom background in Microsoft Paint, and so forth.

3. Log off and then log on as **VIAMONSTRA\Administrator**.

4. Verify that you have write access to the **MDT01\MigData$** share.

5. Execute **MDT01\MDTProduction$\Scripts\LiteTouch.vbs**.

6. Complete the **Windows Deployment Wizard** using the following settings:

   a.   Select a task sequence to execute on this computer:
        Backup Only Task Sequence

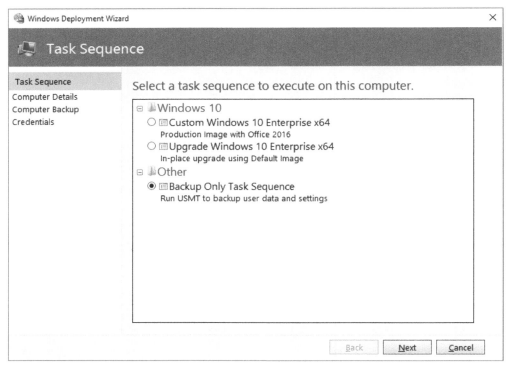

Selecting the Backup Only Task Sequence.

b.   Specify where to save your data and settings: **Specify a location**

Location: **\\MDT01\MigData$\PC0002**

Note: Make sure not to add a trailing backslash (\) to the location, which will break the backup.

c.   Specify where to save a complete computer backup:

Do not back up the existing computer

Note: Again, this is the optional full WIM backup you skip. The USMT backup will still run.

d.   Password: **P@ssw0rd**

The task sequence now runs USMT (Scanstate.exe) to capture user data and settings of the machine.

Real World Note: If you add WipeDisk=YES to your rules, MDT will also do a secure wipe of the old machine. Secure wipe in this case is not a US Department of Defense (DoD) approved secure wipe, but is using the format /p:3 feature that overwrites every sector with zeros, three times. You can also create your own action to wipe the disk using other tools like DaRT from MDOP 2015 to accomplish that.

7. Verify that you have an **USMT.MIG** compressed backup file in the
   \\MDT01\MigData$\PC0002\USMT folder.

Deploy the PC0005 Virtual Machine

1. Create a virtual machine with the following settings:

   a. Name: **PC0005**

   b. Location: **C:\VMs**

   c. Memory: **2048 MB**

   d. Network: **Internal**

   e. Hard disk: **60 GB** (dynamic disk)

   f. Installation options: **Install an operating system from a network-based
      installation server.**

2. Start the **PC0005** virtual machine, press **Enter** and allow it to boot WinPE (PXE), and
   complete the **Windows Deployment Wizard** using the following settings:

   a. Password: **P@ssw0rd**

   b. Select a task sequence to execute on this computer:
      Custom Windows 10 Enterprise x64

   c. Computer Name: **PC0005**

   d. Move Data and Settings: **Do not move user data and settings**

Real World Note: This option is used when using the offline USMT backup, enabling you to
capture USMT data from WinPE.

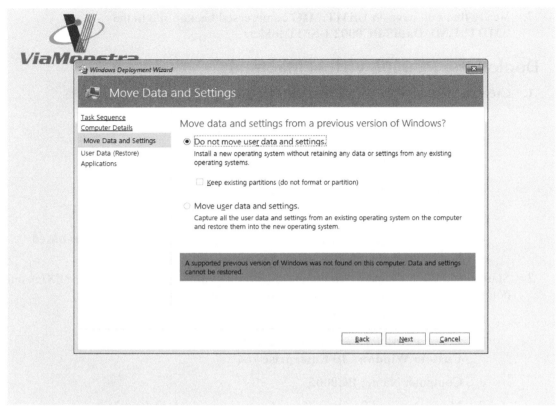

The Offline USMT Backup option.

> e. Specify whether to restore user data: **Specify a location**
>
>   Location: **\\MDT01\MigData$\PC0002**
>
> f. Applications: Select the following applications:
>
>   ▪ **Install - Adobe Acrobat Reader DC**
>
>   ▪ **Install - Oracle Java 8**
>
> g. Do not enable BitLocker for this computer: **Selected**

The setup starts and does the following:

> a. Installs the Windows 10 operating system
>
> b. Joins the corp.viamonstra.com domain
>
> c. Installs the selected applications
>
> d. Restores the backup previously captured from PC0002

3. When the setup is completed, log on as **VIAMONSTRA\frank.sheep** and verify that the customizations you did on **PC0002** have been restored.

Chapter 15

Enable Remote Connection

In this chapter, you learn about implementing an optional, but very useful, remote connection. If your organizations have signed a new Software Assurance agreement after August 1st, 2015, it includes MDOP by default. For older agreements, there is still an extra MDOP per-seat fee.

Included in MDOP is Microsoft Diagnostics and Recovery Toolset (DaRT), which contains tools that can help you troubleshoot MDT deployments, as well as troubleshoot Windows itself.

Real World Note: The coolest feature in DaRT is no doubt the remote connection capabilities that allow you to connect to WinPE remotely.

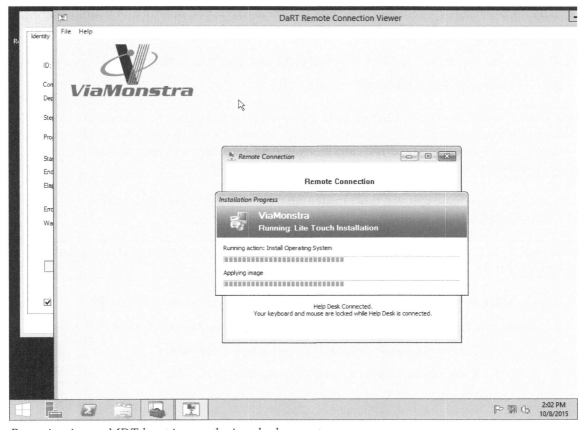

Remoting into a MDT boot image during deployment.

Step-by-Step Guide Requirements

If you want to run the step-by-step guides in this chapter, you need a lab environment configured as outlined in Chapter 1 and Appendix A. In this chapter, you use the following virtual machines:

DC01   MDT01   WSUS01   PC0006

The VMs used in this chapter (you create the PC0006 VM in this chapter).

Add DaRT 10 to the Boot Images

If you have access to DaRT, you can add it to the boot images using the steps in this section. If you don't have access to DaRT, or don't want to use it, simple skip to the next chapter ("Enabling BitLocker"). To enable the remote connection feature in MDT, you need to do the following:

1. Install DaRT 10

2. Copy the two tools CAB files (Toolsx86.cab and Toolsx64.cab) to the deployment share

3. Configure the deployment share to add DaRT

> **Real World Note:** You don't need to enable the normal monitoring to use remote connection. The connection information can be found in the bdd.log file, but it really helps to have the normal monitoring enabled because then you can simply double-click the machine you want to remote into and connect to it directly from the Deployment Workbench.

In these steps, we assume that you downloaded MDOP 2015 and copied DaRT 10 to C:\Setup\DL\DaRT 10 on MDT01.

> **Note:** MDOP 2015 is available for Software Assurance customers and can be downloaded from the Volume Licensing Service Center (VLCS).

1. On **MDT01**, install **DaRT 10 (MSDaRT100.msi)** using the default settings.

2. Using **File Explorer**, navigate to the **C:\Program Files\Microsoft DaRT\v10** folder.

3. Copy the **Toolsx64.cab** file to **E:\MDTProduction\Tools\x64**.

4. Copy the **Toolsx86.cab** file to **E:\MDTProduction\Tools\x86**.

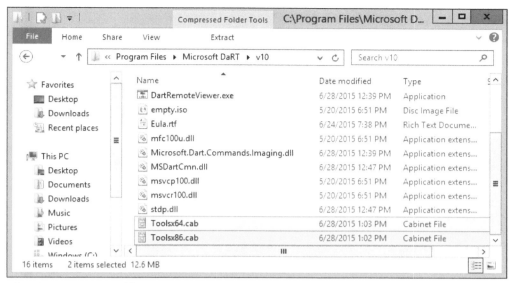

The DaRT 10 CAB files.

5. Using the **Deployment Workbench**, right-click the **MDT Production** deployment share and select **Properties**.

6. In the **Windows PE** tab, in the **Platform** drop-down list, make sure **x86** is selected.

7. In the **Features** sub-tab, select the **Microsoft Diagnostics and Recovery Toolkit (DaRT)** check box.

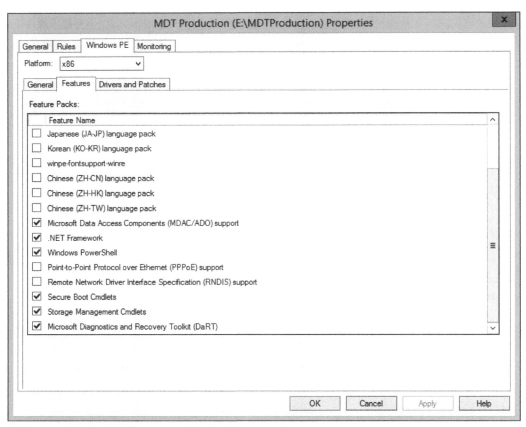

Selecting the DaRT feature in the deployment share.

8. In the **Windows PE** tab, in the **Platform** drop-down list, select **x64**.

9. In the **Features** sub-tab, select the **Microsoft Diagnostics and Recovery Toolkit (DaRT)** check box.

10. Click **OK**.

Update the Deployment Share

When you make boot image changes, the deployment share needs to be updated after it has been configured:

1. Right-click the **MDT Production** deployment share and select **Update Deployment Share**.

2. Use the default options for the **Update Deployment Share** wizard.

Note: The update process takes 5–10 minutes.

Update the Boot Image in WDS

Since the boot image has been updated, you also need to replace the boot image in WDS:

1. Using the **WDS console**, in the **Boot Images** node, right-click the **MDT Production x64** boot image and select **Replace Image**.

2. Browse to the **E:\MDTProduction\Boot\LiteTouchPE_x64.wim** file and add the image with the default settings.

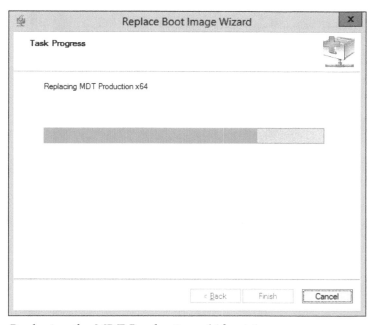

Replacing the MDT Production x64 boot image.

Deploy the PC0006 Virtual Machine

1. Create a virtual machine with the following settings:

   a. Name: **PC0006**

   b. Location: **C:\VMs**

   c. Memory: **2048 MB**

   d. Network: **Internal**

   e. Hard disk: **60 GB** (dynamic disk)

   f. Installation options: Install an operating system from a network-based installation server.

2. Start the **PC0006** virtual machine, press **Enter**, allow it to boot WinPE (PXE), and then complete the **Windows Deployment Wizard** using the following settings:

199

a.   Password: **P@ssw0rd**

b.   Select a task sequence to execute on this computer:
     Custom Windows 10 Enterprise x64

c.   Computer name: **PC0006**

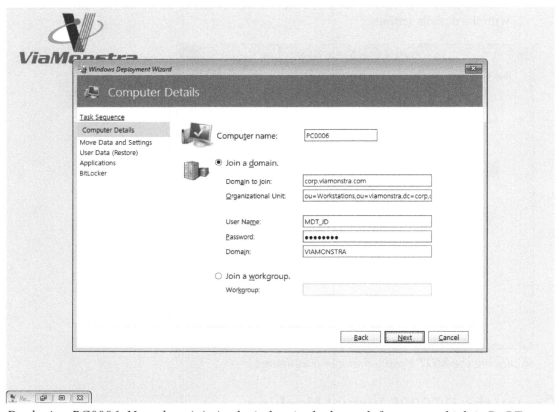

Deploying PC0006. Note the minimized window in the lower left corner, which is DaRT.

d.   Move Data and Settings: **Do not move user data and settings**

e.   Specify whether to restore user data: **Do not restore user data and settings**

f.   Applications: Select the following applications:

   ▪   **Install - Adobe Acrobat Reader DC**

   ▪   **Install – Oracle Java 8**

g.   Do not enable BitLocker for this computer: **Selected**

3.   Start the deployment, and then switch over to **MDT01**.

4.   On **MDT01**, using the **Deployment Workbench**, navigate to **MDT Production /
     Monitoring** and double-click **PC0006**.

5. In the **PC0006 properties** window, select **DaRT Remote Control**.

You are now connected to PC0006 remotely.

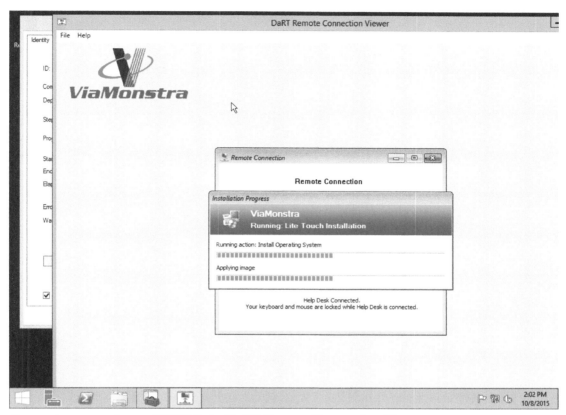

Remotely connecting to PC0006 via DaRT Remote Connection Viewer.

The setup continues and does the following:

    a.   Installs the Windows 10 operating system

    b.   Joins the corp.viamonstra.com domain

    c.   Installs the selected applications

Chapter 16

Enabling BitLocker

BitLocker is the disk volume encryption built into the Windows 10 Pro and Enterprise editions. From an operating system deployment point of view, BitLocker requires two things:

- A protector, which can be stored in the Trusted Platform Module (TPM) chip or stored as a password. Technically, you also can use a USB stick to store the protector, but that's not a very good solution at all. Please use TPM and/or password.

- Multiple partitions on the hard drive.

Real World Note: Even though it's not a BitLocker requirement, we recommend configuring BitLocker to store the recovery key and TPM owner information in Active Directory. In Chapter 7, you learned how to enable this for the ViaMonstra environment. For additional detailed information about these features, see: http://tinyurl.com/ylrhssa.

Step-by-Step Guide Requirements

If you want to run the step-by-step guides in this chapter, you need a lab environment configured as outlined in Chapter 1 and Appendix A. In this chapter, you use the following virtual machines:

DC01   MDT01   WSUS01   PC0007

The VMs used in this chapter. (The PC0007 machine is a physical machine used for BitLocker.)

MDT and BitLocker

Dealing with multiple partitions is not a problem because it's handled by MDT. However, enabling the TPM can be tricky because it involves configuring the computer BIOS. Fortunately, most major vendors offer tools that allow you to enable the TPM chip as part of your deployment.

To configure the ViaMonstra environment for BitLocker, you need to do the following:

1. Configure Active Directory for BitLocker (already done in Chapter 7).

2. Download the various BitLocker scripts and tools.

203

3. Configure the operating system deployment task sequence for BitLocker.

4. Configure the rules (CustomSettings.ini) for BitLocker.

Add BIOS Configuration Tools

If you want to automate enabling the TPM chip as part of the deployment process, you need to download the various vendor tools and run them as a Run Command Line action in the task sequence, add them an application in MDT, or put them into a wrapper script (that also can be added as an application).

Each vendor typically has its own individual tool, for example, for the Dell XPS 13 machine, you use the Dell Command | Configure which in turn is part of the Dell Client Command Suite.

> **Real World Note:** If you wonder where the old Dell Client Configuration Toolkit (CCTK) tool is, just look in the Dell Command | Configure installation folder and you'll find it.

The Dell Command | Configure toolset allows you to create a configuration very easily and then export it as an INI, CCTK, or EXE file. This can then be added to your deployment process to run fully automated as part of the Windows 10 deployment.

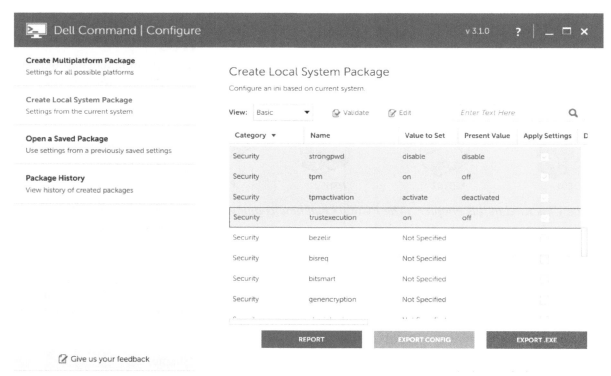

Creating a configuration package for the Dell XPS 13.

Verify That the TPM Chip Is Enabled and Activated

In the book sample files, we include a script, ZTICheckforTPM_v2.wsf, that allows you to verify that TPM is enabled and activated during the deployment. The script was graciously provided by Tim Mintner (https://twitter.com/tmintner). He allowed us to include the script in the book sample files, but you also can find the original script, including additional documentation, at the following Deployment Guys blog post: http://tinyurl.com/ZTICheckforTPM.

Configure the Windows 10 Task Sequence to Enable BitLocker

In these steps, you configure the task sequence to run the check TPM script and to enable BitLocker:

1. On **MDT01**, using the **Deployment Workbench**, right-click the **MDT Production** deployment share and select **Properties**.

2. In the **Rules** tab, add the following lines to the **Default** section, and click **OK**.

   ```
   BDEInstall=TPM
   BDERecoveryKey=AD
   ```

3. On **MDT01**, using the **Deployment Workbench**, right-click the **Custom Windows 10 Enterprise x64** task sequence and select **Properties**.

4. On the **Task Sequence** tab, configure the following settings:

   a. In the **State Restore** group, before the **Enable BitLocker** action, add a new group with the following settings:

      i. Name: **BitLocker**.

      ii. Options: Add a **Task Sequence Variable** condition with the following settings:

         - Variable: **BDEInstallSuppress**
         - Condition: **not equals**
         - Value: **YES**

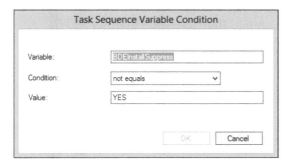

Adding the condition for the BitLocker Configuration group.

b. In the **BitLocker** group, add a **Run Command Line** action with the following settings:

- Name: **Check TPM Status**

- Command line:
  cscript.exe "%DeployRoot%\scripts\ZTICheckforTPM_v2.wsf"

- Options / Continue on error: **Selected**

c. In the **State Restore** group, select the **Enable BitLocker** action and move it after the **Check TPM Status** action. Then configure the options for the **Enable BitLocker** action with the following settings:

  i. Add an **if statement** set to **All conditions**.

  ii. Select **if all conditions are true**, and add a **Task Sequence Variable** condition with the following settings:

  - Variable: **TPMReady**

  - Condition: **equals**

  - Value: **TRUE**

  iii. Select **Task sequence variable TPMReady equals TRUE**, and add a **Task Sequence Variable** condition with the following settings:

  - Variable: **TPMActivated**

  - Condition: **equals**

  - Value: **TRUE**

d. In the **State Restore** group, after the **Apply Local GPO Package** action, add a **Run Command Line** action with the following settings:

- Name: **Remove BDE Recovery File**

- Command line (the command is wrapped and should be one line):
  PowerShell.exe -ExecutionPolicy Bypass -File "%SCRIPTROOT%\Remove-BDERecoveryFile.ps1"

- Options / Continue on error: **Selected**

e. Then click **OK**.

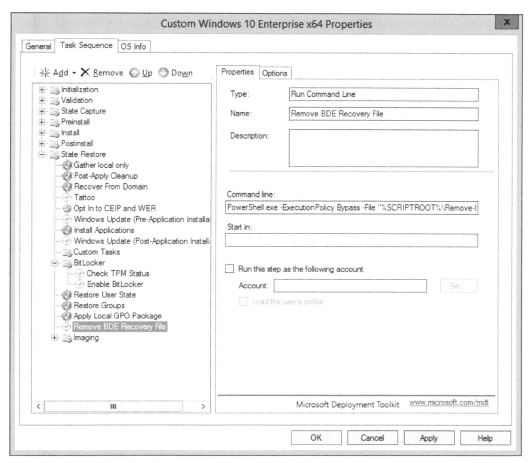

The Windows 10 task sequence configured for BitLocker.

Deploy the PC0007 Machine

In this guide, you deploy a new machine with the modified task sequence. If you want to verify that the BitLocker configuration works correctly, you need to run this on a machine that has a TPM chip enabled and activated. In our example, we used a Dell XPS 13 for testing.

Real World Note: In Windows Server 2016 TP4 or Windows 10 v.1511 or later, you also have a virtual TPM chip you that enables you to use BitLocker, with TPM protection, in virtual machines.

1. Configure the machine (**PC0007**) on which you are testing BitLocker to have **TPM** enabled.

2.   Start the machine, press **Enter** and allow it to boot WinPE (PXE), and complete the **Windows Deployment Wizard** using the following settings:

   a.   Password: **P@ssw0rd**

   b.   Select a task sequence to execute on this computer: **Custom Windows 10 Enterprise x64**

   c.   Computer name: **PC0007**

   d.   Move Data and Settings: **Do not move user data and settings**

   e.   Specify whether to restore user data: **Do not restore user data and settings**

   f.   Applications: Select the following applications:

   ▪   **Install - Adobe Acrobat Reader DC**

   ▪   **Install – Oracle Java 8**

   g.   Specify the BitLocker configuration: **Enable BitLocker**

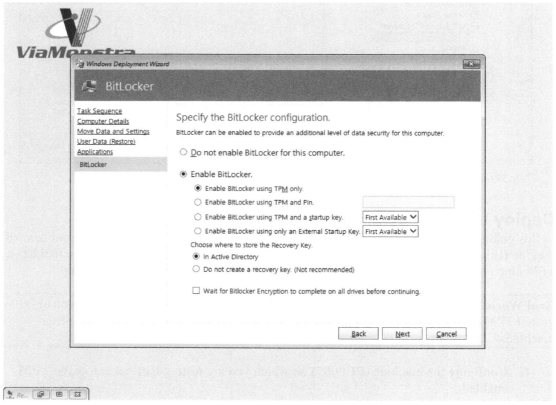

The BitLocker settings.

The setup starts and does the following:

    a.   Installs the Windows 10 operating system

    b.   Joins the corp.viamonstra.com domain

    c.   Installs the selected applications

    d.   Enables BitLocker

Chapter 17

Enabling Dynamic Deployment

When using MDT, you quickly learn that the rules engine is a powerful ally. Most of the settings used for operating system deployments are indeed retrieved and assigned via the rules engine. Using the rules engine to feed instructions to the task sequences is how you can truly achieve a dynamic deployment process.

Step-by-Step Guide Requirements

If you want to run the step-by-step guides in this chapter, you need a lab environment configured as outlined in Chapter 1 and Appendix A. In this chapter, you use the following virtual machines:

DC01   MDT01   PC0002

The VMs used in this chapter.

Bending the Rules

As you learned in previous chapters, the rules engine in its simplest form is just a text file, the CustomSettings.ini text file. So far you have only stored settings directly in this file, but in this chapter, you learn how to configure the rules engine to support additional settings, to reach out to external scripts, and to configure a rules engine simulation environment.

Assigning Settings

When using MDT, you can assign settings in three distinct ways: You can prestage the information before deployment, prompt the user or technician for information, or have MDT generate the settings automatically.

Sample Configurations

Before adding the more advanced components like databases and web services (Chapters 18 and 19), it makes sense to give you a few samples of commonly used configurations so you can see for yourself the power the rules engine gives you.

Set Computer Name by MAC Address

If you have a small test environment, or simply want to assign settings to a very limited number of machines, you can edit the rules to assign settings directly for a given MAC address. If you have many machines, it makes sense to use the database instead.

```
[Settings]
Priority=MacAddress, Default

[Default]
OSInstall=YES

[00:15:5D:85:6B:00]
OSDComputerName=PC00075
```

In the preceding sample, you set the PC00075 computer name for a machine with a MAC address of 00:15:5D:85:6B:00.

Set Computer Name by Serial Number

Another way to assign a computer name is to identify the machine via its serial number.

```
[Settings]
Priority=SerialNumber, Default

[Default]
OSInstall=YES

[CND0370RJ7]
OSDComputerName=PC00075
```

In this sample, you set the PC00075 computer name for a machine with a serial number of CND0370RJ7.

Generate a Computer Name Based on a Serial Number

You also can configure the rules engine to use a known property, like a serial number, to generate a computer name on the fly.

```
[Settings]
Priority=Default

[Default]
OSInstall=YES
OSDComputerName=PC-%SerialNumber%
```

In this sample, you configure the rules to set the computer name to a prefix (PC-) and then the serial number. If the serial number of the machine is CND0370RJ7, the preceding configuration sets the computer name to PC-CND0370RJ7.

Real World Note: Be careful when using the serial number to assign computer names. A serial number can contain more than 15 characters, and the Windows setup becomes quite upset if you try to use a computer name with more than 15 characters.

Generate a Limited Computer Name Based on a Serial Number

To avoid a computer name longer than 15 characters, you can configure the rules even further by adding VBScript functions directly to the rules.

```
[Settings]
Priority=Default

[Default]
OSInstall=YES
OSDComputerName=PC-#Left("%SerialNumber%",12)#
```

In the preceding sample, you still configure the rules to set the computer name to a prefix (PC-) and then the serial number. However, by adding the Left VBScript function, you configure the rule to use only the first 12 serial number characters for the name.

Install an Application Only on Laptops

In the rules, you find built-in properties that determine (using a WMI query) whether the machine you are deploying is a laptop, desktop, or server. In this sample, we assume you want to deploy the Install - Adobe Acrobat Reader DC application, but only if the machine is a laptop.

To assign applications in MDT, you need to know the application GUID, which you can find by simply viewing the application properties in the Deployment Workbench.

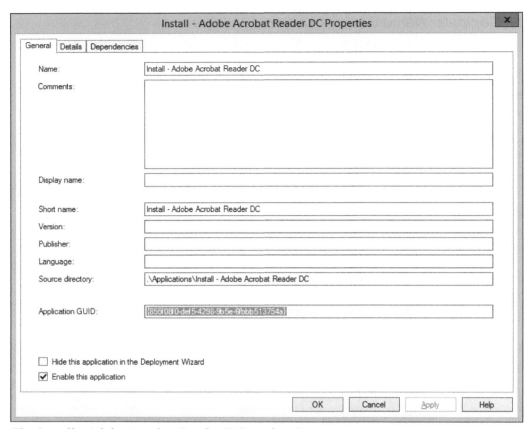

The Install - Adobe Acrobat Reader DC application properties.

In this example the Install - Adobe Acrobat Reader DC application has the GUID {855f08f0-def5-4298-9b5e-6fbbb513754a}.

```
[Settings]
Priority=ByLaptopType, Default

[Default]
SLShare=\\MDT01\Logs$

[ByLaptopType]
Subsection=Laptop-%IsLaptop%

[Laptop-True]
Applications001={855f08f0-def5-4298-9b5e-6fbbb513754a}
```

The IsLaptop property requires you to use a subsection in the rules. This is why there are two sections to relate to the configuration, the ByLaptopType and the Laptop-True sections.

Real World Note: The Applications property, when used in combination with the Deployment Wizard, shows the application as selected, but it is still possible to deselect it. If you want to select the application, but don't want the user or technician to be able to deselect it, you can use the MandatoryApplications property instead.

UserExit Scripts

MDT supports calling external VBScripts as part of the Gather process; these scripts are referred to as UserExit scripts. In this section, you configure the rules to use a UserExit script to generate computer names based on a prefix and the computer MAC address. The script also removes the colons in the MAC address.

Configuring the Rules to Call a UserExit Script

You can call a UserExit script by simply referencing the script in your rules. Then you can configure a property so it is set to the result of a VBScript function. In this example, we have a VBScript named Setname.vbs (provided in the book sample files, in the UserExit folder).

```
[Settings]
Priority=Default

[Default]
OSINSTALL=YES
UserExit=Setname.vbs
OSDComputerName=#SetName("%MACADDRESS%")#
```

The UserExit=Setname.vbs calls the script and then assigns the computer name to what the SetName function in the script returns. As you can see, in this sample, the %MACADDRESS% variable is passed to the script.

The Setname.vbs UserExit Script

The Setname.vbs script takes the MAC address passed from the rules. The script then does some string manipulation to add a prefix (PC) and then remove the semicolons from the MAC address.

```
Function UserExit(sType, sWhen, sDetail, bSkip)

  UserExit = Success

End Function

Function SetName(sMac)

  Dim re

  Set re = new RegExp
  re.IgnoreCase = true
  re.Global = true
  re.Pattern = ":"
  SetName = "PC" & re.Replace(sMac, "")

End Function
```

The first three lines of the script just make up a header that all UserExit scripts have. The interesting part is the lines between Function and End Function. Those lines do the magic of adding a prefix (PC), removing the colons from the MAC address, and returning the value to the rules by setting the SetName value.

Note: The purpose of this sample is not to recommend that you use the MAC address as a base for computer naming, but rather to show you how to take a variable from MDT, pass it to an external script, make some changes to it, and then return the new value to the deployment process.

The AliasUserExit.vbs UserExit Script

The AliasUserExit.vbs script takes the make and model, as well as other values derived from WMI. The purpose is to change the vendor's hardware name to a friendlier name. Some vendors like Intel do not provide a name at all as the SMBIOS computer model and, therefore, driver management becomes more difficult. In this book, you use this script, and that is also why you don't use %Model%. Instead you use %ModelAlias% because it is what the AliasUserExit.vbs script returns. You can see the usage of the script in the following example:

```
[Settings]
Priority=HardwareInfo, Default
Properties=ModelAlias
```

```
[HardwareInfo]
UserExit=AliasUserExit.vbs
ModelAlias=#SetModelAlias()#

[Default]
OSINSTALL=YES
```

Running PowerShell via UserExit Scripts

MDT does not have a built-in feature that supports running PowerShell scripts, but we (well, Mikael Nystrom actually) put together a nice blog post on how to run PowerShell scripts in a UserExit in MDT: http://tinyurl.com/nb3bzhz.

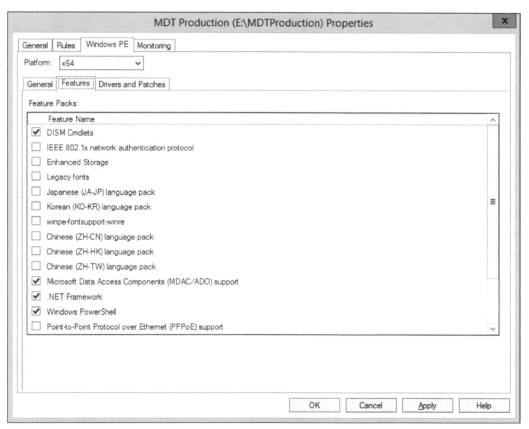

Of course, PowerShell needs to be enabled in WinPE.

Simulating a Deployment in a Test Environment

When working with advanced settings and rules, especially things like database calls, it's very efficient to be able to test the settings without having to run through a complete deployment. Luckily, MDT enables you to perform a simulated deployment by running the Gather process by itself. The simulation works best when you are using a domain-joined machine (client or server). In the following example, you use the PC0002 Windows 10 x64 client.

Create the Test Environment

In these steps, we assume that you have either downloaded the free ConfigMgr 2012 R2 Toolkit, or copied CMTrace if you have access to the ConfigMgr 2012 media.

1. On **PC0002**, log on as **VIAMONSTRA\Administrator** using a password of **P@ssw0rd**.

2. Using **Computer Management**, add the **VIAMONSTRA\MDT_BA** user account to the local **Administrators** group.

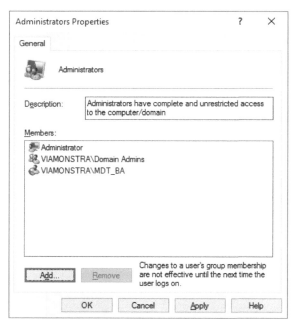

Adding the MDT_BA account to the local Administrators group on PC0002.

3. Log off, and then log on to **PC0002** as **VIAMONSTRA\MDT_BA**.

4. If you don't have access to **CMTrace**, install the **ConfigMgr 2012 R2 Toolkit** using the default settings, start **CMTrace**, and click **Yes** to accept the question about using **CMTrace** to view log files.

5. Using **File Explorer**, create a folder named **C:\MDT**.

6. From the book sample files, copy the **Gather.ps1** file from the **MDTTestEnvironment** folder to **C:\MDT**.

7. From the **\\MDT01\MDTProduction$\Scripts** folder, copy the following files to **C:\MDT**:

    o **ZTIDataAccess.vbs**

    o **ZTIGather.wsf**

    o **ZTIGather.xml**

    o **ZTIUtility.vbs**

    o **AliasUserExit.vbs**

8. From the **\\MDT01\MDTProduction$\Control** folder, copy the **CustomSettings.ini** file to **C:\MDT**.

9. In the **C:\MDT** folder, create a subfolder named **X64**.

10. From the **\\MDT01\MDTProduction$\Tools\X64** folder, copy the **Microsoft.BDD.Utility.dll** file to **C:\MDT\X64**.

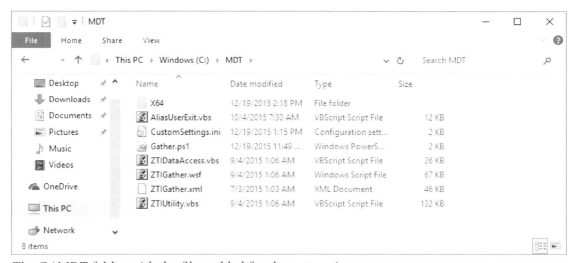

The C:\MDT folder with the files added for the test environment.

11. Using an elevated **PowerShell prompt** (run as administrator), run the following commands (pressing **Enter** after each command):

```
Set-ExecutionPolicy -ExecutionPolicy RemoteSigned -Force
Set-Location C:\MDT
.\Gather.ps1
```

12. Review the **ZTIGather.log** in the **C:\MININT\SMSOSD\OSDLOGS** folder.

Note: Don't worry about warnings or errors with regard to the Wizard.hta. They are expected. If the log file looks okay, you are ready to try a real deployment. Good luck!

The ZTIGather.log file from PC0002 displaying its hardware capabilities.

Add Properties on the Command Line

A little known feature of the test environment is that you can test a different CustomSettings.ini file, or simply override a few values, directly on the ZTIGather.wsf command line. Here is a Gather.ps1 file in which another CustomSettings.ini file is selected:

```
Cls
if (Test-Path -Path "C:\MININT") {Write-Host "C:\MININT exists,
deleting...";Remove-Item C:\MININT -Recurse}
cscript.exe ZTIGather.wsf /debug:true
/inifile:"\\MDT01\MDTBuildLab$\Control\CustomSettings.ini"
```

Here is another example in which another property, OSDComputerName, is configured at runtime:

```
Cls
if (Test-Path -Path "C:\MININT") {Write-Host "C:\MININT exists,
deleting...";Remove-Item C:\MININT -Recurse}
cscript.exe ZTIGather.wsf /debug:true
/OSDComputerName:PC00075
```

Test PowerShell Scripts

What about testing PowerShell scripts with full access to the MDT environment? Check out this post by Nicolas Lacour (https://twitter.com/Diagg) in which he explains how to create a rich simulation for PowerShell scripts: http://www.osd-couture.com/2014/07/mdt-2013-create-simulation-environment.html.

Chapter 18

Prestage Computer Information

The MDT database allows you to prestage information on your deployment in a SQL database, rather than have all the information in a text file (CustomSettings.ini).

As an example of the MDT database use, you can add all clients you want to deploy and specify their computer names, IP addresses, applications to be deployed, and all other sorts of settings for the machines.

Step-by-Step Guide Requirements

If you want to run the step-by-step guides in this chapter, you need a lab environment configured as outlined in Chapter 1 and Appendix A. In this chapter, you use the following virtual machines:

DC01   MDT01   PC0002

The VMs used in this chapter.

Selecting a Database

MDT can use either SQL Server Express or full SQL Server, but because the deployment database doesn't get that big, even in large enterprise environments, we decided to use the free SQL Server 2014 Express database in our environment.

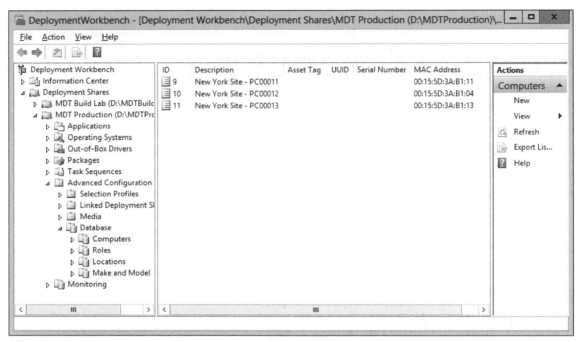

The Computers node in the MDT database showing a few clients.

Install SQL Server 2014 SP1 Express with Tools

In this guide, we assume you have copied the book sample files and SQL Server 2014 SP1 Express with Tools to C:\Setup on MDT01.

1. On **MDT01**, log on as **VIAMONSTRA\Administrator** using a password of **P@ssw0rd**.

2. Install **SQL Server 2014 SP1 Express SP1 with Tools** by running the following command from an elevated **PowerShell prompt** (the command is wrapped and should be one line):

```
C:\Setup\Scripts\Invoke-VIAInstallSQLServerExpress.ps1
-Setup
"C:\Setup\DL\SQL_2014_Express_SP1\SQLEXPRWT_x64_ENU.exe"
-SQLINSTANCENAME "SQLExpress" -SQLINSTANCEDIR "E:\SQLDB"
```

3. Check whether **SQL Server** has started by running the following command:

```
Get-Process -Name *SQL*
```

Configure the Firewall for the SQL Server 2014 Browser Service

When using SQL Server 2014 SP1 Express, the setup creates a separate instance named SQLEXPRESS. Because we are using a separate instance, you need the have SQL Server Browser service to be fully operational.

The SQL Server Browser service is blocked by the Windows Firewall by default, and to have the MDT database working, you need to allow inbound traffic for this service on MDT01. The SQL Server Browser service uses port 1434 UDP, so you open that port for inbound traffic.

1. On **MDT01**, start an elevated **PowerShell prompt**.

2. Configure the firewall by running the following command:

   ```
   C:\Setup\Scripts\Set-VIASQLFirewall.ps1
   ```

Configuring the firewall rules.

Create the Deployment Database

The MDT database is by default created and managed from the Deployment Workbench.

1. On **MDT01**, using the **Deployment Workbench**, navigate to **MDT Production / Advanced Configuration**, right-click **Database**, and select **New Database**.

2. In the **New DB Wizard**, on the **SQL Server Details** page, enter the following settings and click **Next**:

   a. SQL Server Name: **MDT01**

   b. Instance: **SQLEXPRESS**

   c. Port: <blank>

   d. Network Library: **Named Pipes**

3. On the **Database** page, select **Create a new database**; in the **Database** field, type **MDT** and click **Next**.

4. On the **SQL Share** page, in the **SQL Share** field, type **MDTProduction$** and click **Next**. Click **Next** again and then click **Finish**.

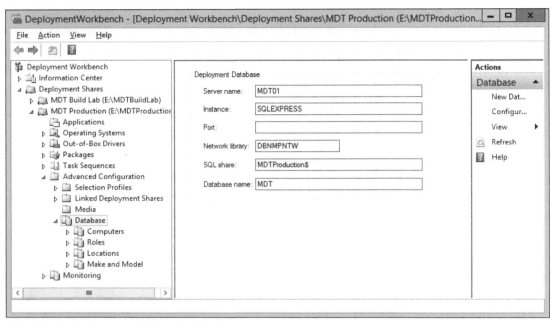

The MDT database added to MDT01.

Configure Database Permissions

After creating the database, you need to assign permissions to it for the account you use to run your deployments.

1. On **MDT01**, start **SQL Server 2014 Management Studio**.

Real World Note: In this environment, the VIAMONSTRA\Administrator account is already an SQL administrator, but often you need to run the SQL Server 2014 Management Studio elevated to make sure you have administrator permissions.

2. In the **Connect to Server** dialog box, in the **Server name** list, select **MDT01\SQLEXPRESS** and click **Connect**.

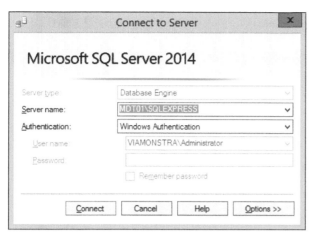

Connecting to the MDT database in SQL Server 2014 Management Studio.

3. In the **Object Explorer** pane, expand the top **Security** node, right-click **Logins**, and select **New Login**.

4. On the **Login – New** page, in the **Login name** field, type **VIAMONSTRA\MDT_BA**. Then in the left pane, select **User Mapping**. Select the **MDT** database, and assign the following roles:

    o   **db_datareader**

    o   **db_datawriter**

    o   **public** (default)

5. Click **OK**, and close **SQL Server 2014 Management Studio**.

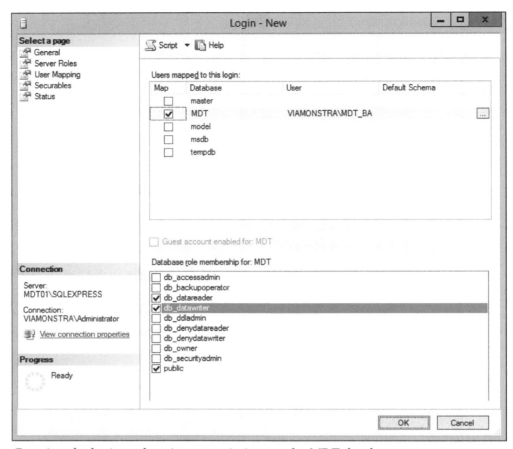

Creating the login and settings permissions to the MDT database.

Create an Entry in the Database

To start using the database, you add a computer entry and assign a description and computer name. As the identifier, you use the computer's MAC address like you did with the text file earlier.

1. On **MDT01**, using the **Deployment Workbench**, navigate to **MDT Production / Advanced Configuration / Database**.

2. Right-click **Computers**, select **New**, and add a computer entry with the following settings:

   a.   Description: **New York Site - PC0002**

   b.   MacAddress: <PC0002's MAC address in the 00:00:00:00:00:00 format>

Note: Replace the MAC address with the real MAC address from PC0002. In our example, it was 00:15:5D:0A:6A:F8.

      c.   Details tab / OSDComputerName: **PC0002**

3.   Click **OK**.

Adding the PC0002 computer to the database.

> **Real World Note:** Adding a single entry manually is all right. However, if you want to add multiple entries, we recommend that you use the SQL Server 2014 Express import features, or perhaps use PowerShell to bulk import your clients. Here is a list of resources for different ways of bulk importing data into the MDT database:
>
> "Deploying Windows 7 - Part 22: Bulk Populating the MDT Database Using PowerShell," by Mitch Tulloch: http://tinyurl.com/mdtbulkimport1
>
> "Manipulating the Microsoft Deployment Toolkit database using PowerShell," by Michael Niehaus: http://tinyurl.com/mdtbulkimport2

"VBScript Bulk Import for MDT," by Skatterbrainz (David M. Stein):
http://tinyurl.com/mdtbulkimport3

Assigning Applications Using Roles

In addition to using computer-specific entries in the database, you can use roles to group settings together. In this section, you learn to add applications to a role in the database and then assign the role to a computer.

Create and Assign a Role Entry in the Database

1. On **MDT01**, using the **Deployment Workbench**, navigate to **MDT Production / Advanced Configuration / Database**.

2. In the **Database** node, right-click **Role**, select **New**, and create a role entry with the following settings:

    a. Role name: **Standard PC**

    b. Applications / Lite Touch Applications:

        ▪ **Install - Adobe Acrobat Reader DC**

        ▪ **Install - Install - Oracle Java 8**

3. Click **OK**.

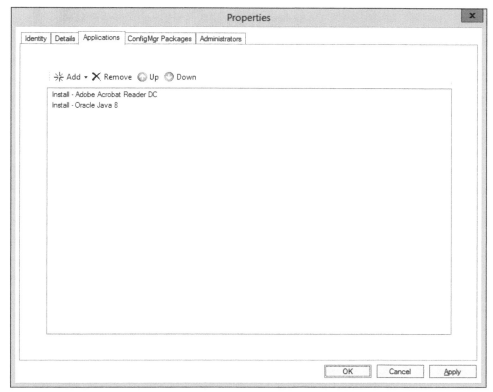

The Standard PC role with the applications added.

Associate the Role with a Computer in the Database

After creating the role, you can associate it with one or more computer entries:

1. Using the **Deployment Workbench**, navigate to **MDT Production / Advanced Configuration / Database / Computers**.

2. In the **Computers** node, double-click the **New York Site - PC0002** entry, and add the following setting:

    Roles: **Standard PC**

3. Click **OK**.

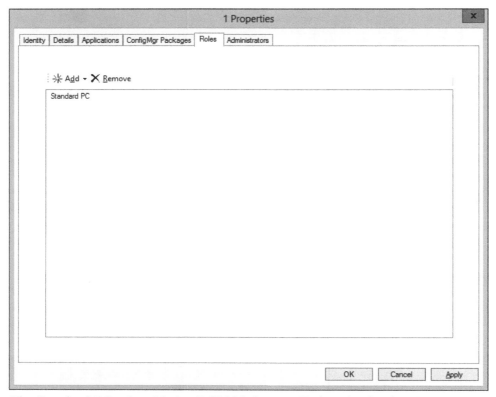

The Standard PC role added to PC0002 (having ID 1 in the database).

Verify the Deployment in the Test Environment

When the database is populated, you can use the test environment to simulate a deployment. The applications are not installed, but you can see which applications would be installed if you did a full deployment of the computer. In these steps, we assume you have copied the book sample files to C:\Setup on PC0002.

1. On **PC0002**, log on as **VIAMONSTRA\MDT_BA**.

2. Copy the **CustomSettings.ini** file from **C:\Setup\Database** to the **C:\MDT** folder (replacing the existing file).

3. Start an elevated **PowerShell prompt** (run as administrator), navigate to the **C:\MDT** folder, and then run the **Gather.ps1** script.

4. In **C:\MININT\SMSOSD\OSDLOGS\ZTIGather.log**, verify that the applications are being assigned.

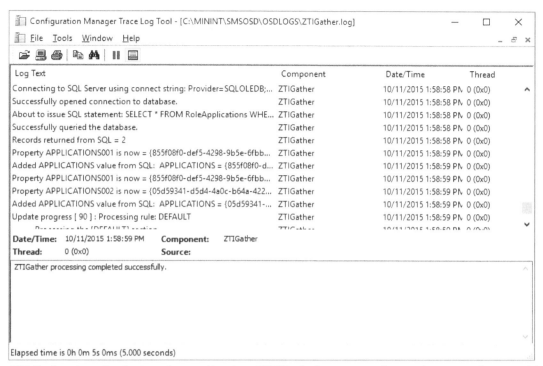

ZTIGather.log displaying the application GUIDs belonging to the applications that would have been installed if you deployed this machine.

Chapter 19

Moving the Computer Object during Deployment

Another powerful way of assigning settings to the deployment is to use web services. Web services are, simply put, web applications that run code on the server side, and MDT has built-in functions to call these web services. In this chapter, you use a sample developed by Maik Koster to move a computer object in Active Directory during deployment. His free web services are named the Deployment Webservice, and the version included in the book sample files is version 7.3.

Credit: Maik Koster kindly granted us permission to use his Deployment Webservice in this book. The full documentation is available on Codeplex: http://mdtcustomizations.codeplex.com.

In the following sections, you learn to use a web service that interacts with Active Directory. The function you use when interacting with Active Directory is the MoveComputerToOU function, which allows you to move computer accounts between OUs during deployment. This is very useful when you start Windows 10 pilot projects and want to have your Windows 10 machines in a new OU structure.

Step-by-Step Guide Requirements

If you want to run the step-by-step guides in this chapter, you need a lab environment configured as outlined in Chapter 1 and Appendix A. In this chapter, you use the following virtual machines:

DC01   MDT01   PC0002

The VMs used in this chapter.

Installing and Configuring the Deployment Webservice

In this section, you install the Deployment Webservice and then set up MDT to use them. The steps are the following:

1. Create a service account and assign permissions.
2. Create an application pool and add the web application.
3. Install the web server (IIS).
4. Test the web services.

Create a Service Account and Assign Permissions

1. On **DC01**, log on as **Administrator** in the **VIAMONSTRA** domain using a password of **P@ssw0rd**, and open an elevated **PowerShell prompt**.
2. Create the MDT web service account by running the following command (the command is wrapped and should be one line):

    ```
    C:\Setup\Scripts\New-VIAServiceAccount.ps1 -AccountName
    MDT_WS -AccountDescription "MDT Web Service Account"
    -AccountType ServiceAccount -Password "P@ssw0rd"
    ```

3. Verify the configuration via **PowerShell** by running the following command:

    ```
    Get-ADUser -Filter 'Name -like "*MDT*"'
    ```

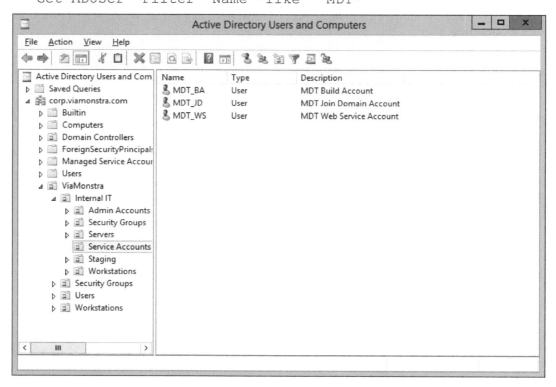

The MDT service accounts in Active Directory, including the new MDT_WS account.

Configure Active Directory Permissions

The MDT_WS account needs to have permissions to the organizational units. In these steps, you run a script that assigns the correct permissions.

1. On **DC01**, log on as **VIAMONSTRA\Administrator**, and open an elevated **PowerShell prompt**.

2. Set the Active Directory permissions for the Workstations OU by running the following command (the command is wrapped and should be one line):

   ```
   C:\Setup\Scripts\Set-VIAOUPermissions.ps1
   -Account MDT_WS
   -TargetOU "OU=Workstations,OU=ViaMonstra"
   ```

3. Set the Active Directory permissions for the Staging OU by running the following command (the command is wrapped and should be one line):

   ```
   C:\Setup\Scripts\Set-VIAOUPermissions.ps1
   -Account MDT_WS
   -TargetOU "OU=Staging,OU=Internal IT,OU=ViaMonstra"
   ```

Install the Web Server (IIS)

1. On **MDT01**, log on as **VIAMONSTRA\Administrator**, and open an elevated **PowerShell prompt**.

2. Install the web server (IIS) by running the following command:

   ```
   C:\Setup\Scripts\Install-VIARoles.ps1 -Role WEB
   ```

Copy the Deployment Webservice and Enable Only Required Functions

By default the Deployment Webservice has most functions enabled, but there is no need to enable more functions that you actually are using.

1. On **MDT01**, using **File Explorer**, navigate to the **C:\Setup** folder and copy the **DeploymentWebService** folder to **E:**.

2. Using **File Explorer**, assign **Modify** permissions for the **VIAMONSTRA\MDT_WS** account to **E:\DeploymentWebService** (NTFS Permissions).

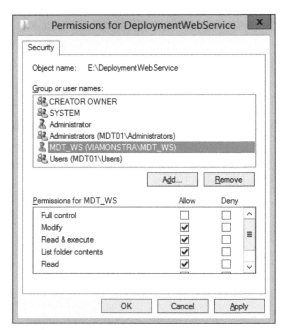

Configuring permissions for the DeploymentWebService folder.

3. Using **Notepad**, modify the **E:\DeploymentWebService\Web.config** file per the following (leave other lines per default):

```
<add key="IncludeFunctions" value=""/>
<add key="IncludeADFunctions" value="MoveComputerToOU"/>
```

Configuring the web.config file.

Create an Application Pool for Deployment Webservice

1. On **MDT01**, using **Internet Information Services (IIS) Manager**, expand the **MDT01 (VIAMONSTRA\Administrator)** node. If prompted with the "Do you want to get started with Microsoft Web Platform…" question, select the **Do not show this message** check box and then click **No**.

2. Right-click **Application Pools**, select **Add Application Pool**, and configure the new application pool with the following settings:
   a. Name: **DeploymentWebService**
   b. .NET CLR version: **.NET CLR 4.0.30319**
   c. Manage pipeline mode: **Integrated**
   d. Select the **Start application pool immediately** check box.
   e. Click **OK**.

3. In the **Application Pools** node, right-click the **DeploymentWebService** application pool and select **Advanced Settings**.

4. Click the **Identity** line and click the browse "…" button.

5. Select **Custom account** and click **Set**. Use the following settings for the **Set Credentials** dialog box:

   a. Username: **VIAMONSTRA\MDT_WS**

   b. Password and confirm password: **P@ssw0rd**

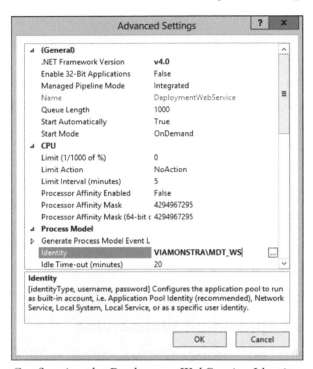

Configuring the DeploymentWebService Identity account.

6. Using **Internet Information Services (IIS) Manager**, expand **Sites**, right-click **Default Web Site**, and select **Add Application**. Use the following settings for the application:

   o Alias: **DeploymentWebService**

   o Application pool: **DeploymentWebService**

   o Physical Path: **E:\DeploymentWebService**

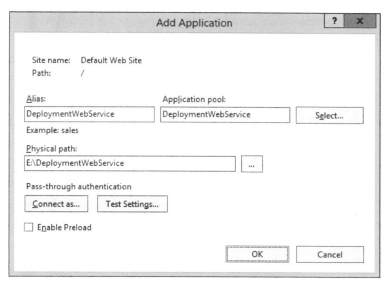

Adding the DeploymentWebService web application.

7.   In the **Default Web Site** node, select the **DeploymentWebService** web application, and in the right pane, double-click **Authentication**. Verify that the following configuration is set in the **Authentication** pane:

      o   Anonymous Authentication: **Enabled**

      o   ASP .NET Impersonation: **Disabled**

      o   Forms Authentication: **Disabled**

      o   Windows Authentication: **Disabled**

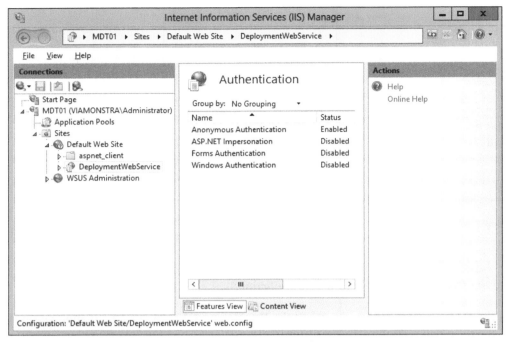

Configuring authentication for the Deployment Webservice.

Using the MoveComputerToOU Function

When you set up the Deployment Webservice, you enabled the MoveComputerToOU function. The following sections provide the steps to test the function and then configure the Windows 10 task sequence to use the function.

Real World Note: If you feel that testing should be done using PowerShell, it is absolutely possible. In this blog post, you can learn how to perform actions against web services directly using PowerShell: http://tinyurl.com/of8gcvr.

Test the MoveComputerToOU Function

1. On **DC01**, using **Active Directory User and Computers**, in the **ViaMonstra /
    Workstations** OU, create a computer object named **PC0008**.

2. On **PC0002**, using **Internet Explorer**, navigate to the following:
    http://MDT01/DeploymentWebService/ad.asmx.

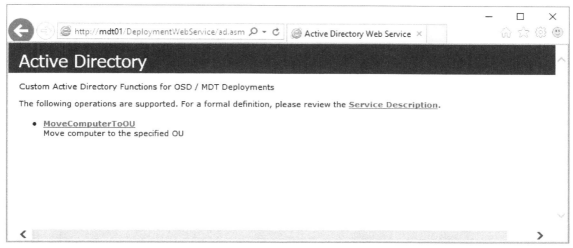

The Active Directory web service, showing the only enabled function.

3.   On the **Active Directory** page, select the **MoveComputerToOU** function.

4.   Use the following settings:

   a.   ComputerName: **PC0008**

   b.   OUPath: **OU=Staging,OU=Internal IT,OU=ViaMonstra,DC=corp, DC=viamonstra,DC=com**

   c.   Click **Invoke**.

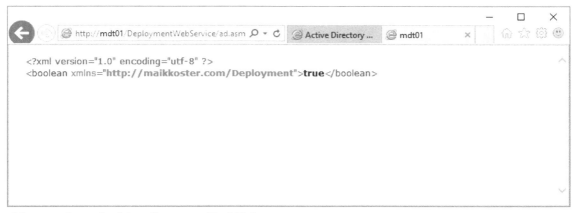

After invoking the MoveComputerToOU function.

5.   On **DC01**, using **Active Directory User and Computers**, select the **ViaMonstra / Internal IT / Staging** OU, and press **F5**. The **PC0008** computer should now be in this OU.

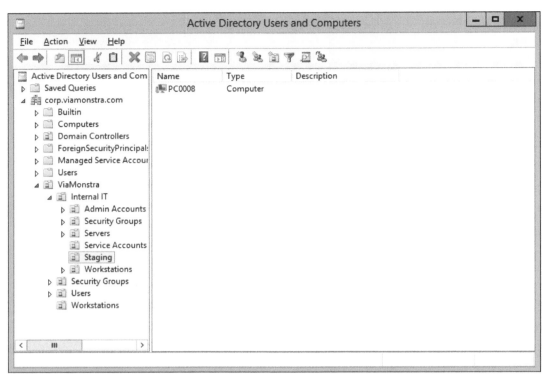

The PC0008 computer after being moved to the Staging OU by the web service.

Enable the MoveComputerToOU Function for Deployments

To enable the MoveComputerToOU function, you need to have a custom property named StagingOU in the rules and then add a few actions to the task sequence that actually moves the computer to another OU:

1. On **MDT01**, start an elevated **PowerShell prompt** and start **Notepad** from it.

2. Using **Notepad**, open the **CustomSettings.ini** file in the **E:\MDTProduction\Control** folder:

    a. Verify that the **StagingOU** value is in the **Properties** line looks like this:

```
[Settings]
Priority=ByIsOnBattery, HardwareInfo, Default
Properties=ModelAlias,StagingOU
...
```

b. Verify that the **StagingOU** value in the **Default** section looks like this:

```
[Default]
_SMSTSORGNAME=ViaMonstra
OSInstall=YES
UserDataLocation=AUTO
TimeZoneName=Pacific Standard Time
AdminPassword=P@ssw0rd
JoinDomain=corp.viamonstra.com
DomainAdmin=VIAMONSTRA\MDT_JD
DomainAdminPassword=P@ssw0rd
StagingOU=ou=Staging,ou=Internal IT,ou=ViaMonstra,dc=corp,
dc=viamonstra,dc=com
MachineObjectOU=ou=Workstations,ou=viamonstra,dc=corp,
dc=viamonstra,dc=com
. . .
```

3. Verify that the following section is available:

```
[MoveComputerToOU]
WebService=http://mdt01/DeploymentWebService/ad.asmx/
MoveComputerToOU
Parameters=OSDComputerName,MachineObjectOU
OSDComputerName=ComputerName
MachineObjectOU=OUPath
```

4. On **MDT01**, using the **Deployment Workbench**, navigate to **MDT Production / Task Sequences / Windows 10**, right-click **Custom Windows 10 Enterprise x64**, and select **Properties**.

5. In the **Task Sequence** tab, configure the following settings:

   a. In the **State Capture / Refresh only** group, before the **Disable BDE Protectors** action, add a **Run Command Line** action with the following settings:

      ▪ Name: **Move Computer to Staging OU**

      ▪ Command line:
      cscript.exe "%SCRIPTROOT%\Z_MoveComputer_StagingOU.wsf"

      ▪ Options / Continue on error: **Selected**

   b. In the **State Restore** group, after the **Apply Local GPO Package** action, add a new group named **Finalize**.

   c. In the **Finalize** group, add a **Run Command Line** action with the following settings:

- Name: **Swap Staging OU**
- Command line (the command is wrapped and should be one line): **cscript.exe "%SCRIPTROOT%\Z_MoveComputer_SwapOUValues.wsf"**
- Options / Continue on error: **Selected**

   d. In the **Finalize** group, after the **Swap Staging OU** action, add a **Run Command Line** action with the following settings:

- Name: **Move Computer to Target OU**
- Command line: **cscript.exe "%SCRIPTROOT%\Z_MoveComputer_TargetOU.wsf"**
- Options / Continue on error: **Selected**

   e. Click **OK**.

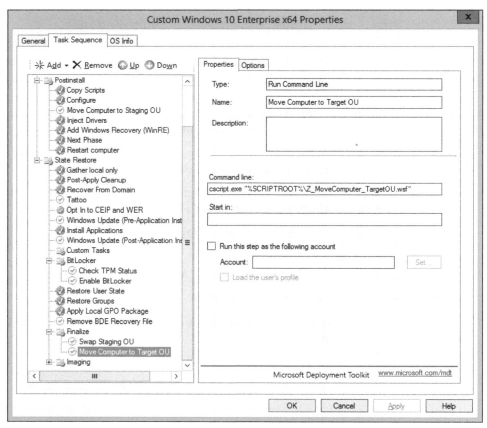

The Windows 10 task sequence configured to use the web service.

If you use this task sequence to refresh an existing machine, it first moves the computer to the staging OU. Then, at the end of the task sequence, the computer object is moved to the target OU.

This configuration also is useful to add to the Windows 10 upgrade task sequence.

Real World Note: By now you probably realize the true power of web services. However, please note that some of the web service functions can be pretty dangerous if they can be used by anyone. For a guide to securing the Deployment Webservice, see http://tinyurl.com/ws73sec.

Appendix A

Using the Hydration Kit to Build the PoC Environment

Hydration is the concept of using a deployment solution, like MDT, to do a fully automated build of an entire lab, or proof-of-concept environment. This appendix is here to help you quickly spin up a lab environment that matches up with all the guides you use in this book.

We recommend using Hyper-V in Windows Server 2012 R2 as your virtual platform, but we have tested the hydration kit on the following virtual platforms:

- Hyper-V in Windows 10 and Windows Server 2012 R2
- VMware Workstation 11.0
- VMware ESXi 5.5

As you learned in Chapter 1, to set up a virtual environment with all the servers and clients, you need a machine with at least 16 GB of RAM. Also make sure you are using a SSD drive for your storage. A single 480 GB SSD is enough to run all the scenarios in this book.

> **Real World Note:** Don't go cheap on the disk drive. If using a normal laptop or desktop when doing the step-by-step guides in this book, please, please, please use a SSD drive for your virtual machines. Using normal spindle-based disks are just too slow for a decent lab and test environment. Also, please note that most laptops support at least 16 GB RAM these days, even if many vendors do not update their specifications with this information.

The Base Servers

Using the hydration kit, you build the following list of servers.

New York Site Servers (192.168.1.0/24)

- **DC01.** Windows Server 2012 R2, Domain Controller, DNS, and DHCP
- **GW01.** Windows Server 2012 R2 and Router (optional virtual machine)
- **MDT01.** Windows Server 2012 R2, SQL Server 2014 Express, and MDT Server
- **MDT02.** Optional Windows Server 2012 R2, and MDT Server
- **WSUS01.** Windows Server 2012 R2, SQL Server 2014 Express, and WSUS Server

The Base Clients

In addition to the servers, you also use a few clients throughout the book guides.

New York Site Clients (192.168.1.0/24)

- **PC0001.** Windows 7 SP1 Enterprise x64

- **PC0002.** Windows 7 SP1 Enterprise x64

Internet Access

Some of the guides in this book require you to have Internet access on the virtual machines. To help you achieve that, and still have the virtual machines on an isolated network for lab and test purposes, we provide instructions on how to set up the GW01 virtual machine so it is configured as a virtual router.

If your virtual platform is already configured to provide Internet access to your VMs, or if you are on a dedicated lab network that allows you to run your own DHCP server, you can skip creating the GW01 virtual machine.

> **Real World Note:** You also can use a Linux-based system for routing the network traffic. For detailed guidance on setting up a Linux-based virtual router for your lab environment, see this article: http://tinyurl.com/usingvirtualrouter.

Setting Up the Hydration Environment

Again, to enable you to quickly set up the servers and clients used for the step-by-step guides in this book, we provide you with a hydration kit (part of the book sample files) that builds all the servers and clients. The sample files are available for download at http://deploymentfundamentals.com.

How Does the Hydration Kit Work?

The hydration kit that you download is just a folder structure and some scripts. The hydration kit scripts help you create the MDT Lite Touch offline media, and the folder structure is there for you to add your own software and licenses when applicable. In addition to the scripts to set up the MDT offline media, you also use other PowerShell scripts to perform post-deployment OS configuration on the virtual machines once they are deployed. The overview steps are the following:

1. Download the needed software.

2. Install MDT 2013 Update 2 and Windows ADK 10.

3. Create an MDT deployment share.

4. Populate the folder structure with your media and any license information.

5. Generate the MDT media item.

6. Create a few virtual machines, boot them on the media item, and select which servers they should become, and then about one hour later you have the lab environment ready to go.

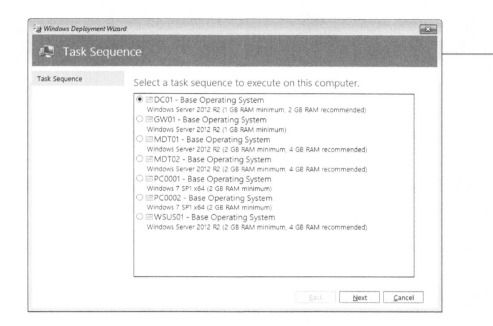

The end result: You boot a VM from the ISO and simply select which server to build.

Preparing the Setup Folder

These steps should be performed on the Windows machine that you use to manage Hyper-V or VMware. If you are using Hyper-V or VMware Workstation, this machine also can be the host machine.

Download the Software

1. On the Windows machine that you use to manage Hyper-V or VMware, create the **C:\Setup** folder.

2. Download the book sample files from **http://deploymentfundamentals.com** and extract them to **C:\Setup**.

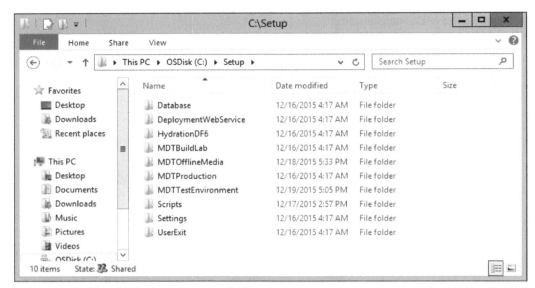

The sample files (ISO) extracted to C:\Setup.

3. Download the necessary software from Microsoft by running the following command in an elevated **PowerShell prompt**:

```
C:\Setup\Scripts\Get-DF6Downloads.ps1
```

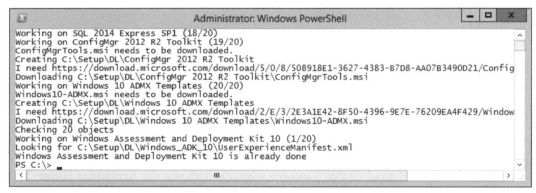

Consuming bandwidth using PowerShell.

4. The preceding script downloads all the necessary files except the core Windows operating systems, so in addition to running the script, you also need to download ISO files of the following operating systems from Microsoft:

   o   Windows Server 2012 R2 Standard (trial or full version)

   o   Windows 7 SP1 Enterprise x64 (trial or full version)

> **Note:** When downloading the Windows Server 2012 R2 installation media, make sure to get the latest version. (Starting with Windows 8.1 and Windows Server 2012 R2, Microsoft provides installation media that already contain rollup updates, like the April 2014 or November 2014 updates.) In general, VLCS and MSDN media are more frequently updated then evaluation media.

5. After the downloads are compete, copy the **Windows Server 2012 R2** installation files (the content of the ISO, not the actual ISO) to the following folder:

    C:\Setup\DL\Windows_Server_2012_R2

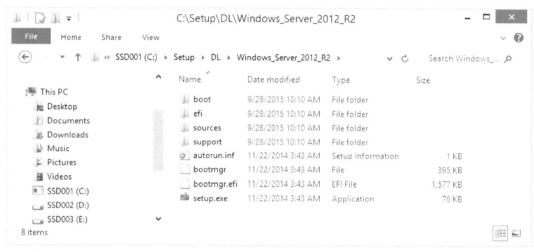

Windows Server 2012 R2, including the November 2014 rollup update.

6. Copy the **Windows 7 SP1 Enterprise x64** installation files (again, the content of the ISO, not the actual ISO) to the following folder:

    C:\Setup\DL\Windows_7_SP1_Enterprise_x64

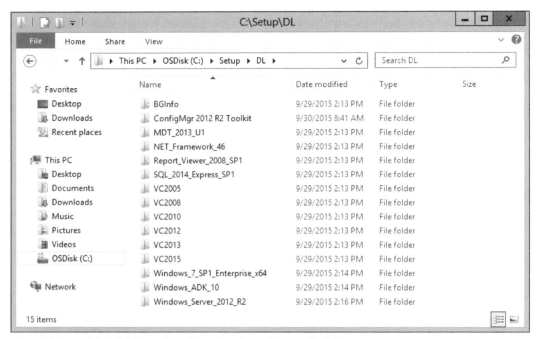

The C:\Setup\DL folder after downloading the needed files.

Preparing the Hydration Environment

The Windows machine that you use to manage Hyper-V or VMware needs to have PowerShell installed.

> **Note:** MDT requires local administrator rights/permissions. You need to have at least 60 GB of free disk space on C:\ for the hydration kit and about 500 GB of free space for the volume hosting your virtual machines. Also make sure to run all commands from an elevated PowerShell prompt.

Create the Hydration Deployment Share

In this guide, you install some of the applications you downloaded to C:\Setup\DL using the PowerShell script:

1. On the Windows machine that you use to manage Hyper-V or VMware, install **MDT 2013 Update 2 (MicrosoftDeploymentToolkit2013_x64.msi)** with the default settings.

2. Install **Windows ADK 10 (adksetup.exe)** selecting only the following components:

   o **Deployment Tools**

   o **Windows Preinstallation Environment (Windows PE)**

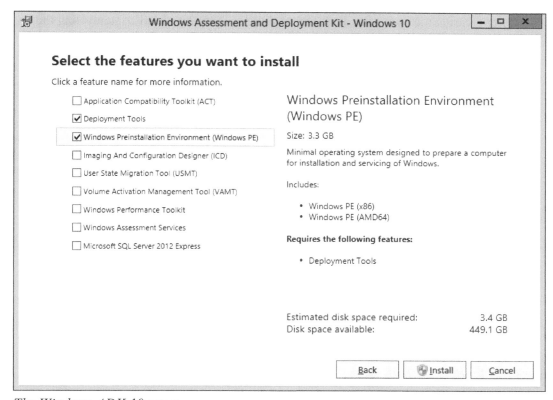

The Windows ADK 10 setup.

3. In an elevated **PowerShell prompt**, create the hydration deployment share by running the following command:

```
C:\Setup\Scripts\New-HydrationDeploymentShare.ps1
```

4. After creating the hydration deployment share, review the added content using the **Deployment Workbench** (installed as part of the MDT setup).

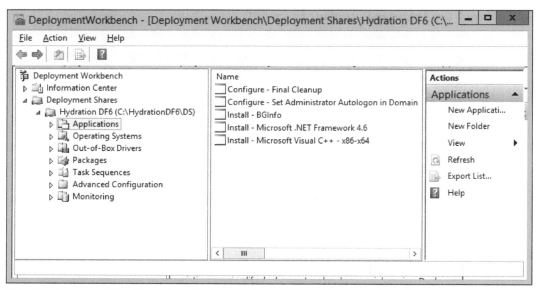

The Deployment Workbench with the ready-made applications listed.

Create the Hydration ISO (MDT Update Offline Media Item)

1. Using the **Deployment Workbench** (available on the **Start screen**), navigate to **Deployment Shares / Hydration DF6**.

2. Review the various nodes. The **Applications**, **Operating Systems**, and **Task Sequences** nodes should all have some content in them.

3. Navigate to **Advanced Configuration / Media**.

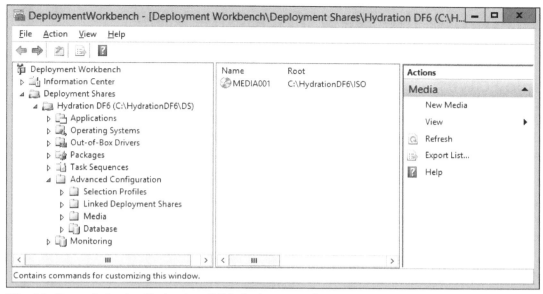

The Media node in the Hydration DF6 deployment share.

4.   In the right pane, right-click **MEDIA001** and select **Update Media Content**.

Note: The most common reason for failures in the hydration kit are related to antivirus software preventing the ISO from being generated correctly. If you see any errors in the update media content process, disable (or uninstall) your antivirus software, and then try the update again. Anyway, the media update takes a while to run, so it's a perfect time for a coffee break. ☺

After the media update, you have a big ISO (HydrationDF6.iso) in the C:\HydrationDF6\ISO folder. The ISO will be between 7 and 8 GB in size depending on which Windows media you have been using. (You have probably noticed that Microsoft offers Windows Server 2012 R2 ISO files with updates already installed, and these ISO files are larger.)

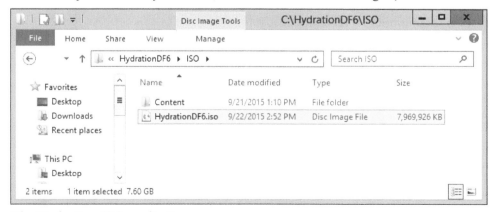

The Hydration ISO media item.

Deploying the New York Site VMs

In these steps, you deploy and configure the virtual machines for the New York site.

Deploy GW01

GW01 is an optional server used as a virtual router. Again, this allows for having the other virtual machines on an isolated network but still being able to access the Internet. If your virtual platform is already configured to provide Internet access to your VMs (for example, you are using the NAT network feature in VMware Workstation, or you are on a dedicated lab network that allows you to run your own DHCP server), you can skip creating the GW01 virtual machine.

> **Note:** If you have Hyper-V installed on your host PC or server and have created a virtual switch named Internal, you can use the New-DF6LAB.ps1 script from the book sample files for the fully automated creation of the various virtual machines you need for the guides in this book. If you review the script, you can see, for example, that the following PowerShell script is used to create the DC01 virtual machine:
>
> C:\Setup\Scripts\CreateNew-VM.ps1 -VMName DF6-DC01 -VMMem 1GB -VMvCPU 2 -VMLocation C:\VMs -DiskMode Empty -EmptyDiskSize 100GB -VMSwitchName Internal -ISO C:\Setup\ISO\HydrationDF6.iso -VMGeneration 2

1. Using **Hyper-V Manager** or **VMware Sphere**, create a virtual machine with the following settings:

   a. Name: **GW01**

   b. Memory: **1 GB** (minimum, 2 GB recommended)

   c. Hard drive: **100 GB** (dynamic disk)

   d. Network: The virtual network you use for the virtual machines

   e. Image file (ISO): **C:\HydrationDF6\ISO\HydrationDF6.iso**

   f. vCPUs: **2** (minimum, 4 recommended)

2. Start the **GW01** virtual machine. After booting from **HydrationDF6.iso**, and after WinPE has loaded, select the **GW01** task sequence.

> **Note:** It might take some time before the task sequence list is displayed. WinPE tries really hard to get an IP address from the DHCP, but because we don't have one, we'll just wait.

3. Wait until the setup is complete and you see the **Hydration completed** message in the final summary. Verify that there is no ISO file mounted in the **GW01** virtual machine, and leave virtual machine running.

GW01 Post-Deployment OS Configurations

After the initial deployment of GW01 is completed, you need to do additional post-deployment OS configurations like adding a second virtual network adapter and installing Routing and Remote Access (RRAS).

Add a Second Virtual Network Adapter

Because the purpose of GW01 is to route Internet traffic, you need to add a second virtual network adapter and connect it to the external network on your host PC or server. In this guide, you learn how to do it in Hyper-V. When using VMware, you have to do the equivalent VMware operations:

1. Using **Hyper-V Manager**, create a virtual switch that is connected to the external network (your network card). In our sample, we named the virtual network switch UplinkSwitch.

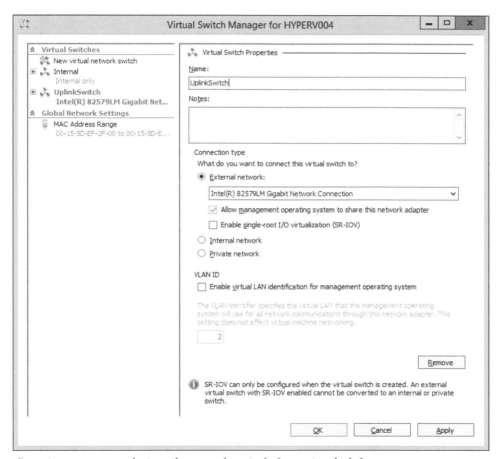

Creating an external virtual network switch for a simple lab setup.

2. Unless you are using Windows 10 as your Hyper-V host, shut down the **GW01** virtual machine before you continue. (Windows 10 allows you to add virtual network adapters while the virtual machine is running.)

3. Right-click the **GW01** virtual machine and select **Settings**.

4. In the **Hardware / Add Hardware** node, add a second virtual network adapter and connect it to the **UplinkSwitch** virtual network.

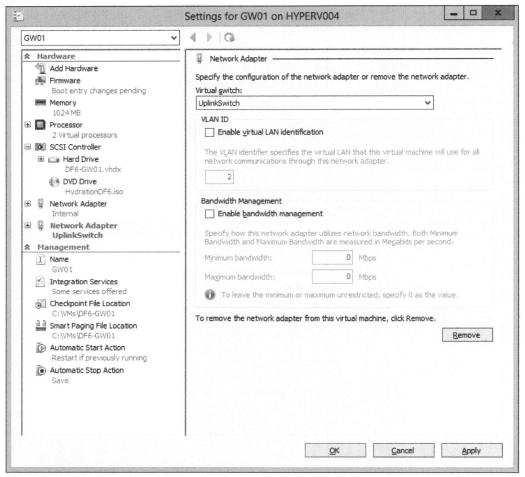

Adding a second virtual network adapter to GW01.

5. If you turned off the **GW01** virtual machine in this guide, now start it again.

Install Routing and Remote Access

In this guide, we assume you have copied the book sample files to C:\Setup on GW01.

> **Real World Note:** In addition to copying the files over the network, or via RDP (slow), one easy way to copy setup or sample files to a virtual machine is simply to mount the ISO file on the virtual machine. If you don't have an ISO file, but have Windows ADK 10 installed on a machine, you can open a Deployment and Imaging Tools Environment prompt and run the following command to create an ISO file: oscdimg.exe -u2 C:\Setup C:\ISO\SetupFiles.iso.

1. On **GW01**, log on as **Administrator**, and open an elevated **PowerShell prompt**.

2. Verify that the second virtual network adapter got an IP address from the external network by running the following command:

   ```
   Get-NetIPAddress | FT
   ```

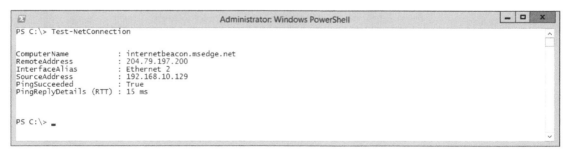

```
Administrator: Windows PowerShell

PS C:\> Get-NetIPAddress | FT

ifIndex IPAddress                               PrefixLength PrefixOrigin SuffixOrigin AddressState PolicyStore
------- ---------                               ------------ ------------ ------------ ------------ -----------
23      fe80::ace0:8745:974e:7924%23                      64 WellKnown    Link         Preferred    ActiveStore
12      fe80::5dde:b07e:b58c:286d%12                      64 WellKnown    Link         Preferred    ActiveStore
27      fe80::5efe:192.168.10.129%27                     128 WellKnown    Link         Deprecated   ActiveStore
13      fe80::5efe:192.168.1.1%13                        128 WellKnown    Link         Deprecated   ActiveStore
1       ::1                                              128 WellKnown    WellKnown    Preferred    ActiveStore
23      192.168.10.129                                    24 Dhcp         Dhcp         Preferred    ActiveStore
12      192.168.1.1                                       24 Manual       Manual       Preferred    ActiveStore
1       127.0.0.1                                          8 WellKnown    WellKnown    Preferred    ActiveStore

PS C:\>
```

Verifying IP configuration using PowerShell.

3. Verify that **GW01** has Internet access by running the following command:

   ```
   Test-NetConnection
   ```

```
Administrator: Windows PowerShell

PS C:\> Test-NetConnection

ComputerName            : internetbeacon.msedge.net
RemoteAddress           : 204.79.197.200
InterfaceAlias          : Ethernet 2
SourceAddress           : 192.168.10.129
PingSucceeded           : True
PingReplyDetails (RTT)  : 15 ms

PS C:\>
```

Verifying Internet access using PowerShell.

4. Install **RRAS** by running the following command:

   ```
   C:\Setup\Scripts\Install-VIARoles.ps1 -Role RRAS
   ```

261

Configure Routing and Remote Access

Routing and Remote Access is now installed but needs to be configured. During the configuration, the server will be a router with Network Address Translation functionality.

1. On **GW01**, open an elevated **PowerShell prompt**.

2. Configure **RRAS** by running the following command (the command is wrapped and should be one line):

```
C:\Setup\Scripts\Set-VIARRASNetworking.ps1 -InternalIP
"192.168.1.1"
```

3. Restart **GW01** by running the following command:

```
Restart-Computer -Force
```

4. After the **GW01** virtual machine is restarted, log in again and start Routing and Remote Access to review the configuration.

> **Real World Note:** First, restarting GW01 is not really required because of the Routing and Remote Access configuration, but it's nice to do a final reboot after completing the configuration and make sure everything starts properly. Also, please note that Routing and Remote Access service is configured with a delayed start, so give it some time to start. A service configured for delayed start starts two minutes after the last "automatic" service has started.

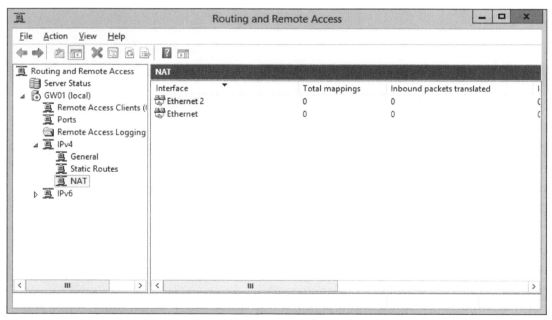

Routing and Remote Access configured via PowerShell. Ethernet 2 is the public NAT interface.

Deploy DC01

This is the primary domain controller used in the environment, and it also runs DNS and DHCP.

1. Using **Hyper-V Manager** or **VMware Sphere**, create a virtual machine with the following settings:

    a. Name: **DC01**

    b. Memory: **1 GB** (minimum, 2 GB recommended)

    c. Hard drive: **100 GB** (dynamic disk)

    d. Network: The virtual network you use for the virtual machines

    e. Image file (ISO): **C:\HydrationDF6\ISO\HydrationDF6.iso**

    f. vCPUs: **2**

2. Start the **DC01** virtual machine. After booting from **HydrationDF6.iso**, and after WinPE has loaded, select the **DC01** task sequence.

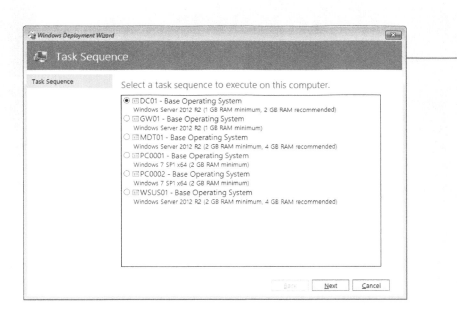

Selecting the DC01 task sequence.

3. Wait until the setup is complete and you see the **Hydration completed** message in the final summary. Verify that there is no ISO file mounted on the **DC01** virtual machine, and leave the virtual machine running.

> **Real World Note:** Using a dynamic disk is really useful for a lab and test environment because the host PC uses only the actually consumed space on the virtual hard drive and not the size that you enter like a fixed disk would.

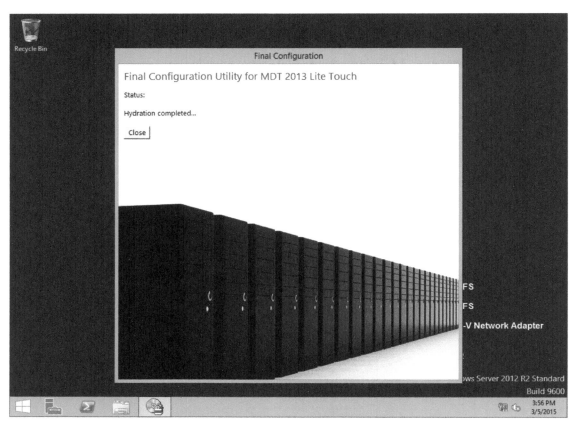

The initial deployment of DC01 completed, showing the custom final summary screen.

DC01 Post-Deployment OS Configurations

When the initial deployment of DC01 is complete, you need to do some additional post-deployment OS configurations like set up Active Directory, Time Service, DNS, and DHCP.

Install Active Directory Domain Services

In this guide, we assume you have copied the book sample files to C:\Setup on DC01.

1. On **DC01**, log on as **Administrator**, and open an elevated **PowerShell prompt**.

2. Install **ADDS** by running the following command:

   ```
   C:\Setup\Scripts\Install-VIARoles.ps1 -Role ADDS
   ```

Configure Active Directory and DNS

Active Directory and DNS are now installed but need to be configured. During the configuration, the server will be a domain controller in the corp.viamonstra.com domain.

1. On **DC01**, open an elevated **PowerShell prompt**.

2. Configure **ADDS** and **DNS** by running the following command (the command is wrapped and should be one line):

   ```
   C:\Setup\Scripts\Set-VIAADDSFDCConfig.ps1 -Password
   "P@ssw0rd" -FQDN "corp.viamonstra.com" -NetBiosDomainName
   "VIAMONSTRA"
   ```

> **Note:** During the configuration of Active Directory and DNS, a decent number of warnings pop up. The warnings are warnings regarding changes in Active Directory that prevent NT domain controllers from joining in. That should *not* be a problem for you.

3. Restart **DC01** by running the following command:

   ```
   Restart-Computer -Force
   ```

4. After **DC01** reboots, log on as **VIAMONSTRA\Administrator**, and open an elevated **PowerShell prompt**.

5. Verify the configuration via **PowerShell** by running the following command:

   ```
   Get-ADDomain
   ```

```
Administrator: Windows PowerShell                                    _ □ x

PS C:\> Get-ADDomain

AllowedDNSSuffixes                 : {}
ChildDomains                       : {}
ComputersContainer                 : CN=Computers,DC=corp,DC=viamonstra,DC=com
DeletedObjectsContainer            : CN=Deleted Objects,DC=corp,DC=viamonstra,DC=com
DistinguishedName                  : DC=corp,DC=viamonstra,DC=com
DNSRoot                            : corp.viamonstra.com
DomainControllersContainer         : OU=Domain Controllers,DC=corp,DC=viamonstra,DC=com
DomainMode                         : Windows2012R2Domain
DomainSID                          : S-1-5-21-1871993781-1107036147-166890822
ForeignSecurityPrincipalsContainer : CN=ForeignSecurityPrincipals,DC=corp,DC=viamonstra,DC=com
Forest                             : corp.viamonstra.com
InfrastructureMaster               : DC01.corp.viamonstra.com
LastLogonReplicationInterval       :
LinkedGroupPolicyObjects           : {CN={31B2F340-016D-11D2-945F-00C04FB984F9},CN=Policies,CN=System,DC=corp,DC=viamon
                                     stra,DC=com}
LostAndFoundContainer              : CN=LostAndFound,DC=corp,DC=viamonstra,DC=com
ManagedBy                          :
Name                               : corp
NetBIOSName                        : VIAMONSTRA
ObjectClass                        : domainDNS
ObjectGUID                         : 2d5e7d5a-83fd-4806-adf4-a143df03ffd3
ParentDomain                       :
PDCEmulator                        : DC01.corp.viamonstra.com
QuotasContainer                    : CN=NTDS Quotas,DC=corp,DC=viamonstra,DC=com
ReadOnlyReplicaDirectoryServers    : {}
ReplicaDirectoryServers            : {DC01.corp.viamonstra.com}
RIDMaster                          : DC01.corp.viamonstra.com
SubordinateReferences              : {DC=ForestDnsZones,DC=corp,DC=viamonstra,DC=com,
                                     DC=DomainDnsZones,DC=corp,DC=viamonstra,DC=com,
                                     CN=Configuration,DC=corp,DC=viamonstra,DC=com}
SystemsContainer                   : CN=System,DC=corp,DC=viamonstra,DC=com
UsersContainer                     : CN=Users,DC=corp,DC=viamonstra,DC=com


PS C:\> _
```

The Get-ADDomain output.

Create Active Directory Sites

The default site name is "Default-First-Site-Name," but we prefer to have a more suitable name, like NewYork. You also need configure the subnet for that site. These scripts do exactly that.

1. On **DC01**, open an elevated **PowerShell prompt**.

2. Configure the Active Directory sites by running the following command:

    ```
    C:\Setup\Scripts\Set-VIAADDSSiteName.ps1 -SiteName "NewYork"
    ```

3. Configure the Active Directory site subnet by running the following command (the command is wrapped and should be one line):

    ```
    C:\Setup\Scripts\Set-VIAADSiteSubnet.ps1 -SiteName "NewYork"
    -ADSubnets "192.168.1.0/24"
    ```

Real World Note: If you want to add multiple subnets to a site, you can specify them as an array: -ADSubnets "192.168.1.0/24","192.168.2.0/24"

---

4. Verify the site configuration by running the following command:

    ```
    Get-ADReplicationSite
    ```

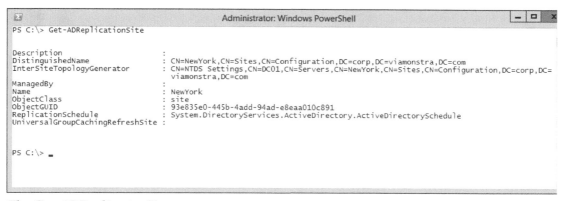

The Get-ADReplicationSite output.

Configure DNS Client Settings

After you install Active Directory and DNS, we recommend that you configure the DNS client settings per the Best Practice Analyzer (BPA):

1. On **DC01**, open an elevated **PowerShell prompt**.

2. Create the DNS zone by running the following command (the command is wrapped and should be one line):

```
C:\Setup\Scripts\Set-VIAADClientDNSSettings.ps1
-ClientDNSServerAddr "127.0.0.1","192.168.1.200"
```

Create DNS Zones

After you install Active Directory and DNS, we recommend that you create a DNS Reverse Lookup Zone.

1. On **DC01**, open an elevated **PowerShell prompt**.

2. Create the DNS zone by running the following command (the command is wrapped and should be one line):

```
Add-DnsServerPrimaryZone 1.168.192.in-addr.arpa
-ReplicationScope Domain
```

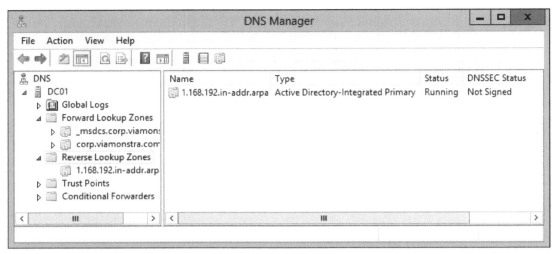

The created DNS zone, here displayed in DNS Manager.

Additional DNS Server Configuration

To make sure the DNS Server is running optimally, we recommend that no DNS forwarders are configured by default.

1.   On **DC01**, open an elevated **PowerShell prompt**.

2.   Remove any DNS forwarders by running the following command:

```
C:\Setup\Scripts\Remove-VIADNSForwarders.ps1
```

Configure Time Sync

In Active Directory, the domain controller holding the PDC Emulator role (DC01 in the ViaMonstra environment) is responsible for time synchronization. Therefore, it's critical that its time is correct. In this guide, you configure DC01 to sync against a known accurate time source. However, since this VM is virtualized, you need to partially disable the Hyper-V time synchronization provider. The script you are about to run handles all the settings needed for a virtual time provider to work.

1.   On **DC01**, open an elevated **PowerShell prompt**.

2.   Configure the time sync by running following command (the command is wrapped and should be one line):

```
C:\Setup\Scripts\Set-VIATimeSync.ps1
-TimeSource "se.pool.ntp.org"
```

Real World Note: You may want to change the command to use a time server pool close to your location. Check http://www.pool.ntp.org for a list for your country.

Install DHCP

DC01 also should run the DHCP service. In this guide, you run a script that installs and configures the DHCP server.

> **Note:** If you have another DHCP server running in your network, now is a good time to disable it.

1. On **DC01**, open an elevated **PowerShell prompt**.

2. Install **DHCP** by running the following command:

    ```
    C:\Setup\Scripts\Install-VIARoles.ps1 -Role DHCP
    ```

3. Authorize DHCP in Active Directory and configure the DHCP security group by running the following command:

    ```
    C:\Setup\Scripts\Set-VIARoles.ps1 -Role DHCP
    ```

4. Create the DHCP scope by running the following command (the command is wrapped and should be one line):

    ```
    C:\Setup\Scripts\Set-VIADHCP.ps1 -OSDAdapter0Net
    "192.168.1.0" -OSDAdapter0SubnetMaskPrefix "24"
    -DHCPScopeStart "100" -DHCPScopeEnd "199" -ScopeFQDN
    "corp.viamonstra.com" -ScopeDNS1 "192.168.1.200"
    -ScopeRouter "192.168.1.1"
    ```

5. Verify the setup by opening **DHCP Manager** and reviewing the settings.

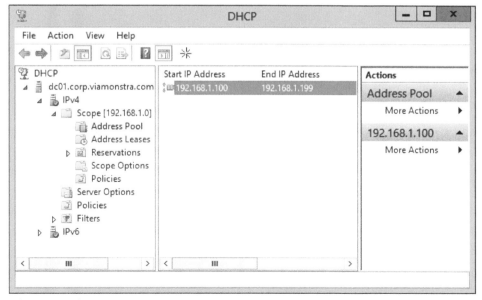

The created scope in DHCP Manager.

Verify the Network Profile on DC01

Before continuing, it's a good idea to make sure the network profile on DC01 is set to Domain. Due to timing issues with the NLS service, it's common for virtual domain controllers to have their networks set to Public. See the following screenshot.

DC01 network profile set to Public.

To have DC01 rediscover the network and configure it to Domain, simply perform the following steps:

1. On **DC01**, open an elevated **PowerShell prompt**.

2. Configure the **NLS Service** for delayed start by running the following command:

    ```
    sc.exe config NlaSvc start=delayed-auto
    ```

3. Restart the **NLS Service** by running the following command:

    ```
    Restart-Service -Name NlaSvc -Force
    ```

DC01 network profile set to Domain (as it should be).

Create the ViaMonstra OU Structure

Throughout the book, you use a sample OU structure which needs to be created:

1. On **DC01**, open an elevated **PowerShell prompt**.

2. Create the ViaMonstra base OU by running the following command:

   ```
   C:\Setup\Scripts\New-VIAADBaseOU.ps1 -BaseOU "ViaMonstra"
   ```

3. Create the ViaMonstra OU structure by running the following command (the command is wrapped and should be one line):

   ```
   C:\setup\Scripts\Set-VIAADDSOuStructure.ps1 -BaseOU
   "ViaMonstra" -SettingsFile C:\Setup\Settings\Settings.xml
   ```

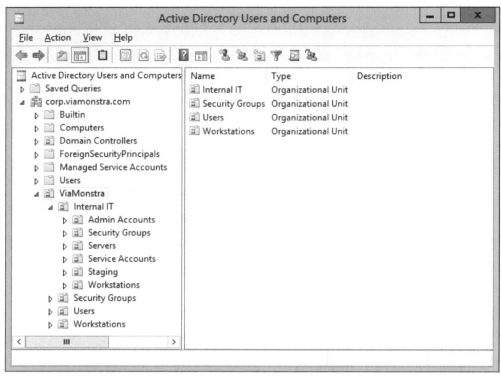

The OU structure created by the PowerShell scripts.

Deploy MDT01

MDT01 is the server used for MDT and WDS.

1. Using **Hyper-V Manager** or **VMware Sphere**, create a virtual machine with the following settings:

   a. Name: **MDT01**

   b. Memory: **2 GB** (minimum, 4 GB recommended)

   c. Hard drive: **300 GB** (dynamic disk)

   d. Network: The virtual network you use for the virtual machines

   e. Image file (ISO): **C:\HydrationDF6\ISO\HydrationDF6.iso**

   f. vCPUs: **2** (minimum, 4 recommended)

2. Make sure the **DC01** virtual machine is running, and then start the **MDT01** virtual machine. After booting from **HydrationDF6.iso**, and after WinPE has loaded, select the **MDT01** task sequence. Wait until the setup is complete and you see the **Hydration completed** message in the final summary. Verify that there is no ISO file mounted on the **MDT01** virtual machine.

Deploy MDT02

MDT02 is an optional server used for the distributed environment topic covered in Appendix B. You need this server only if you want to try that scenario.

1. Using **Hyper-V Manager** or **VMware Sphere**, create a virtual machine with the following settings:

    a. Name: **MDT02**

    b. Memory: **2 GB** (minimum, 4 GB recommended)

    c. Hard drive: **300 GB** (dynamic disk)

    d. Network: The virtual network you use for the virtual machines

    e. Image file (ISO): **C:\HydrationDF6\ISO\HydrationDF6.iso**

    f. vCPUs: **2** (minimum, 4 recommended)

2. Make sure the **DC01** virtual machine is running, and then start the **MDT02** virtual machine. After booting from **HydrationDF6.iso**, and after WinPE has loaded, select the **MDT02** task sequence. Wait until the setup is complete and you see the **Hydration completed** message in the final summary. Verify that there is no ISO file mounted on the **MDT02** virtual machine.

Deploy WSUS01

WSUS01 is the server used for Windows Software Update Services.

1. Using **Hyper-V Manager** or **VMware Sphere**, create a virtual machine with the following settings:

    a. Name: **WSUS01**

    b. Memory: **2 GB** (minimum, 4 GB recommended)

    c. Hard drive: **300 GB** (dynamic disk)

    d. Network: The virtual network you use for the virtual machines

    e. Image file (ISO): **C:\HydrationDF6\ISO\HydrationDF6.iso**

    f. vCPUs: **1** (minimum, 2 recommended)

2. Make sure the **DC01** virtual machine is running, and then start the **WSUS01** virtual machine. After booting from **HydrationDF6.iso**, and after WinPE has loaded, select the **WSUS01** task sequence. Wait until the setup is complete and you see the **Hydration completed** message in the final summary. Verify that there is no ISO file mounted on the **WSUS01** virtual machine.

Deploy PC0001

This is a client running Windows 7 SP1 Enterprise x64 in the domain.

1. Using **Hyper-V Manager** or **VMware Sphere**, create a virtual machine with the following settings:

   a. Name: **PC0001**

   b. Memory: **2 GB**

   c. Hard drive: **60 GB** (dynamic disk)

   d. Network: The virtual network you use for the virtual machines

   e. Image file (ISO): **C:\HydrationDF6\ISO\HydrationDF6.iso**

   f. vCPUs: **1** (minimum, 2 recommended)

2. Start the **PC0001** virtual machine. After booting from **HydrationDF6.iso**, and after WinPE has loaded, select the **PC0001** task sequence. Wait until the setup is complete and you see the **Hydration completed** message in the final summary. Verify that there is no ISO file mounted on the **PC0001** virtual machine.

Deploy PC0002

This is an extra client running Windows 7 SP1 Enterprise x64 in the domain.

1. Using **Hyper-V Manager** or **VMware Sphere**, create a virtual machine with the following settings:

   a. Name: **PC0002**

   b. Memory: **2 GB**

   c. Hard drive: **60 GB** (dynamic disk)

   d. Network: The virtual network you use for the virtual machines

   e. Image file (ISO): **C:\HydrationDF6\ISO\HydrationDF6.iso**

   f. vCPUs: **1** (minimum, 2 recommended)

2. Start the **PC0002** virtual machine. After booting from **HydrationDF6.iso**, and after WinPE has loaded, select the **PC0002** task sequence. Wait until the setup is complete and you see the **Hydration completed** message in the final summary. Verify that there is no ISO file mounted on the **PC0002** virtual machine.

Appendix B

Building a Distributed Environment

What about distributed environments? Is it possible to deploy over WAN links? Should you put up a separate server? How is this done? In this appendix, you set up a replication from MDT01 to MDT02, which will serve as a file server for a deployment share. Also, if you need to set up a deployment server in another site, you most likely want to add the PXE services to it through WDS.

> **Note:** This Appendix assumes that you have configured MDT01 for production deployments as outlined in Chapter 10: "Setting Up MDT for Production Deployment".

Replicating Deployment Shares

Replicating the content between MDT01 and MDT02 can be done in a number of different ways. The most common content replication solutions with MDT are to use either the MDT-linked deployment share feature or Distributed File System Replication (DFS-R). We have even seen some organizations use a simple Robocopy script for replication of the content.

> **Real World Note:** Even if Robocopy seems to be a simple solution, it actually can work quite nicely. Robocopy does have options that allow for synchronization between folders; it has a simple reporting function; it supports transmission retry; and by default, it only copies files from the source that are newer than files on the target.

Linked Deployment Shares in MDT

In MDT, there is a built-in feature for replicating content called linked deployment shares (LDS). However, LDS works really well only if you have great connections. With high-latency links, using LDS across the Atlantic Ocean can be very "challenging," and, furthermore, LDS lacks central monitoring and troubleshooting actions. Unless you are doing replications within the same datacenter, or just want something really quick for a test, we don't recommend using linked deployment shares. We have seen too many organizations struggle with them when there is a much better option: DFS-R.

Why DFS-R Is a Better Option

In a word, when it comes to replicating MDT deployment share(s), using DFS-R is a superior option. But, before going deeper on why and how, we should explain that DFS-R is not a part of

MDT. Rather, it's a component in the Windows Server operating system and has been around since Windows Server 2003 R2. DFS-R works very well, but it does need some administration and monitoring (not much but some).

DFS-R is not only very fast and reliable, it also has central monitoring, bandwidth control, and a great delta replication engine. DFS-R works equally well whether you have only two sites or 90 sites. Currently, we know of about 3000 customers globally who are relying on DFS-R for their MDT replication, but there are likely to be many more out there.

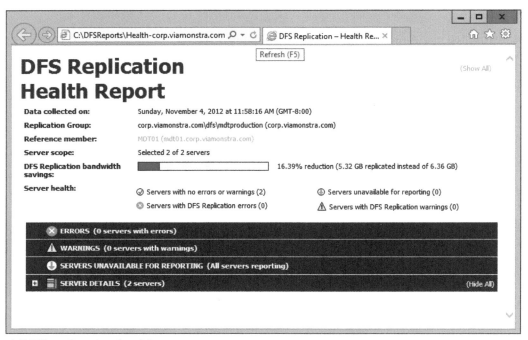

A DFS replication health report.

Use Read-Only Targets

We recommend running your deployment servers on at least Windows Server 2012 R2. In addition, to support replication target(s) as read-only (added in Windows Server 2008 R2), you get the most robust replication platform when running on Windows Server 2012 R2. When using read-only targets, you can have your master deployment share centralized and replicate out changes as they happen. DFS-R quickly picks up changes at the central deployment share in MDT01 and replicates the delta changes to MDT02.

Setting Up DFS-R

Setting up DFS-R for replication is a quick and straightforward process. You start by adding DFS to the deployment servers, creating a DFS namespace, creating targets (two), and then selecting which type of replication you want. Done!

Prepare MDT01 and MDT02 for DFS-R

1. On **MDT01,** using an elevated **PowerShell prompt**, prepare **MDT01** by running the following command (the command is wrapped and should be one line):

```
C:\setup\scripts\Install-VIARoles.ps1 -Role FILE
```

2. On **MDT01,** using an elevated **PowerShell prompt**, prepare **MDT02** by running the following command (the command is wrapped and should be one line):

```
Invoke-Command -ComputerName MDT02
-FilePath C:\Setup\Scripts\Install-VIARoles.ps1
-ArgumentList FILE
```

Create the Replication Group Using PowerShell

1. On **MDT01,** using an elevated **PowerShell prompt**, create the replication group by running the following command (the command is wrapped and should be one line):

```
C:\Setup\Scripts\New-VIADFSReplica.ps1 -GroupName MDT
-FolderName MDTProduction -SourceComputer MDT01
-DestinationComputer MDT02 -SourceFolder E:\MDTProduction
-DestinationFolder E:\MDTProduction
```

2. You can verify replication health using the **UI** (See "Verify Replication" later n this appendix for more information) or **PowerShell**. Here is a simple PowerShell command to generate an HTML report in the C:\DFSReports folder (the command is wrapped and should be one line, also the C:\DFSReports folder must exist):

```
Write-DfsrHealthReport -GroupName "MDT"
-ReferenceComputerName "MDT01" -Path C:\DFSReports
```

3. The output gives a file location that you then can open using **PowerShell**:

```
Invoke-Item -Path C:\DFSReports\Health-MDT-xyzzyx.html
```

Real World Note: It takes quite a bit of time for the replication configuration to be picked up by the replication members (MDT01 and MDT02), and of course the initial sync also takes some time, depending on the WAN link speed between the sites. Even in a lab and test environment, the initial configuration may take an hour to complete. After that, delta changes are replicated quickly.

Configure the Deployment Share

When you have multiple deployment servers sharing the same content, you need to configure the Bootstrap.ini file with information on which server to connect to, based on which site the client is in. In MDT, that can be done by using the DefaultGateway property. So, if MDT02 is located on another site (with another subnet), you would modify Bootstrap.ini to look something like this:

```
[Settings]
Priority=DefaultGateway, Default

[DefaultGateway]
192.168.1.1=NewYork
192.168.2.1=Stockholm

[NewYork]
DeployRoot=\\MDT01\MDTProduction$

[Stockholm]
DeployRoot=\\MDT02\MDTProduction$

[Default]
UserDomain=VIAMONSTRA
UserID=MDT_BA

SkipBDDWelcome=YES
```

With these settings, a client on the NewYork network uses the NewYork deployment share, and a client on the Stockholm network uses the deployment share in Stockholm.

Real World Note: You also can use the MDT database to store information on what server to connect to. You learn about the MDT database in Chapter 18.

Appendix C

Creating an Office 2016 MSI Setup

In Chapter 5, you learned how to deploy Office 2016 via the Office 365 process. Here is a short guide to creating an application in MDT for the MSI-based setup of Office 2016.

Creating the Install - Microsoft Office 2016 Pro Plus - x86 Application

In these steps, we assume you have copied the Office 2016 Professional Plus x86 volume license installation files to the C:\Setup\DL\Microsoft Office 2016 Pro Plus x86 folder.

Add the Microsoft Office 2016 Pro Plus x86 Installation Files

1. On **MDT01**, using the **Deployment Workbench**, expand the deployment share to which you want to add Office 2016 and navigate to **Applications**.

2. Right-click **Applications** and select **New Application**. Use the following settings for the **New Application Wizard**:

   a. **Application with source files**

   b. Publisher: **<blank>**

   c. Application name: **Install - Microsoft Office 2016 Pro Plus - x86**

   d. Version: **<blank>**

   e. Source directory: **C:\Setup\DL\Microsoft Office 2016 Pro Plus x86**

   f. Specify the name of the directory that should be created: **Install - Microsoft Office 2016 Pro Plus - x86**

   g. Command line: **Setup.exe**

   h. Working directory: **<default>**

Automate the Microsoft Office 2016 Pro Plus x86 Setup

After adding the Microsoft Office 2016 Pro Plus x86 application, you then automate its setup by running the Office Customization Tool. In fact, MDT detects that you added the Microsoft Office 2016 Pro Plus x86 application and creates a shortcut for doing this.

You also can customize the Office installation using a Config.xml file. But we recommend that you use the Office Customization Tool as described in following steps, as it provides a much richer way of controlling Office 2016 settings.

1. Using the **Deployment Workbench**, in the deployment share you are using, expand **Applications** and double-click the **Install - Microsoft Office 2016 Pro Plus - x86** application.

2. In the **Office Products** tab, click **Office Customization Tool**, and click **OK** in the **Information** dialog box.

> **Note:** If you don't see the Office Products tab, verify that you are using a volume license version of Office 2016.

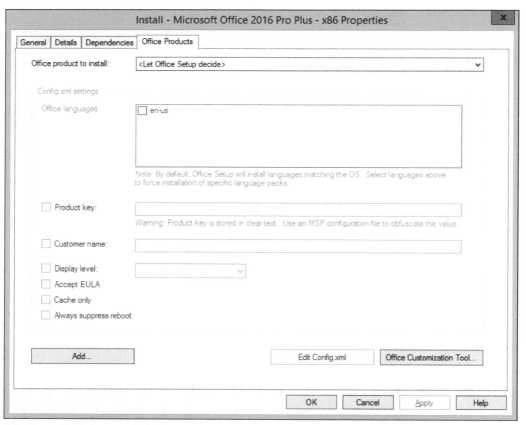

The Install - Microsoft Office 2016 Pro Plus - x86 application properties.

3. In the **Office Customization Tool** dialog box, select the **Create a new Setup customization file for the following product** option, select the **Microsoft Office Professional Plus 2016 (32-bit)** product, and click **OK**.

4. Use the following settings to configure the Office 2016 setup to be fully unattended:

    a. Install location and organization name

        Organization name: **ViaMonstra**

    b. Licensing and user interface

        ▪ **Use KMS client key**

        ▪ Select: **I accept the terms in the License Agreement**

        ▪ Display Level: **None**

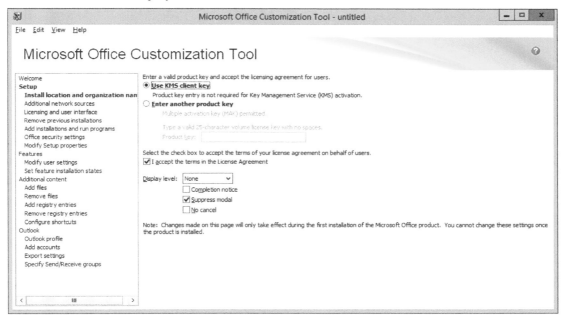

The licensing and user interface screen in the Microsoft Office Customization Tool.

    c. Modify Setup properties

        Add the **SETUP_REBOOT** property and set the value to **Never**.

    d. Modify user settings

        In the **Microsoft Office 2016** node, expand **Privacy**, select **Trust Center**, and enable the **Disable Opt-in Wizard on first run** setting.

5. In the **File** menu, select **Save**, and save the configuration as **0_Office2016ProPlusx86.msp** in the **<Deployment Share>\ Install - Microsoft Office 2016 Pro Plus - x86\Updates** folder.

> **Real World Note:** The reason for naming the file with a 0 (zero) at the beginning is that the Updates folder also handles Microsoft Office updates, and they are installed in alphabetical order. The Office 2016 setup works best if the customization file is installed before any updates.

6. Close the **Office Customization Tool**, click **Yes** in the dialog box and in the **Install - Microsoft Office 2016 Pro Plus - x86 Properties** window, and click **OK**.

> **Real World Note:** If you also want to use the Config.xml file that Office 2016 supports, for example, for language settings, you need to do an "interesting" series of actions ☺. First, you need to close the Office application properties and open them again, but before clicking the Office Products tab to do the configuration, you need to click each tab in order: General, Details, Dependencies, and then Office Products. If you don't do this, the install command will not change.

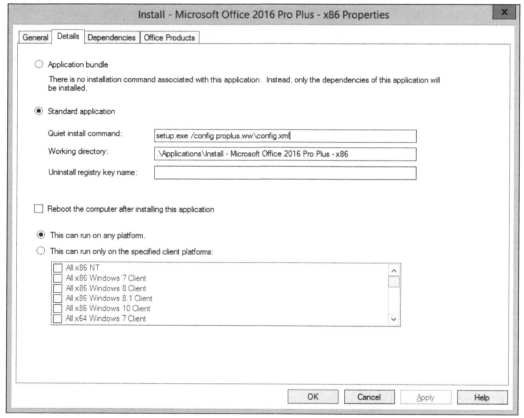

Using the Office 2016 Config.xml file.

Index

Beyond the Book – Meet the Experts

If you liked their book, you will love to hear them in person.

Live Presentations
Johan and Mikael frequently speak at Microsoft conferences around the world, such as Microsoft Management Summit (MMS) and TechEd. For current tour dates and presentations, see our blogs:

- Mikael Nyström: http://deploymentbunny.com
- Johan Arwidmark: http://deploymentresearch.com

Video Training
For video-based training, see the following site:

http://deploymentartist.com

Live Instructor-led Classes
Johan and Mikael present scheduled instructor-led classes in the US and in Europe. For current dates and locations, see the following sites:

- http://labcenter.se
- http://truesec.com
- http://deploymentartist.com

Twitter
Johan and Mikael also tweet on the following aliases:

- Mikael Nyström: @mikael_nystrom
- Johan Arwidmark: @jarwidmark

Lightning Source UK Ltd.
Milton Keynes UK
UKOW07f1826130116

266329UK00001B/1/P